# WEST-E

## Health/Fitness (029)

# SECRETS

## Study Guide
### Your Key to Exam Success

WEST-E Test Review for the
Washington Educator Skills
Tests - Endorsements

Dear Future Exam Success Story:

First of all, **THANK YOU** for purchasing Mometrix study materials!

Second, congratulations! You are one of the few determined test-takers who are committed to doing whatever it takes to excel on your exam. **You have come to the right place.** We developed these study materials with one goal in mind: to deliver you the information you need in a format that's concise and easy to use.

In addition to optimizing your guide for the content of the test, we've outlined our recommended steps for breaking down the preparation process into small, attainable goals so you can make sure you stay on track.

We've also analyzed the entire test-taking process, identifying the most common pitfalls and showing how you can overcome them and be ready for any curveball the test throws you.

Standardized testing is one of the biggest obstacles on your road to success, which only increases the importance of doing well in the high-pressure, high-stakes environment of test day. Your results on this test could have a significant impact on your future, and this guide provides the information and practical advice to help you achieve your full potential on test day.

### Your success is our success

**We would love to hear from you!** If you would like to share the story of your exam success or if you have any questions or comments in regard to our products, please contact us at **800-673-8175** or **support@mometrix.com**.

Thanks again for your business and we wish you continued success!

Sincerely,
The Mometrix Test Preparation Team

**Need more help? Check out our flashcards at:** <u>http://MometrixFlashcards.com/WEST</u>

# TABLE OF CONTENTS

# Introduction

**Thank you for purchasing this resource**! You have made the choice to prepare yourself for a test that could have a huge impact on your future, and this guide is designed to help you be fully ready for test day. Obviously, it's important to have a solid understanding of the test material, but you also need to be prepared for the unique environment and stressors of the test, so that you can perform to the best of your abilities.

For this purpose, the first section that appears in this guide is the **Secret Keys**. We've devoted countless hours to meticulously researching what works and what doesn't, and we've boiled down our findings to the five most impactful steps you can take to improve your performance on the test. We start at the beginning with study planning and move through the preparation process, all the way to the testing strategies that will help you get the most out of what you know when you're finally sitting in front of the test.

We recommend that you start preparing for your test as far in advance as possible. However, if you've bought this guide as a last-minute study resource and only have a few days before your test, we recommend that you skip over the first two Secret Keys since they address a long-term study plan.

If you struggle with **test anxiety**, we strongly encourage you to check out our recommendations for how you can overcome it. Test anxiety is a formidable foe, but it can be beaten, and we want to make sure you have the tools you need to defeat it.

# Secret Key #1 – Plan Big, Study Small

There's a lot riding on your performance. If you want to ace this test, you're going to need to keep your skills sharp and the material fresh in your mind. You need a plan that lets you review everything you need to know while still fitting in your schedule. We'll break this strategy down into three categories.

## Information Organization

Start with the information you already have: the official test outline. From this, you can make a complete list of all the concepts you need to cover before the test. Organize these concepts into groups that can be studied together, and create a list of any related vocabulary you need to learn so you can brush up on any difficult terms. You'll want to keep this vocabulary list handy once you actually start studying since you may need to add to it along the way.

## Time Management

Once you have your set of study concepts, decide how to spread them out over the time you have left before the test. Break your study plan into small, clear goals so you have a manageable task for each day and know exactly what you're doing. Then just focus on one small step at a time. When you manage your time this way, you don't need to spend hours at a time studying. Studying a small block of content for a short period each day helps you retain information better and avoid stressing over how much you have left to do. You can relax knowing that you have a plan to cover everything in time. In order for this strategy to be effective though, you have to start studying early and stick to your schedule. Avoid the exhaustion and futility that comes from last-minute cramming!

## Study Environment

The environment you study in has a big impact on your learning. Studying in a coffee shop, while probably more enjoyable, is not likely to be as fruitful as studying in a quiet room. It's important to keep distractions to a minimum. You're only planning to study for a short block of time, so make the most of it. Don't pause to check your phone or get up to find a snack. It's also important to **avoid multitasking**. Research has consistently shown that multitasking will make your studying dramatically less effective. Your study area should also be comfortable and well-lit so you don't have the distraction of straining your eyes or sitting on an uncomfortable chair.

The time of day you study is also important. You want to be rested and alert. Don't wait until just before bedtime. Study when you'll be most likely to comprehend and remember. Even better, if you know what time of day your test will be, set that time aside for study. That way your brain will be used to working on that subject at that specific time and you'll have a better chance of recalling information.

Finally, it can be helpful to team up with others who are studying for the same test. Your actual studying should be done in as isolated an environment as possible, but the work of organizing the information and setting up the study plan can be divided up. In between study sessions, you can discuss with your teammates the concepts that you're all studying and quiz each other on the details. Just be sure that your teammates are as serious about the test as you are. If you find that your study time is being replaced with social time, you might need to find a new team.

# Secret Key #2 – Make Your Studying Count

You're devoting a lot of time and effort to preparing for this test, so you want to be absolutely certain it will pay off. This means doing more than just reading the content and hoping you can remember it on test day. It's important to make every minute of study count. There are two main areas you can focus on to make your studying count:

## Retention

It doesn't matter how much time you study if you can't remember the material. You need to make sure you are retaining the concepts. To check your retention of the information you're learning, try recalling it at later times with minimal prompting. Try carrying around flashcards and glance at one or two from time to time or ask a friend who's also studying for the test to quiz you.

To enhance your retention, look for ways to put the information into practice so that you can apply it rather than simply recalling it. If you're using the information in practical ways, it will be much easier to remember. Similarly, it helps to solidify a concept in your mind if you're not only reading it to yourself but also explaining it to someone else. Ask a friend to let you teach them about a concept you're a little shaky on (or speak aloud to an imaginary audience if necessary). As you try to summarize, define, give examples, and answer your friend's questions, you'll understand the concepts better and they will stay with you longer. Finally, step back for a big picture view and ask yourself how each piece of information fits with the whole subject. When you link the different concepts together and see them working together as a whole, it's easier to remember the individual components.

Finally, practice showing your work on any multi-step problems, even if you're just studying. Writing out each step you take to solve a problem will help solidify the process in your mind, and you'll be more likely to remember it during the test.

## Modality

*Modality* simply refers to the means or method by which you study. Choosing a study modality that fits your own individual learning style is crucial. No two people learn best in exactly the same way, so it's important to know your strengths and use them to your advantage.

For example, if you learn best by visualization, focus on visualizing a concept in your mind and draw an image or a diagram. Try color-coding your notes, illustrating them, or creating symbols that will trigger your mind to recall a learned concept. If you learn best by hearing or discussing information, find a study partner who learns the same way or read aloud to yourself. Think about how to put the information in your own words. Imagine that you are giving a lecture on the topic and record yourself so you can listen to it later.

For any learning style, flashcards can be helpful. Organize the information so you can take advantage of spare moments to review. Underline key words or phrases. Use different colors for different categories. Mnemonic devices (such as creating a short list in which every item starts with the same letter) can also help with retention. Find what works best for you and use it to store the information in your mind most effectively and easily.

# Secret Key #3 – Practice the Right Way

Your success on test day depends not only on how many hours you put into preparing, but also on whether you prepared the right way. It's good to check along the way to see if your studying is paying off. One of the most effective ways to do this is by taking practice tests to evaluate your progress. Practice tests are useful because they show exactly where you need to improve. Every time you take a practice test, pay special attention to these three groups of questions:

- The questions you got wrong
- The questions you had to guess on, even if you guessed right
- The questions you found difficult or slow to work through

This will show you exactly what your weak areas are, and where you need to devote more study time. Ask yourself why each of these questions gave you trouble. Was it because you didn't understand the material? Was it because you didn't remember the vocabulary? Do you need more repetitions on this type of question to build speed and confidence? Dig into those questions and figure out how you can strengthen your weak areas as you go back to review the material.

Additionally, many practice tests have a section explaining the answer choices. It can be tempting to read the explanation and think that you now have a good understanding of the concept. However, an explanation likely only covers part of the question's broader context. Even if the explanation makes sense, **go back and investigate** every concept related to the question until you're positive you have a thorough understanding.

As you go along, keep in mind that the practice test is just that: practice. Memorizing these questions and answers will not be very helpful on the actual test because it is unlikely to have any of the same exact questions. If you only know the right answers to the sample questions, you won't be prepared for the real thing. **Study the concepts** until you understand them fully, and then you'll be able to answer any question that shows up on the test.

It's important to wait on the practice tests until you're ready. If you take a test on your first day of study, you may be overwhelmed by the amount of material covered and how much you need to learn. Work up to it gradually.

On test day, you'll need to be prepared for answering questions, managing your time, and using the test-taking strategies you've learned. It's a lot to balance, like a mental marathon that will have a big impact on your future. Like training for a marathon, you'll need to start slowly and work your way up. When test day arrives, you'll be ready.

Start with the strategies you've read in the first two Secret Keys—plan your course and study in the way that works best for you. If you have time, consider using multiple study resources to get different approaches to the same concepts. It can be helpful to see difficult concepts from more than one angle. Then find a good source for practice tests. Many times, the test website will suggest potential study resources or provide sample tests.

# Practice Test Strategy

When you're ready to start taking practice tests, follow this strategy:

## Untimed and Open-Book Practice

Take the first test with no time constraints and with your notes and study guide handy. Take your time and focus on applying the strategies you've learned.

## Timed and Open-Book Practice

Take the second practice test open-book as well, but set a timer and practice pacing yourself to finish in time.

## Timed and Closed-Book Practice

Take any other practice tests as if it were test day. Set a timer and put away your study materials. Sit at a table or desk in a quiet room, imagine yourself at the testing center, and answer questions as quickly and accurately as possible.

Keep repeating timed and closed-book tests on a regular basis until you run out of practice tests or it's time for the actual test. Your mind will be ready for the schedule and stress of test day, and you'll be able to focus on recalling the material you've learned.

# Secret Key #4 – Pace Yourself

Once you're fully prepared for the material on the test, your biggest challenge on test day will be managing your time. Just knowing that the clock is ticking can make you panic even if you have plenty of time left. Work on pacing yourself so you can build confidence against the time constraints of the exam. Pacing is a difficult skill to master, especially in a high-pressure environment, so **practice is vital**.

Set time expectations for your pace based on how much time is available. For example, if a section has 60 questions and the time limit is 30 minutes, you know you have to average 30 seconds or less per question in order to answer them all. Although 30 seconds is the hard limit, set 25 seconds per question as your goal, so you reserve extra time to spend on harder questions. When you budget extra time for the harder questions, you no longer have any reason to stress when those questions take longer to answer.

Don't let this time expectation distract you from working through the test at a calm, steady pace, but keep it in mind so you don't spend too much time on any one question. Recognize that taking extra time on one question you don't understand may keep you from answering two that you do understand later in the test. If your time limit for a question is up and you're still not sure of the answer, mark it and move on, and come back to it later if the time and the test format allow. If the testing format doesn't allow you to return to earlier questions, just make an educated guess; then put it out of your mind and move on.

On the easier questions, be careful not to rush. It may seem wise to hurry through them so you have more time for the challenging ones, but it's not worth missing one if you know the concept and just didn't take the time to read the question fully. Work efficiently but make sure you understand the question and have looked at all of the answer choices, since more than one may seem right at first.

Even if you're paying attention to the time, you may find yourself a little behind at some point. You should speed up to get back on track, but do so wisely. Don't panic; just take a few seconds less on each question until you're caught up. Don't guess without thinking, but do look through the answer choices and eliminate any you know are wrong. If you can get down to two choices, it is often worthwhile to guess from those. Once you've chosen an answer, move on and don't dwell on any that you skipped or had to hurry through. If a question was taking too long, chances are it was one of the harder ones, so you weren't as likely to get it right anyway.

On the other hand, if you find yourself getting ahead of schedule, it may be beneficial to slow down a little. The more quickly you work, the more likely you are to make a careless mistake that will affect your score. You've budgeted time for each question, so don't be afraid to spend that time. Practice an efficient but careful pace to get the most out of the time you have.

# Secret Key #5 – Have a Plan for Guessing

When you're taking the test, you may find yourself stuck on a question. Some of the answer choices seem better than others, but you don't see the one answer choice that is obviously correct. What do you do?

The scenario described above is very common, yet most test takers have not effectively prepared for it. Developing and practicing a plan for guessing may be one of the single most effective uses of your time as you get ready for the exam.

In developing your plan for guessing, there are three questions to address:

- When should you start the guessing process?
- How should you narrow down the choices?
- Which answer should you choose?

## When to Start the Guessing Process

Unless your plan for guessing is to select C every time (which, despite its merits, is not what we recommend), you need to leave yourself enough time to apply your answer elimination strategies. Since you have a limited amount of time for each question, that means that if you're going to give yourself the best shot at guessing correctly, you have to decide quickly whether or not you will guess.

Of course, the best-case scenario is that you don't have to guess at all, so first, see if you can answer the question based on your knowledge of the subject and basic reasoning skills. Focus on the key words in the question and try to jog your memory of related topics. Give yourself a chance to bring the knowledge to mind, but once you realize that you don't have (or you can't access) the knowledge you need to answer the question, it's time to start the guessing process.

It's almost always better to start the guessing process too early than too late. It only takes a few seconds to remember something and answer the question from knowledge. Carefully eliminating wrong answer choices takes longer. Plus, going through the process of eliminating answer choices can actually help jog your memory.

**Summary: Start the guessing process as soon as you decide that you can't answer the question based on your knowledge.**

- 7 -

# How to Narrow Down the Choices

The next chapter in this book (**Test-Taking Strategies**) includes a wide range of strategies for how to approach questions and how to look for answer choices to eliminate. You will definitely want to read those carefully, practice them, and figure out which ones work best for you. Here though, we're going to address a mindset rather than a particular strategy.

Your chances of guessing an answer correctly depend on how many options you are choosing from.

| How many choices you have | How likely you are to guess correctly |
|---|---|
| 5 | 20% |
| 4 | 25% |
| 3 | 33% |
| 2 | 50% |
| 1 | 100% |

You can see from this chart just how valuable it is to be able to eliminate incorrect answers and make an educated guess, but there are two things that many test takers do that cause them to miss out on the benefits of guessing:

- Accidentally eliminating the correct answer
- Selecting an answer based on an impression

We'll look at the first one here, and the second one in the next section.

To avoid accidentally eliminating the correct answer, we recommend a thought exercise called **the $5 challenge**. In this challenge, you only eliminate an answer choice from contention if you are willing to bet $5 on it being wrong. Why $5? Five dollars is a small but not insignificant amount of money. It's an amount you could afford to lose but wouldn't want to throw away. And while losing $5 once might not hurt too much, doing it twenty times will set you back $100. In the same way, each small decision you make—eliminating a choice here, guessing on a question there—won't by itself impact your score very much, but when you put them all together, they can make a big difference. By holding each answer choice elimination decision to a higher standard, you can reduce the risk of accidentally eliminating the correct answer.

The $5 challenge can also be applied in a positive sense: If you are willing to bet $5 that an answer choice *is* correct, go ahead and mark it as correct.

**Summary: Only eliminate an answer choice if you are willing to bet $5 that it is wrong.**

# Which Answer to Choose

You're taking the test. You've run into a hard question and decided you'll have to guess. You've eliminated all the answer choices you're willing to bet $5 on. Now you have to pick an answer. Why do we even need to talk about this? Why can't you just pick whichever one you feel like when the time comes?

The answer to these questions is that if you don't come into the test with a plan, you'll rely on your impression to select an answer choice, and if you do that, you risk falling into a trap. The test writers know that everyone who takes their test will be guessing on some of the questions, so they intentionally write wrong answer choices to seem plausible. You still have to pick an answer though, and if the wrong answer choices are designed to look right, how can you ever be sure that you're not falling for their trap? The best solution we've found to this dilemma is to take the decision out of your hands entirely. Here is the process we recommend:

**Once you've eliminated any choices that you are confident (willing to bet $5) are wrong, select the first remaining choice as your answer.**

Whether you choose to select the first remaining choice, the second, or the last, the important thing is that you use some preselected standard. Using this approach guarantees that you will not be enticed into selecting an answer choice that looks right, because you are not basing your decision on how the answer choices look.

This is not meant to make you question your knowledge. Instead, it is to help you recognize the difference between your knowledge and your impressions. There's a huge difference between thinking an answer is right because of what you know, and thinking an answer is right because it looks or sounds like it should be right.

**Summary: To ensure that your selection is appropriately random, make a predetermined selection from among all answer choices you have not eliminated.**

# Test-Taking Strategies

This section contains a list of test-taking strategies that you may find helpful as you work through the test. By taking what you know and applying logical thought, you can maximize your chances of answering any question correctly!

It is very important to realize that every question is different and every person is different: no single strategy will work on every question, and no single strategy will work for every person. That's why we've included all of them here, so you can try them out and determine which ones work best for different types of questions and which ones work best for you.

## Question Strategies

### Read Carefully

Read the question and answer choices carefully. Don't miss the question because you misread the terms. You have plenty of time to read each question thoroughly and make sure you understand what is being asked. Yet a happy medium must be attained, so don't waste too much time. You must read carefully, but efficiently.

### Contextual Clues

Look for contextual clues. If the question includes a word you are not familiar with, look at the immediate context for some indication of what the word might mean. Contextual clues can often give you all the information you need to decipher the meaning of an unfamiliar word. Even if you can't determine the meaning, you may be able to narrow down the possibilities enough to make a solid guess at the answer to the question.

### Prefixes

If you're having trouble with a word in the question or answer choices, try dissecting it. Take advantage of every clue that the word might include. Prefixes and suffixes can be a huge help. Usually they allow you to determine a basic meaning. Pre- means before, post- means after, pro - is positive, de- is negative. From prefixes and suffixes, you can get an idea of the general meaning of the word and try to put it into context.

### Hedge Words

Watch out for critical hedge words, such as *likely, may, can, sometimes, often, almost, mostly, usually, generally, rarely,* and *sometimes*. Question writers insert these hedge phrases to cover every possibility. Often an answer choice will be wrong simply because it leaves no room for exception. Be on guard for answer choices that have definitive words such as *exactly* and *always*.

### Switchback Words

Stay alert for *switchbacks*. These are the words and phrases frequently used to alert you to shifts in thought. The most common switchback words are *but, although,* and *however*. Others include *nevertheless, on the other hand, even though, while, in spite of, despite, regardless of*. Switchback words are important to catch because they can change the direction of the question or an answer choice.

## Face Value

When in doubt, use common sense. Accept the situation in the problem at face value. Don't read too much into it. These problems will not require you to make wild assumptions. If you have to go beyond creativity and warp time or space in order to have an answer choice fit the question, then you should move on and consider the other answer choices. These are normal problems rooted in reality. The applicable relationship or explanation may not be readily apparent, but it is there for you to figure out. Use your common sense to interpret anything that isn't clear.

# Answer Choice Strategies

### Answer Selection

The most thorough way to pick an answer choice is to identify and eliminate wrong answers until only one is left, then confirm it is the correct answer. Sometimes an answer choice may immediately seem right, but be careful. The test writers will usually put more than one reasonable answer choice on each question, so take a second to read all of them and make sure that the other choices are not equally obvious. As long as you have time left, it is better to read every answer choice than to pick the first one that looks right without checking the others.

### Answer Choice Families

An answer choice family consists of two (in rare cases, three) answer choices that are very similar in construction and cannot all be true at the same time. If you see two answer choices that are direct opposites or parallels, one of them is usually the correct answer. For instance, if one answer choice says that quantity $x$ increases and another either says that quantity $x$ decreases (opposite) or says that quantity $y$ increases (parallel), then those answer choices would fall into the same family. An answer choice that doesn't match the construction of the answer choice family is more likely to be incorrect. Most questions will not have answer choice families, but when they do appear, you should be prepared to recognize them.

### Eliminate Answers

Eliminate answer choices as soon as you realize they are wrong, but make sure you consider all possibilities. If you are eliminating answer choices and realize that the last one you are left with is also wrong, don't panic. Start over and consider each choice again. There may be something you missed the first time that you will realize on the second pass.

### Avoid Fact Traps

Don't be distracted by an answer choice that is factually true but doesn't answer the question. You are looking for the choice that answers the question. Stay focused on what the question is asking for so you don't accidentally pick an answer that is true but incorrect. Always go back to the question and make sure the answer choice you've selected actually answers the question and is not merely a true statement.

### Extreme Statements

In general, you should avoid answers that put forth extreme actions as standard practice or proclaim controversial ideas as established fact. An answer choice that states the "process should be used in certain situations, if..." is much more likely to be correct than one that states the "process should be discontinued completely." The first is a calm rational statement and doesn't even make a definitive, uncompromising stance, using a hedge word *if* to provide wiggle room, whereas the second choice is a radical idea and far more extreme.

## Benchmark

As you read through the answer choices and you come across one that seems to answer the question well, mentally select that answer choice. This is not your final answer, but it's the one that will help you evaluate the other answer choices. The one that you selected is your benchmark or standard for judging each of the other answer choices. Every other answer choice must be compared to your benchmark. That choice is correct until proven otherwise by another answer choice beating it. If you find a better answer, then that one becomes your new benchmark. Once you've decided that no other choice answers the question as well as your benchmark, you have your final answer.

## Predict the Answer

Before you even start looking at the answer choices, it is often best to try to predict the answer. When you come up with the answer on your own, it is easier to avoid distractions and traps because you will know exactly what to look for. The right answer choice is unlikely to be word-for-word what you came up with, but it should be a close match. Even if you are confident that you have the right answer, you should still take the time to read each option before moving on.

# General Strategies

## Tough Questions

If you are stumped on a problem or it appears too hard or too difficult, don't waste time. Move on! Remember though, if you can quickly check for obviously incorrect answer choices, your chances of guessing correctly are greatly improved. Before you completely give up, at least try to knock out a couple of possible answers. Eliminate what you can and then guess at the remaining answer choices before moving on.

## Check Your Work

Since you will probably not know every term listed and the answer to every question, it is important that you get credit for the ones that you do know. Don't miss any questions through careless mistakes. If at all possible, try to take a second to look back over your answer selection and make sure you've selected the correct answer choice and haven't made a costly careless mistake (such as marking an answer choice that you didn't mean to mark). This quick double check should more than pay for itself in caught mistakes for the time it costs.

## Pace Yourself

It's easy to be overwhelmed when you're looking at a page full of questions; your mind is confused and full of random thoughts, and the clock is ticking down faster than you would like. Calm down and maintain the pace that you have set for yourself. Especially as you get down to the last few minutes of the test, don't let the small numbers on the clock make you panic. As long as you are on track by monitoring your pace, you are guaranteed to have time for each question.

## Don't Rush

It is very easy to make errors when you are in a hurry. Maintaining a fast pace in answering questions is pointless if it makes you miss questions that you would have gotten right otherwise. Test writers like to

- 12 -

include distracting information and wrong answers that seem right. Taking a little extra time to avoid careless mistakes can make all the difference in your test score. Find a pace that allows you to be confident in the answers that you select.

## Keep Moving

Panicking will not help you pass the test, so do your best to stay calm and keep moving. Taking deep breaths and going through the answer elimination steps you practiced can help to break through a stress barrier and keep your pace.

# Final Notes

The combination of a solid foundation of content knowledge and the confidence that comes from practicing your plan for applying that knowledge is the key to maximizing your performance on test day. As your foundation of content knowledge is built up and strengthened, you'll find that the strategies included in this chapter become more and more effective in helping you quickly sift through the distractions and traps of the test to isolate the correct answer.

Now it's time to move on to the test content chapters of this book, but be sure to keep your goal in mind. As you read, think about how you will be able to apply this information on the test. If you've already seen sample questions for the test and you have an idea of the question format and style, try to come up with questions of your own that you can answer based on what you're reading. This will give you valuable practice applying your knowledge in the same ways you can expect to on test day.

**Good luck and good studying!**

# Factors Affecting Growth and Development

## Major Muscles

### Head, Neck, Shoulders, and Chest

The **head and neck** include the epicranius frontalis at the cranium's front; epicranius occipitalis at its back; orbicularis oculi around the eye; orbicularis oris around the mouth; buccinator in the cheek; zygomaticus in the cheekbone; platysma in the neck; masseter in the side of the face, connecting and controlling the jaws in chewing; temporalis in the side of the head (also used in chewing); sternocleidomastoid, running from the sternum (chest) along the side of the neck to behind the ear (mastoid) at the base of the skull; splenius capitis in the back of the neck, connecting to the skull's base; and semispinalis capitis in the upper back neck between shoulder and head, rotating the neck. **Shoulders and chest** include the trapezius, a triangle covering the neck, shoulder, and back; rhomboideus major connecting the shoulder blade (scapula) to the vertebrae; levator scapulae; serratus anterior; pectoralis major and minor in the chest; teres major and minor in the shoulder, connecting the upper arm (humerus) to the scapula; latissimus dorsi in the outer sides of the back, connecting to the arms; supraspinatus, a rotator cuff muscle in the shoulder; infraspinatus, a lower-shoulder abductor/external rotator; and deltoid on shoulder top/upper arm.

### Abdomen, Arms, Thighs and Hips, and Lower Legs

**Abdominal muscles** include, outer-to-inner, external (downward/forward) and internal (upward/forward) oblique, transversus abdominis (horizontal/forward), and rectus abdominis. The **arms** contain the biceps brachii (upper-arm front); triceps brachii (upper-arm back); forearm brachioradialis, flexing at the elbow; forearm flexor carpi radialis and flexor carpi ulnaris, flexing and respectively abducting and adducting the hand; extensor carpi ulnaris, extending and adducting the wrist; and extensor digitorum, controlling the middle four fingers. The **thighs and hips** include the rectus femoris, vastus medialis, vastus lateralis, and vastus intermedius, the four quadriceps (front thigh) muscles; sartorius, the body's longest muscle running from the spine along the thigh to the knee; gracilis, running along the inner thigh from pubic bone to tibia; adductor longus, a hip muscle in the inner thigh controlling inward and sideways movement; gluteus maximus, medius, and minimus, three of four buttock muscles—gluteus maximus being the body's largest, strongest muscle; tensor fasciae latae, the fourth, smallest buttock muscle, to the front and side of the others in the thigh; and biceps femoris, semitendinosus, and semimembranosus, the hamstring muscles in the back thigh. The **lower leg** includes the gastrocnemius, plantaris, and soleus in the calf; and tibialis anterior, a dorsal foot flexor.

## Human Skeleton

The human adult skeleton has 206 bones forming a framework that protect and support the internal organs, and work with the muscles to effect movement. The skeleton has two parts: the **axial skeleton**, containing the skull bones, hyoid bone, spinal vertebrae, ribs, and sternum; and the **appendicular skeleton**, containing the pectoral girdle bones, pelvic girdle bones, and extremities, i.e., upper and lower limbs. The **cranial** (skull) bones include the frontal (front), parietal (side), occipital (back), sphenoid (middle) and ethmoid (between the eyes, above the nose) bones. The **facial** bones include the zygomatic (cheekbone), lacrimal (inner eye near the tear duct), and maxilla (several fused upper jaw) and mandible (lower jaw) bones. The **vertebral** bones include the atlas, or first cervical vertebra, supporting the skull; the axis, or second cervical vertebra; the third through seventh cervical vertebrae, i.e., the back bones at the neck level; the 12 thoracic vertebrae, i.e., the back bones at the upper back level; the five lumbar vertebrae, i.e., the back bones at the lower back level; and the sacrum or five sacral vertebrae, the back

- 14 -

bones at the level of the pelvis and hips; and three to five small, often fused bones comprising the coccyx or tailbone.

## Upper and Lower Limbs

Bones of the human **upper limbs** include the clavicle, or collarbone; scapula, or shoulder blade; humerus, or upper arm bone; radius and ulna, or forearm bones; carpal or wrist bones; metacarpal or hand bones; and phalanges, or finger bones. The bones of the human **lower limbs** include the os coxa or hip bone, composed of the ilium at the top, pubis at the lower front, and ischium at the lower back, which are fused together. The left and right os coxae form the pelvic girdle. The pelvis is made up of the os coxae, sacrum, and coccyx or tailbone. The femur is the thigh bone, which includes a head, neck, greater trochanter, and shaft. The patella is the knee bone, including a base, medial and lateral facets that articulate (connect) with the femur, and apex. The tibia is the shinbone, to which the thinner fibula (pin) is connected; they connect to the femur. The metatarsal and tarsal bones are the ankle and foot bones; the calcaneus is the heel bone.

## Major Human Body Systems

The **skeletal system** provides the body's structural framework of bones to support it, protects the soft vital organs from harm, collaborates with muscles to produce body movement, stores calcium in the bones, and produces red blood cells in the bone marrow. The **integumentary system** includes the hair, nails, glands, nerves, and especially skin, which is the body's largest sensory organ. It provides tactile sensation, including pain, heat, cold, pressure, and pleasure; regulates loss of blood and other fluids; synthesizes vitamin D; and protects deeper tissues. The **muscular system** maintains body posture, creates body movements with the support of the bones, generates heat, and consumes energy. The **immune system** is composed of parts of many other systems, including parts of the lymphatic system, the cardiovascular system, the respiratory system, the gastrointestinal system, etc. It works to protect and defend the body against disease organisms and other foreign elements.

The **lymphatic system** retrieves fluids that leak from the capillaries (small blood vessels), and contains the white blood cells, hence supporting parts of the immune system. The **cardiovascular system** transports nutrients containing oxygen and other necessities throughout the bloodstream, transports gaseous wastes for elimination, and supports immune functions. The **urinary system** regulates balances of fluids, electrolytes, and pH; and removes nitrogenous wastes from the blood. The **digestive system** breaks foods down into proteins, sugars, amino acids, and other building blocks for the body's metabolic processes, growth, replenishment, and repair. The **respiratory system** performs gas exchanges by taking in, warming, and moistening environmental air, delivering oxygen, and expelling carbon dioxide. The **nervous system** provides sensory input, interprets the sensory information, evokes and signals responses, and coordinates muscle functions. The **endocrine system** secretes hormones that regulate the body's growth, metabolism, and general functionality. The **reproductive system** produces hormones enabling reproduction; and creates, nurtures, and delivers offspring.

## Jean Piaget's Theory of Cognitive Development

## Sensorimotor Stage

From birth to around 2 years, infants are in what psychologist **Jean Piaget** termed the **sensorimotor stage** because they learn about the world through sensory input and motor output. They see, hear, smell, taste, and feel; and they move their body parts in response to these sensory perceptions. They learn about the environment through looking, listening, sucking, and grasping things around them. During this stage, babies develop object permanence: the realization that things out of sight still exist. Piaget divided the sensorimotor stage into six substages. (1) **Reflexes** (0-1 month): inborn reflexive actions like sucking and looking. (2) **Primary circular reactions** (1-4 months): babies form new schemas (concepts),

- 15 -

intentionally repeating accidental actions they find rewarding, e.g., thumb-sucking. (3) **Secondary circular reactions** (4-8 months): babies purposefully repeat actions to cause environmental effects, e.g., picking objects up to suck them. (4) **Coordination of reactions** (8-12 months): children combine schemas to accomplish goals; imitate others' behaviors; act intentionally; and understand objects, e.g., that rattles make sounds if shaken. (5) **Tertiary circular reactions** (12-18 months): children perform trial-and-error experiments, e.g., sounds and movements to get parental attention. (6) **Early representational thought** (18-24 months): children use symbols to represent other things, e.g., make-believe and pretend play, developing understanding not just via actions but mental operations.

## Preoperational Stage

Jean Piaget called the stage from around 2-7 years **preoperational** because children cannot yet perform logical, formal mental operations. Children extend the symbolic representation they began to develop in the previous sensorimotor stage, playing adult roles, using toys as animals, etc. They develop language. Piaget defined preoperational children as **egocentric**, i.e., they cannot see others' points of view—literally and physically as well as abstractly. Piaget found children could easily select the picture among three showing a scene they had observed; but asked to select the picture of what people sitting in a different location saw, they would still select the picture of what they themselves saw. They neither manipulate ideas or information mentally nor comprehend logic concerning concrete objects. Piaget's experiments with conservation of volume, quantity, number, length, weight, and mass showed preoperational children who did not understand these properties were conserved regardless of changes in shape, arrangement, or appearance—e.g., objects numbered the same whether clustered together or spread out; or liquid was the same amount despite container shapes. Piaget also characterized preoperational thinking as **intuitive** (non-logical), **magical** (believing their thoughts cause events), and **animistic** (ascribing human emotions and motivations to inanimate objects).

## Concrete Operations Stage

Jean Piaget described concrete operations in children aged 7-11 as developing logical thought, but only about concrete events and objects; he found they still had difficulty understanding hypothetical and/or abstract ideas. **Concrete operational children** are better at inductive logic (i.e., moving from a specific event to a general principle) than deductive logic (i.e., moving from a general principle to predict a specific outcome). A milestone of this stage is developing **reversibility**, i.e., that actions and categories can be reversed. Whereas preoperational children focused on only one aspect of a problem at a time, which Piaget termed **centration** (e.g., they thought more liquid was in a taller, thinner container than a shorter, wider container even though it was the same amount because they focused only on container height), in concrete operations, Piaget found children **decentrate**, considering multiple components of a problem simultaneously. The egocentrism of preoperational thinking gives way to **sociocentrism**, i.e., children now realize others have different viewpoints from their own. However, they may not yet know what is included in others' perspectives, though they know they exist. Children can think logically in this stage if they have concrete objects and events to observe and manipulate.

## Formal Operations Stage

What Jean Piaget called formal operations occurs around ages 11-12 and continues into adulthood. Piaget found that pre-adolescents and adolescents develop the ability to think logically without needing concrete objects as they did in the previous concrete operations stage; perform deductive reasoning; plan systematically; and understand abstract concepts like justice, morality, democracy, etc. In **formal operations**, people can manipulate information mentally, reason through hypothetical situations, and determine specific outcomes from general principles (deductive reasoning), which mathematics and sciences often require. Whereas concrete operational children rely on their actual experiences, in formal operations they develop the ability to consider **potential consequences** of actions and possible outcomes, which is necessary for long-term planning. Rather than solving problems through trial-and-

- 16 -

error, they use logic to develop organized, **methodical approaches**. Considering and rejecting ineffective solutions without attempting them enhances their efficiency. Thinking abstractly without objects and imagining hypothetical outcomes enables adolescents to engage in the systematic decision-making and future planning required of them at their ages.

## Howard Gardner's Multiple Intelligences as Different Learning Styles

Students with strong **visual-spatial intelligence** are very aware of their environments. They conceptualize in terms of physical space, as sailors and architects do. They enjoy reading maps, drawing, completing jigsaw puzzles, and visually daydreaming. Good teaching materials and methods for them include models, drawings, charts, graphics, photos, physical and verbal imagery, 3-D models, videos, videoconferencing, multimedia, TV, and texts with many illustrations, diagrams, and graphs. Students with strong **bodily-kinesthetic intelligence** are highly aware of their bodies and effectively use them, like surgeons and dancers. They like moving, touching things, and making things. They communicate effectively via body language. They learn well through hands-on learning, acting out concepts, physical activity, role-playing, and being taught using real objects and equipment. Students with strong **musical intelligence** are sensitive to sound and rhythm. In addition to loving music, they respond to all environmental sounds. Playing music in the background may help them study. They learn well by learning verbal information as song lyrics, using rhythmic speech, and beating or tapping out rhythms. Compatible teaching uses audio recordings, live music, musical instruments, radios, and multimedia presentations.

Students with high **logical-mathematical intelligence** excel at calculations and reasoning, thinking abstractly and conceptually. They detect and explore patterns and relationships, ask cosmic questions, enjoy solving puzzles, and conducting experiments. Before addressing details of a problem, they must learn and formulate concepts. Compatible teaching strategies include offering mysteries, investigations, and logic games. Students with strong **linguistic intelligence** are effective with words. Their auditory skills are highly developed. They often think in words, not pictures, feelings, sounds, etc. They enjoy reading, writing, and playing word games. Teaching methods and tools include reading books with them, encouraging them to see and pronounce words, lectures, books, computers, multimedia materials, voice recorders, and spoken-word recordings. Students with high **intrapersonal intelligence** tune into their own feelings and are "loners," avoiding social interaction. They are independent, confident, strong-willed, motivated, opinionated, intuitive, and wise. Introspective reflection and independent study, journals, diaries, books, creative materials, time, and privacy are useful instructional methods and materials. Students with strong **interpersonal intelligence** are social, interactive, empathetic, and "street-smart." Group activities, dialogues, seminars, telephones, audio- and video-conferencing or Skyping, and email are good teaching methods and tools.

## Early Childhood Physical Growth and Development

From birth to 3 years, children typically grow to twice their height and gain four times their weight. Whereas infants' heads are nearly one-fourth of their full body length, toddlers develop more balanced proportions similar to those of adults. They overcome the disequilibrium of changing so rapidly: generally, children usually start walking around 1 year, climb stairs holding banisters around 18 months, and master running around 2 years. Three-year-olds have normally mastered sitting, walking, toilet training, eating with spoons, scribbling, and demonstrating enough eye-hand coordination to throw and catch a ball. Most children develop sufficient gross motor skills for balancing on one foot and skipping; fine motor skills for controlling scissors, crayons, and pencils; and further refinement of their body proportions between 5 and 8 years old. Implications of the period from birth to 8 years include its being a critical time for developing many **fundamental skills**; hence it is also a critical time for **developmental delays** to be identified and to receive early intervention, which has proven more effective than later intervention.

- 17 -

## Physical Growth and Development During Middle Childhood

When contrasted with the rapid, obvious, and dramatic changes of early childhood, **middle childhood** is a period of slower physical growth and development. Children continue to grow, but at a slower and steadier rate than when they were younger. In middle childhood, muscle mass develops and children grow stronger. Their **strength** and **coordination in motor skills** advance, evidenced by gradually improving skills for tasks like accurately throwing baseballs; walking on tiptoes; broad-jumping; skipping; lacing and tying shoes; cutting and pasting paper; and drawing people including heads, bodies, arms, and legs. Children can typically dress themselves unassisted, skip using both feet, ride bicycles, skate, and bounce a ball four to six times by the time they are 6. By the time they are around 9, children usually can learn to sew and build models; by age 10, children are capable of catching fly balls. Their hair darkens slightly, and their skin appearance and texture more closely approximate those of adults. Girls and boys in middle childhood are usually similar in height until **puberty**, which frequently begins near the end of middle childhood, averaging around 10 years in girls and 11 years in boys.

## Physical Growth and Development in Adolescence

The most salient physical growth and development aspects of adolescence undoubtedly involve **puberty**. Girls today develop the first signs of puberty, breast buds, before adolescence in late middle childhood, at an average of 10 years within a range between 8 and 13 years; peak growth in height, weight, muscle mass, etc. is around a year after puberty's onset and menarche about two years after, averaging before age 13. Boys begin puberty around a year later than girls, averaging around 11 years within a range of 9-14 years, with peak growth around two years after onset. The first signs are testicular enlargement and scrotal reddening and thinning. Both girls and boys go through a series of **stages** that make up puberty. These stages incorporate changes to almost all of their body systems, including most notably the **skeletal, muscular, and reproductive systems**. Voices deepen, and body hair and other secondary sex characteristics develop. Acne often plagues adolescents. Whereas girls and boys are about the same heights in middle childhood, girls frequently become taller in their early teens. However, boys catch up within one or two years, typically growing taller than girls. Puberty accounts for around 25 percent of individual growth in height.

## Basic Principles of Genetics

Humans have 23 pairs of **chromosomes** (bundles of DNA and genes) in the nucleus of body cells, with half of each pair coming from each parent. The chromosomes in each cell contain 35,000 or more **genes**, which carry instructions for producing proteins. Chromosomes carry the blueprint for the individual, including traits inherited from the parents. There are two types of chromosomes:

- **Autosomal**: Pairs 1 to 22, ranked in size according to the number of base pairs they each contain with 1 being the largest and 22 being the smallest.
- **Allosomal** (Sex): Pair 23. XX for female and XY for male.

Genetic disorders occur when there is a **mutation** (spontaneous or transmitted) in one or more genes. Diseases are classified as **autosomal recessive** if both parents must carry the defective autosomal gene in order to pass it on to offspring, and they are classified as **autosomal dominant** if only one parent must carry the defective gene. Genetic disorders may also be X-linked recessive or dominant and Y-linked.

## Factors That Can Affect Heredity

**Inheritance** is complex. In some cases, a disorder is directly inherited through transmission of defective **genes**, such as with sickle cell disease; however, in other cases, people may inherit a defective gene that increases risk but does not necessarily result in disease. These include the BRCA1 and BRCA2 gene mutations that increase risk of breast and ovarian cancer as well as the HER2 gene mutation associated with estrogen-progesterone-positive breast cancers. Many **environmental factors** may spur the development of diseases with a genetic component or may cause genetic mutations. Most **sporadic genetic mutations** are harmless, but some result in disease. Environmental factors that may affect outcomes include stress, smoking, poor diet, exposure to second-hand smoke, exposure to ultraviolet (UV) radiation, excessive drinking, poor air quality, some viruses, and exposure to toxic substances. Researchers have theorized that there may be a genetic component to many common disorders.

> **Review Video: Gene Mutation**
> Visit mometrix.com/academy and enter code: 955485

## Hereditary Disorders and Their Characteristics

### Autosomal Recessive

If a disease is inherited in the autosomal recessive pattern, each parent must be a carrier and pass on the defective gene to the offspring, resulting in a 25% chance that an offspring will develop the disease (two defective copies) and a 50% chance that the offspring will be a carrier (one defective copy). Common autosomal recessive disorders include the following:

- **Cystic fibrosis** - Chronic progressive disease of the mucous glands, causing blockage in the respiratory system and gastrointestinal system and affecting most body systems. Blockage in the pancreatic ducts results in impaired digestion of fats and proteins and malabsorption. Respiratory infections, pneumonia, constipation, and bowel obstructions are common.
- **Sickle cell disease (SCD)** - Disease that results in sickle-shaped red blood cells, which clump together and occlude vessels, causing severely painful occlusive crises. Patients are chronically anemic and often require routine transfusions and medications. Onset within six months of birth. SCD affects primarily African Americans and people of South American descent.

### Autosomal Dominant

If a disease is inherited in the autosomal dominant pattern, only one parent must pass on the defective gene and each pregnancy carries a 50% risk that the child will inherit the disease. There is no carrier state. Common autosomal dominant disorders include the following:

- **Achondroplasia (dwarfism)** - Disorder in which the body can't respond normally to growth factors, resulting in short stature; large, prominent forehead; and short arms, legs, and fingers. Some may develop hydrocephalus. Chronic otitis media, lordosis (swayback), and orthopedic problems are common.
- **Huntington disease** - This is a progressive fatal neurodegenerative disorder characterized by motor, cognitive, and psychiatric disturbances. Onset is usually between ages 35 and 45, but the juvenile-onset variety has onset before age 20.
- **Marfan syndrome** - Disorder of the connective tissue characterized by elongated head; long arms and legs; scoliosis; crowded teeth; unusual stretch marks; and cardiac abnormalities including aortic enlargement, which can result in rupture and sudden death.
- **Otosclerosis** - Disorder with abnormal bone growth in the middle ear, resulting in hearing loss.

### X-Linked Recessive

Because males have only one X chromosome, X-linked recessive disorders usually affect only males because females have one healthy X chromosome that can compensate for the defective one, although daughters of a mother with the recessive gene have a 50% chance of being carriers. If the father carries the defective gene, sons are unaffected, but all daughters are carriers.

- **Duchenne muscular dystrophy (MD)** - This progressive fatal disease of boys is characterized by degeneration of muscle fibers; muscle wasting; and, frequently, mental retardation. Onset is at age 3 to 4, and most are wheelchair bound by age 12 with death occurring during adolescence. Boys tire easily and exhibit lordosis (swayback) and a waddling gait. Other MD varieties are less common and may be milder or have some different clinical symptoms.
- **Fragile X** - Most common inheritable cause of mental retardation. Condition includes macrocephaly (large head), macroorchidism (large testicles), and low IQ.
- **Hemophilia (A, B, and von Willebrand)** - Disorder is characterized by deficiency of blood-clotting proteins causing bruising and excessive bleeding.

X-Linked Dominant and Y-Linked

X-linked disorders can be inherited by males and females, but they are more common in females. A father with a defective gene on the X-chromosome gives the disorder to all daughters but no sons (who inherit their X chromosome from their mother). A positive mother, however, has a chance of passing the trait to 50% of female and male children.

- **Rett syndrome** - This disorder affects only females and becomes evident at about age 6 to 18 months because of a gene defect that impairs brain development, so the head fails to grow properly, resulting in progress microcephaly and cognitive impairment. Hands and feet are small, and the child often exhibits repetitive hand movements. Autistic-like behavior is common.
- **Incontinentia pigmenti** - This rare disorder, which affects males more than females, is characterized by excessive deposits of melanin in the skin, resulting in unusual patterns of skin discoloration.

**Y-linked disorders** affect only males and are much less common because they result in male infertility and impaired development of male secondary sexual characteristics, so those affected are rarely able to procreate.

**Aging Process**

Infancy to Early Childhood

The stages of aging in infancy, toddlerhood, and early childhood include the following:

- **Infancy** (0–1): The infant is almost completely dependent on adults for his or her needs. The child grows rapidly and begins to develop both fine and gross motor skills as well as an understanding of simple words. The infant begins to display some distinct personality traits.
- **Toddlerhood** (1–3): Growth slows but cognitive ability increases as the child begins to use words and shows beginning problem-solving skills. The toddler begins to enjoy playing side by side with others and has improved fine and gross motor skills. The toddler shows increasing independence and may react negatively if thwarted.
- **Early childhood** (3 to 6): The preschool years are characterized by steady physical growth, increased fine and gross motor skills, and increased visual acuity. The child begins to engage in associative play and interactions with other children. Language skills improve markedly. Personality traits of infancy persist and may be at odds with learning environments.

## Mid-Childhood to Adolescence

The stages of aging in mid-childhood to adolescence include the following:

- **Mid-childhood** (6–8): The child loses baby teeth and begins to mature physically. The child relies on concrete experiences but makes improvements at problem solving. The child begins to enjoy cooperating with others and team sports. The child's temperament remains relatively unchanged, but communication skills improve.
- **Late childhood** (8–12): Girls undergo a growth spurt at about age 9, and boys start a year or so later with the maturing of internal organs and lengthening of the long bones. The child understands the concept of conservation (matter remains unchanged when its form changes) and continues to enjoy group activities and sports. The child may become interested in sexuality and gender differences.
- **Adolescence** (12–18): Sexual maturation occurs, and the adolescent is concerned with identity. The adolescent can reason abstractly and may begin to act independently and to rebel. Peer interactions are especially important. The adolescent may undergo a period of stress before developing a strong identity.

## Adulthood

The stages of aging in adulthood include the following:

- **Early adulthood** (18–35): Physical and social changes emerge slowly as the adult makes choices about a career and sets goals. The person may experiment with lifestyle and sexuality and expands social circles. Problem-solving skills improve, and moral development continues.
- **Middle adulthood** (35–50): This is a period of relative stability and good health, although bad habits such as smoking may begin to cause impairment. The person has many obligations and responsibilities, including family and job, and may experience increased stress. Social relationships are often stable and rewarding.
- **Maturity** (50–80): The person experiences gradual physical decline and may have serious illnesses. Some may show cognitive decline and increased incidence of chronic and acute illnesses. The person may have an improved sense of well-being, self-confidence, and emotional stability.
- **Late adulthood** (80+): The person may have chronic illness and increased dependency on others, such as adult children. Cognition varies, with short-term memory loss being common. Many live alone or in assisted living.

## Methods of Care for the Terminally Ill

Because of advances in the treatment of disease and longer life expectancies, the process of dying for the terminally ill is often prolonged. Methods of care for the terminally ill include the following:

- **Aggressive treatment**: This includes life support, such as tube feedings, transfusions, IVs, and ventilators, and it often involves hospitalization in an effort to prolong life as much as possible, often regardless of the quality of life.
- **Comfort care**: This approach provides only measures that promote comfort, such as adequate pain management and emotional support, with avoidance of life support and extraordinary measures to prolong life, although curative treatments may be used.
- **Hospice care**: This is one model of comfort care in which the person stops curative treatment and remains in the home environment with the assistance of home health hospice caregivers to support the person and family members. Some people may opt for this if their condition is advanced or after aggressive treatment has failed.

## Aspects of Death, Dying, and Grieving Among Various Cultures and Traditions in Society

### Asians and Hispanics

- **Asians (Buddhists)** - Asians often believe that people should not hear bad news about their health, and the family may shield a person from knowledge that he or she is dying. People may be stoic in the face of pain. Buddhists believe in rebirth and may want monks to chant during the dying process to ensure a happy rebirth. The spirit is believed to linger around the body after death, so the body must be treated respectfully. Grieving is usually done privately.
- **Hispanics** - Most are Christian and Catholic and may want a priest present to administer the Sacraments of Reconciliation and Holy Communion (last rites). Males, especially, often believe that admitting to pain is a sign of weakness. Care is often provided by female family members. Family members commonly grieve openly and hold a wake after death to celebrate the person's life and to talk about memories. The funeral usually includes a processional and a Mass.

### Middle Easterners

- **Middle Easterners (Muslims)** - The sick and dying are usually cared for by a female family member in the home, although some may be hospitalized. The person's bed should be facing Mecca, and the person should be assisted with washing prior to prayers as long as the he or she is able. Pain management is acceptable. A Koran should be at the bedside so visitors (often many) can read from it. On death, the eyes are closed and the arms and legs straightened. The family will wash and wrap the body. Muslims are never cremated, and postmortem exams are usually not allowed. Burial should take place within 24 hours. Females are usually prohibited from attending a burial, and demonstrations of grief should not be excessive. The family has three days of mourning after the burial during which they greet visitors. The grave is visited daily or weekly, and prayers are said for 40 days. Grief counseling is often considered to be intrusive.

## Erikson's Theory of Psychosocial Development

### First Stage

Each stage of Erik Erikson's theory of psychosocial development involves a **nuclear conflict**. When this conflict is successfully resolved, Erikson proposed a positive outcome that the individual would realize. Erikson called the stage from birth to around 18 months **basic trust vs. mistrust**. The key event during this stage is **nursing**. When an infant's needs are met fully, consistently, reliably, and with affection and care, the baby develops a basic sense of trust in the world and feels secure and safe. On the other hand, if the baby's needs are not adequately met, met only inconsistently, or the parent or caregiver does not give the infant a sense of love, caring, and affection, then the baby develops a sense of basic mistrust in the world, finds it unpredictable and inconsistent, and feels fearful and insecure. Erikson said the positive outcome of the infant stage of basic trust vs. mistrust is **hope**. Babies nurtured properly develop confidence and optimism through feeling secure and trusting. Those not well cared for develop feelings of worthlessness through feeling insecure and mistrustful.

### Second Stage

Erik Erikson named the nuclear conflict of the toddlerhood (ages 18-36 months) stage as **autonomy vs. shame and self-doubt**. The positive outcome of successfully resolving this conflict, Erikson found, is **will**. The significant event during this stage is **toilet training**. Toddlers, in learning to control their bladders and bowels and to control their bodies for walking, develop autonomy (independence) through developing this self-control. They develop fine motor skills for manipulating small objects as well as gross motor skills. Concurrently with physical skills, they learn right vs. wrong. Developing independence helps develop self-esteem. Properly nurtured children display confidence and pride. Those not well cared for, and/or who may be unable to learn the requisite skills, feel ashamed and doubt themselves. This stage includes the "terrible twos," when children naturally display stubbornness, defiance, and temper tantrums in the process of asserting their individual will. Children who do not develop appropriate autonomy in this stage lack self-confidence, are afraid to try new things, and may be overly dependent on parents.

Third Stage

Erik Erikson named the preschool (ages 3-5) stage for the nuclear conflict **initiative vs. guilt**. He identified the positive outcome of successfully resolving this conflict as **purpose**. Children in this stage engage in pretend and make-believe play, imitating their parents. They also explore the environment, wanting to know why things are as they are and happen as they do. They display initiative by taking action, exerting power and control over their environments. Successful children realize a sense of purpose. Those who exert too much power, causing damage to the environment and incurring parental disapproval, develop guilt feelings. Instead of purpose, they feel frustration about not being able to attain their desires or accomplish their goals. Children's most significant relationships during this stage are with their **immediate family**. Erikson was influenced by Freud, but unlike Freud's psychosexual orientation, Erikson's was **psychosocial**. Freud described the Oedipal conflict: unconsciously desiring the opposite-sex parent and wanting to eliminate the rival same-sex parent, the child resolves this through "identification with the aggressor"—wanting to be like the same-sex parent. Erikson saw this psychosocially as a **child-parent struggle**, resolved via "**social role identification**."

Fourth Stage

Erik Erikson characterized school-aged (6-12 years old) children as being in the stage centered on the nuclear conflict of **industry vs. inferiority**. He found that children who successfully resolved this conflict experienced the positive outcome of **competence**. At this time, children's focus shifts away from being exclusively on the parents, outward to the wider world of the **neighborhood** and the **school**, as they make new friends and learn new academic skills. While parents are still very important to school-age children, they are no longer the ultimate authorities they were in early childhood. As they acquire many types of new knowledge and skills, and create new products, successful children develop a sense of industry. Those who fail academically and/or socially develop feelings of inferiority, comparing themselves unfavorably to their peers. They feel incompetent and their self-esteem suffers. Children who succeed enjoy enhanced self-esteem and feel competent to handle the increased demands of their expanding environments.

Adolescence

Adolescents begin developing a sense of personal identity. In his theory, Erik Erikson named this stage of psychosocial development **identity vs. role confusion**. In the stages previous to this one, Erikson portrayed development in terms of how the parents cared for the child, and how the child reacted to that care or lack thereof. A key change in adolescence is that Erikson depicted this stage in terms of what the child does instead. The nuclear conflict in this stage revolves around the adolescent's efforts to discover his or her own **individual identity**. At the same time, the teenager is learning how to negotiate social interactions, how to fit in with peer groups, and developing an abstract concept of morality beyond the concrete ideas of right and wrong in earlier childhood. Some teens, unready for the responsibilities, withdraw into what Erikson termed **moratorium** to delay entering adulthood. In experimenting with and developing identity, adolescents experience strong ties and dedication to friends, ideals, and causes. Successful resolution of this stage's conflict has the positive outcome of **fidelity**; unsuccessful teens are confused about their roles and identities.

Young Adulthood

Erik Erikson described the stage of young adulthood (18-35 years) as centering on the nuclear conflict of **intimacy vs. isolation**. Young adults are primarily occupied with finding love and companionship through the development of **intimate relationships** with others. Erikson identified the positive outcome of successfully resolving this conflict as **love**. Young adults who do not succeed in finding another individual with whom they can form a satisfying relationship in which they can develop deep intimacy suffer the consequence of isolation. They feel isolated and lonely. At the time when Erikson was formulating his theory, it was more common for young adults also to marry, have children, and start their own families. In recent years, though, this often occurs later in life as many young adults defer domestic matters to pursue advanced educations and/or build and further their careers. Some young adults also spend longer times experimenting socially through dating multiple partners without settling on one; having series of less serious relationships; or a series of serious, intimate relationships which do not ultimately progress to lifetime commitments. Another influence on this stage is that more people are living much longer now, extending the duration of lifetime commitments.

Middle Adulthood

Erik Erikson called the nuclear conflict of middle adulthood (35-55/65 years) **generativity vs. stagnation**. He called the positive outcome of this conflict **care**. The focus in this stage is on work, career, and family. As they mature into increased control and responsibility, middle adults endeavor to create stability, and to produce something of value to society, i.e., **generativity**—they want to establish a legacy that will live beyond them. This can include raising successful children and seeing them have grandchildren; establishing successful businesses or organizations; making creative and industrial products; and discoveries, inventions, scholarships, research, etc. that give meaningful contributions to society and will exist even after they die. Significant relationships are in families, workplaces, local religious institutions, and other community entities. Successful adults feel they are caring for others and generating valuable products. Unsuccessful ones feel self-absorbed and/or stagnant, fearing their lives lack meaning and purposeful activity. Empty nests, career changes, and other major shifts in life are characteristic of this stage.

Eighth Stage and Proposed Ninth Stage

Erik Erikson described late adulthood (55-65 years to death) as involving the nuclear conflict of **ego integrity vs. despair**. Older adults review their lives, reflecting on what they have and/or have not accomplished. The positive outcome of resolving this conflict is **wisdom**. Older adults feeling they contributed value to society and lived meaningful lives experience fulfillment and contentment, i.e., **integrity of self**. They have learned and gained insight and perspective from their life experiences, attaining wisdom. They can accept impending death peacefully. Those feeling they failed to attain their goals, did not accomplish anything significant, had no clear purpose, and/or did not realize meaning in life instead experience regret, bitterness, fear of death, and despair. Erikson, who died just before his 92nd birthday, made notes about a ninth stage, **old age**, which his widow Joan completed. She wrote that the very old revisit all eight previous stages simultaneously, but with negative outcomes dominating positive ones (mistrust vs. trust, etc.) as life presents daily new challenges. The elderly can lose autonomy as abilities and roles diminish. They no longer have the "luxury" of retrospective despair. However, the positive outcome is "**gerotranscendence**"—peaceful readiness to progress to another stage of being.

**Rules For K-12 PE Classes**

Some recommended **rules for K-12 students** when attending PE classes include the following. Students should be prepared for PE class. This includes wearing only athletic shoes, not wearing dresses, and tying back long hair. Students should pay attention. This includes treating their classmates, PE teacher, and equipment the same way they want to be treated themselves, and not eating or bringing food to PE class or chewing gum during class. Students should be safe and respectful. This includes following directions, staying on task, and cooperating with others. Some PE teachers also inform students of consequences for violating rules during PE classes. One method has three steps:

- The PE teacher gives an oral, verbal warning that the student(s) is/are disobeying class rules.
- If the student(s) do/es not comply, the PE teacher gives the student(s) a time-out, i.e., brief individual separation from the class to take time and refocus their attention.
- After this initial time-out, if the student(s) is/are still not following the rules, the PE teacher assigns an additional time-out during which the student(s) must write a response, e.g., identifying which rule(s) he or she broke and what he or she will do to follow the rule(s).

### PE Rules Across the Country

A Maryland teacher uses "Freeze Up": stop, look at the teacher with eyes and ears open and mouth closed; "Move Under Control": avoiding running into persons or objects; "Get Equipment": politely (teacher demonstrates and explains this), carefully, one at a time; and "Reminder for Any Cue": the teacher asks, "What am I looking for?" This teacher also advises consistently praising good work when assisting students at school year's start and periodically after holidays and other school breaks during "refresher courses." An Oregon teacher tells students to "be nice" to one another and try their hardest; he comments that in 23 years of teaching elementary-grade PE, "I have found...pretty much everything can be handled within these two rules." An Illinois teacher adds the rule "Hands Off." He reviews rules often, asking students to identify and explain them; tests fifth through eighth graders on rules; and assigns papers for rule violation to fourth through eighth graders. Another uses the mnemonic acronym **RESPECT**: Right to learn; Effort; Safety; Purpose; Enthusiasm; Challenge; Trust/Team building. She engages students in "meaningful discussion" of these concepts in school's first week and includes the acronym in home letters and newsletters.

### PE Classroom Management Methods

Two Texas elementary teachers, male and female, use the acronym "**PEACE**" for their PE class rules: "Protect PE equipment; Enter and Exit quietly; Attention – follow directions the first time; Cooperation – work well with others; Esteem – respect others." These teachers issue "behavior tickets" to students breaking rules; tickets count against student conduct grades. A Wisconsin teacher writes rules on a stairway drawing for middle school, and posts them on a totem pole made by an art teacher for elementary grades. The stairway basement/pole bottom = "below-the-line" behavior. Step 1/second pole face = self-control. Step 2/third pole face = participation. Step 3/fourth pole face = self-directed learning. Step 4/fifth pole face = "kind and caring." She starts classes discussing these levels for the first two school weeks. She also has students self-assess their behavior quarterly, sending self-assessments to parents. A Pennsylvania elementary teacher uses these rules: "EYES watching, EARS listening, MOUTH quiet, HANDS to yourself, BRAIN thinking, RESPECT others, USE equipment correctly, and SAFETY – Stop, look, and listen." Two New Jersey teachers add "Win without boasting, lose without blaming," and high-fives before leaving to respect self, others, and the environment.

### PE Class Rules

One elementary school in Ohio has four rules: "Safety; Use good manners; Respect self, others and equipment; Have fun and enjoy PE class." They report students created these rules and follow them well. Teachers say that despite being broad, these rules "...for the most part, cover all that can happen in a [PE] class." A Connecticut teacher tells students to "Stop, look, and listen when [the] whistle blows"; "Demonstrate good sportsmanship"; and "Be responsible for gym equipment." His rewards are "1. Praise"; "2. Recreation day"; and "3. Awards." His consequences are "1. Time out"; "2. 'F' for the day"; "3. Letter home"; and "4. Referral to administrator." Another teacher instructs students to find a place in the

- 25 -

gym and prepare for the activities; show kindness to others; "know when to talk"; follow all instructions; and participate for the whole activity. Another teacher at a Maryland elementary school instructs students, "Always try your best. If someone in class is having trouble, HELP instead of laughing. The equipment belongs to all of us – let's take care of it! Keep hands, feet, and objects to yourself. When the teacher or your classmates are talking, you are not."

## Classroom Management Practices

A Wisconsin elementary PE teacher sends lists of expectations and rules to students' parents at the beginning of every school year. She issues students rules to enter the gym, sit on their numbers, and listen for directions; show courtesy and kindness to opponents and teammates; discuss any disputes using words, involving the teacher for unresolved disputes; stop any activity upon a signal; and leave the gym from their numbers, preparing for resuming classroom activities. For each class period, she first gives an "S" warning for violations; second violations get an "I", third violations a "T" = "**SIT**" = students sit out for specified durations until they can verbalize how they will return "ready to learn." This starts over with each class. Violations repeating across class periods incur parent letters. Parents must review the rules with their children and sign the letters for students to be permitted to return to PE class. An Alaska elementary teacher uses "**ABCD**": Act safely; Be prepared and be positive; Cooperate; Do your best"; and the motto "Have Fun – Work Hard – Learn." He comments, "For 18 years...these ABCD guidelines and...motto have served me well."

## Class Management

An elementary PE teacher in Washington state states three rules, all beginning with "**RESPECT**:" "Yourself (by working hard and safely every day to improve your fitness level); Others (always encourage, never put down); Equipment (by using it for intended purposes)." This teacher comments, "These are my posted rules. I haven't found anything I couldn't somehow relate to these rules." Another teacher in Illinois comments, "We believe in using a few simple rules that can cover any situation. These rules are sent to all parents at the beginning of the school year." These rules are: "Follow directions; Actively listen when a teacher is talking; Respect others; "Keep your hands and feet to yourself." An elementary teacher in New York state comments, "I explain each rule in some detail; the older the students, the more detail they get. For example, being a good listener means: eyes on the speaker, hands quiet, voices quiet, and raise your hand to speak." His rules for students are: "Be a good listener; Always follow directions; Treat others with respect; Use equipment correctly; Always try your best."

## Psychological Factors That Affect Learning

**Factors that influence learning** include readiness, i.e., physiological and psychological variables that affect individual ability and interest for learning; motivation, i.e., intrinsic conditions of needs and drives required for individuals to initiate goal-directed activities; reinforcement, i.e., actions, behaviors, and events, positive or negative, augmenting the probability that an individual will repeat the same response to a stimulus; and individual differences, i.e., student abilities, backgrounds, intelligence, personalities, and learning styles. In the cognitive stage of motor learning, learners understand the goal and nature of the activity, and make first attempts, including major errors. In the associative stage, learners practice to master skill timing; errors are more consistent and less numerous. In the autonomous stage, learner movements seem effortless and are well coordinated; errors are minimal; and performance automaticity enables learners to redirect attention to other skill aspects. Peak athletic performance is enabled by optimal individual arousal levels. Attention ranges from narrow to wide, and internal to external. Attentional flexibility is capacity for shifting voluntarily and quickly among different attentional styles according to task demands. Anxiety affects performance by narrowing and internalizing attentional focus.

Physical activity reduces general or non-competition anxiety; pre-competition warmups reduce performance anxiety, as well as prevent injuries and enhance movement.

## Five Conditions for Cooperative Learning

Merely grouping students does not achieve cooperative learning, which requires a common group goal whose achievement the group is rewarded. Conditions required for **cooperative learning** include these five basic elements:

- The students have positive interdependence and clearly perceive this.
- The students engage in substantial amounts of face-to-face, promotive interaction.
- The students are personally and individually accountable and responsible for achieving the goals of the group, and they clearly perceive they are.
- The students often make use of the small-group and interpersonal skills that are pertinent to their cooperative learning activity.
- The students regularly and frequently engage in group processing of their current group functioning to improve the effectiveness of the group in the future.

All effective cooperative relationships, including work groups, partner learning, peer tutoring, peer mediation, families, etc., always incorporate these five fundamental conditions or elements. Cooperative relationships do not necessarily occur naturally through simply grouping students; teachers need to structure and manage them for students.

## Patterns of Group Learning

Students in **cooperative groups** first learn skills, procedures, knowledge, and strategies together. Then they apply this learning individually to show they have mastered it personally. Teachers must evaluate each individual student's contribution to group work; give individual students and groups constructive feedback; help groups eliminate work redundancy by multiple members; and assure all members' responsibility for their final results. Six ways to structure **individual accountability** in cooperative student groups are:

- Keep group size small to increase individual accountability.
- Give each individual student a test.
- Randomly call on individual students to present group work to the teacher or class for oral examinations.
- Observe each student group and record how often each member contributes to the group.
- In each group, assign one student to the function of checker. This student asks other members of his or her group to explain rationales and reasoning behind the group answers they formulate.
- Have individual students teach what they have learned to another. "Simultaneous explaining" is when all students participate in this activity.

## Positive Interdependence

In the shared responsibility termed **positive interdependence**, students perceive they cannot succeed unless their group mates do, and vice versa, and they must coordinate their work with other members' work to accomplish any task. Students perceive that reciprocally, their group mates' work benefits them and their work benefits their group mates. Students maximize the learning of all small-group members when they collaborate by giving each other mutual encouragement and support, sharing resources, and celebrating their group success. When students clearly comprehend positive interdependence, they realize no member of their group gets a free ride: every member's work is indispensable and necessary

- 27 -

for the group to succeed. They also understand that every member of the group has unique roles, responsibilities, and resources; therefore, every member makes a unique contribution to the collective endeavor. In **cooperative learning groups**, all students are responsible for learning the assigned content, and for assuring every member of their group also learns it.

## Structuring Positive Interdependence

- **"Positive Goal Interdependence"**: Students understand that the only way to accomplish their learning goals is if all group members also achieve their learning goals. A shared goal unites the group, giving them a concrete reason for the group's existence. Students must care about how much every other group member learns, and must perceive that they "sink or swim together." To establish this perception, teachers must structure a clear mutual or group goal, incorporated in every lesson. For example, the teacher might assign the goal that each student learns the assigned information, and also makes sure all members of his or her group learn it.
- **"Positive Reward – Celebrate Interdependence"**: The teacher gives every group member the same reward for accomplishing group goals. Teachers may also include joint rewards adding to goal interdependence; for example, each student gets five extra credit points if all group members score 90 percent or higher on the test. Teachers may give students individual test grades, group grades for overall results, and extra credit for all members' meeting test criteria. Experts find cooperation quality enhanced through regularly celebrating group success and effort.

## Organizing Positive Interdependence

- **"Positive Resource Interdependence"**: Every group member only has part of the information, materials, or resources needed to complete a task; therefore, members must combine resources to attain group goals. To accentuate cooperative group relationships, teachers may give students limited resources that they have to share, e.g., one copy of the task or problem for each group; or they can use the "jigsaw procedure," only giving one piece or part of the necessary resources to each group member, and they then must fit their pieces together to make a whole.
- **"Positive Role Interdependence"**: Each group member is assigned a role, specifying responsibilities needed for the group to complete a joint task. Each role is interconnected and complementary with the others. For example, roles include reader, recorder, participation encourager, understanding checker, and knowledge elaborator. Numerous well-controlled, high-quality research studies show checking for understanding correlates significantly with higher student learning and achievement levels.

## External Variables Affecting Performance

**External factors** are things outside ourselves, over which we usually have little or no control but which still have impacts on our physical performance. Weather in outdoor environments can have helpful or detrimental impacts on physical performance, depending on the activity. For example, a strong wind blowing steadily can interfere with performance when playing tennis, but will aid performance when sailing a boat. Equipment is another external variable. Although individual or team performance is aided by better equipment, there is also always a chance of equipment malfunction or failure. Technology is an external variable gaining importance as it develops and advances. Video and computer technology enable more precise and sophisticated analysis of sports and movement techniques. Computer technology also enhances equipment capabilities and use. In sports, other players constitute an external variable. Performance is affected by both teammates and opponents. Poor teammate performance can interfere; good teammate performance can inspire. Poor or good opponent performance can make competing easier and less challenging, or harder and more challenging. Decisions made by referees, umpires, and other officials are external factors that can increase or destroy motivation.

### Relative Availability of Resources

According to research findings, **smaller** PE class sizes and student-teacher ratios improve student safety, activity levels, and learning as well as how much time students participate in PE, whereas **larger** class sizes and student-teacher ratios correlate with decreased physical activity by students. Also, in schools with enough teachers teaching only PE and no other subjects, students receive more PE weekly. Student activity levels and physical fitness knowledge correlate positively with numbers of available, qualified PE teachers. Teachers having to teach both PE and other subjects give shorter lessons, with less student physical activity. Similarly to human resources, material and curricular **resources** affect student physical activity during PE classes, directly influencing how much of class includes student engagement in moderate-to-vigorous physical activity (MVPA). Educational researchers are reaching increasing consensus that standards-based PE curricula augment students' physical activity. Access to safe, appropriate, well-maintained, aesthetically appealing facilities and environments also enhance physical activity. Another resource contributing to greater opportunities for physical activity during PE classes is having enough exercise and sports equipment, suitable for students' sizes and in good condition.

### Amounts of Physically Active Time

Researchers find that one mechanism whereby students are physically active during less of their PE classes is the proportion of time PE teachers must devote to **administrative tasks**. For example, studies have revealed PE teachers may take up to 21 percent of their class time on class management and administrative duties. This can be decreased by providing sufficient resources: high student-teacher ratio and large classes entail more time taking attendance and making transitions between activities. Similarly, equipment selection and transitions among spaces take more time when access to suitable equipment and facilities is inadequate. A positive influence increasing student PE class time spent in physical activity is access to curriculum resources aligned with best PE practices, particularly when physical educators use these resources in focused, organized lesson planning. In some studies, investigators have found that the minority of schools studied offered PE every day, averaging fewer than three days weekly; average lessons lasted less than 47 minutes; and students were very active only during one-fourth of class time, spending over 20 percent of the time walking, over 20 percent sitting, over one-third of the time standing, and lying down a small amount of time.

### Allocation, Organization, Management of Resources

Some studies have revealed that an average of over 23 percent of time in PE classes was used for **class management**. Students were found to be engaging in moderate to vigorous physical activity (MVPA) during 45.3 percent of the time during PE classes, which averaged 21.2 minutes per class and equated to only 10.4 minutes per school day, because most schools studied only offered PE classes 2.47 days per week. Researchers found that of the schools they examined, only 17.4 percent offered PE five days of the week. Elementary school PE teachers were found to spend a significantly larger amount of class time than middle school teachers on class management; hence middle school students received more minutes per day of PE. Students were exposed to more PE daily when schools had more teachers dedicated to teaching only health and PE. Students engaged in MVPA during more of PE class, and teachers used less class time on management, when student-teacher ratios were lower. Higher student MVPA and lower management time were also associated with better access to adequate physical activity facilities and exercise and sports equipment.

### Recommendations vs Actual Activity

The Institute of Medicine has recommended (2005) that children engage in **moderate to vigorous physical activity (MVPA)** for 60 minutes per day. However, researchers found that in the actual schools

- 29 -

they used for their study samples, children had approximately 23 minutes of PE class per day, and were engaged in MVPA for less than half of that time, i.e., around 10 minutes a day. This equates to about one-sixth of the national recommendation. The researchers acknowledge that, obviously, children must be active outside of PE classes to attain the recommended levels of physical activity; but they also advise that to support children in doing so, schools must nevertheless increase the proportions of PE class time when children are active physically. They conclude that a low ratio of students per full-time equivalent (FTE) PE teacher affords significant gains in both PE class duration and proportions of student physical activity during those classes. They find school district allocation of enough resources for hiring and retaining PE teachers with superior skills will enable longer PE classes and student activity.

## Quality of PE Instruction

Although enough exposure to PE of high enough intensity is proven to contribute effectively to healthy lifestyles among children and adults, research finds that many PE programs do not meet national recommendations for either **duration of class time** or **physical activity intensity**. Some researchers (cf. Bevans et al., 2010) differentiate between structural and process factors for predicting levels of student physical activity. For example, among resources that promote student physical activity, adequate facilities, equipment, and quantity and quality of PE teachers are defined as structural factors. Instructional practices by PE teachers are defined as **process factors**. Even though both structural and process factors predict student activity levels, and thus comprehensive approaches for enhancing children's health and well-being through more effective PE must address both of these, the researchers also note the importance of differentiating them for the purposes of differentiating approaches for improving each. Federal, state, and district policies that require allocating sufficient funding for procuring and maintaining facilities and equipment, and for hiring and retaining enough PE teachers for ideal teacher-student ratios, will improve structural factors. PE teacher professional development in techniques for decreasing class management time will improve process factors.

## Individual and Situational Interest

**Individual interest** describes the relatively lasting psychological preference or predisposition of an individual to repeatedly engage with certain categories of events, ideas, or objects over time. It is specific to the content involved, develops gradually and slowly, and is comparatively stable. Individual interest also evolves in relation to the individual's values and knowledge. As such, individual interest figures significantly in students' preferences for engaging in certain activities or tasks over time, and is predictive of their future motivation. In contrast, situational interest describes the momentary affective responses generated by environmental stimuli. The effects of this may be short term, and its influence on individual values and knowledge may be marginal. Appealing or specific environmental features usually stimulate **situational interest**, which can also potentially lead to true interest. Both individual and situational interest influence learning. Although the former proceeds from internal psychological characteristics and the latter from external environmental stimuli, they do not exist separately: they interact and influence each other's development. Situational interest can help long-term individual interest to develop, and strong individual interest can enable an individual to respond differently to stimulating environmental situations than others lacking such interest.

## Increasing Internal Motivation

Research finds that despite ongoing concern and priority for enhancing all Americans' physical activity for its physical and mental health benefits, daily PE for high school students has **decreased**; worse, fewer high school students elect to take available PE courses. Thus, effective PE teachers and programs have critical roles for giving children positive experiences with physical activity early in life. These are accompanied by the necessity of creating environments structured for motivating students to engage in healthy lifestyles with ongoing physical activity. One strategy to increase internal motivation is giving students freedom to choose. Example practices are giving students choices of two or more activities, and involving them in decision-making processes whenever possible. Another strategy is modifying activities and skills, and letting students do so. Example practices are changing the rules, space, or equipment to facilitate student success, and giving students flexibility to be creative in modifying activities to fit their individual needs and interests. A third strategy is giving every student ideal challenges. Practice examples are matching activities to students, and offering students choices among different task difficulty levels, e.g., letting students select among differently shaped balls or scarves in juggling lessons.

## Perceived Physical Competence

According to research into students' reasons for engaging in physical activity, their main **motives** are to enjoy it for its fun, and for how enhancing skills and learning enable a sense of accomplishment. Students' perception of their physical abilities—**perceived physical competence**—frequently determines willingness to try new activities and keep participating. To develop perceived physical competence, students must have chances to learn and practice, without which they can develop negative attitudes regarding physical activity, decreasing its future probability. Teaching frequently requires specific numbers of trials within a time limit, counterproductively inducing students to sacrifice quality of movement for completing required quantities. Giving students certain durations for practice without specifying trial numbers enables focus on correct form. Moreover, practice durations long enough to develop skill, yet short enough to sustain concentrated attention, preserve enthusiasm and motivation. Teachers should let students experiment while learning and perfect processes, and give them positive feedback describing what they did right technically, instead of stressing products—e.g., emphasizing correct basketball-throwing technique rather than making the basket—to enhance motivation to practice.

### Enhancing Perceived Physical Competence

- **Give students enough time to practice**. As an example, teachers can specify a certain length of time to work on skills, but not require them to complete a certain number of trials during that time. This will allow them to concentrate on performing the skills correctly rather than focusing on performing actions enough times without perfecting their technique. Teachers can reduce off-task student behavior by changing or varying the activities assigned.
- **Give students positive, specific instructional feedback**. Teachers can make it easier for students to take on challenges and risks of errors or failing by communicating relevant, meaningful, task-specific and technique-specific instructional feedback to students. For example, when a PE teacher tells a student the way he or she held his or her elbows in or bent his or her arms when throwing or catching was admirable and to keep it up, the student will experience approval, appreciation, and encouragement of his or her efforts and be more motivated to continue practicing and participating.

### Improve Perceived Physical Competence

- Stress personal improvement. PE teachers can instruct students to determine their fitness or activity baselines, e.g., by counting the number of times they can make a chest pass or bounce pass against the wall, and encourage them to establish personal goals, repeating these actions to match or exceed baseline numbers.
- Group students rapidly. If PE teachers quickly group students, they prevent students from comparing peers to choose teams. Teachers can instruct students to move through the space randomly, and upon hearing a specified number of teacher whistle-blows, move into groups with other students in nearest proximity to them. This avoids comparing some students unfavorably to others, which impedes their developing perceived physical competence.

- Ask students their permission in advance to demonstrate skills. When a PE teacher observes a student performing a technique correctly, he or she should ask the student first whether he or she is willing to demonstrate for the class instead of unexpectedly telling the student to demonstrate. Putting a student on the spot is more stressful; offering the student choice and preparation better enables developing perceived physical competence.

## Peer Comparisons Negative Affect

Younger elementary school students, e.g., first and second graders, frequently assume they are competent in all physical activities they perform. However, in third and fourth grades they typically begin noticing some of their peers perform certain skills better than others. Consequently, they start judging their own **physical competence** by comparing it to that of other students. This negative outcome is reinforced by separating individual students or groups by focusing everybody's attention on them, encouraging their perception that their abilities are being judged by others. PE teachers can use a strategy of having students practice in scattered formations, not in a circle where they tend to perceive everybody is watching them, and of not waiting in line to take turns, also exposing each student to an audience, which both make students feel uncomfortable that others are judging them. Even with positive teacher feedback, students become embarrassed over performing unsuccessfully in front of peers, damaging their perceived physical competence. Another strategy is to ask individual students or groups in advance if they are comfortable demonstrating a skill, rather than surprising them.

## TARGET (T, A, and R)

**TARGET** stands for Task, Authority, Recognition, Grouping, Evaluation, and Timing. For **Task**, strategies include giving several activities with varying difficulty levels, and adjusting skills and activities to be developmentally appropriate. For example, PE teachers can instruct first graders to try catching beanbags with their preferred hand, their non-dominant hand, or both hands. For **Authority**, a strategy is to allow students to have some of the responsibility for their choices of activities. For example, PE teachers can tell each student to select his or her favorite among upper-body exercises, and perform their selected exercises while music is playing. For **Recognition**, strategies include recognizing the process rather than the product, focusing on self-improvement rather than outcomes, and helping students focus on self-improvement by establishing an environment that eliminates or reduces peer performance comparisons and by delivering positive feedback. For example, the PE teacher can praise a student in a voice just above a whisper, commenting that he or she can tell the student is working hard because the student is using the other foot or hand, thus complimenting the student's efforts.

## TARGET (G, E, and T)

The **TARGET** acronym represents Task, Authority, Recognition, Grouping, Evaluation, and Timing. For **Grouping**, teaching strategies include using "toe to toe" and other techniques to form groups quickly, avoiding peer comparisons, and augmenting the aspect of social interactions in the PE environment by encouraging students to partner with different classmates often. For example, teachers can instruct students to seat themselves in groups of four following the class rule of one girl and one boy to each group; inform them they will stay in the group for a few minutes and then switch; and thank them for quickly forming groups. For **Evaluation**, strategies include engaging students in self-evaluations targeting self-improvement, and involving students in evaluation processes, ensuring each student's evaluation is private, meaningful, and specific. For example, the teacher tells a student, "Awesome pass! I like how you're making a table and moving your feet, remembering the cues. Excellent work!" For **Timing**, strategies include maximizing learning and practice time, and not introducing competitive play too soon; helping students make time outside class to practice and be physically active; and individualizing teaching and practices so all students have time and motivation for practice. Examples include specific fielding instructions, and suggesting additional practice at home later.

## Responsible Behaviors

**Pre-K/K students** may be expected to show consideration of and cooperation with others, like taking turns and sharing, to maximize activity times. **Grades 1-2** may be expected to show good fitness partnership behaviors, e.g., cooperation, willingness to work with any partner, and giving encouragement. **Grades 3-5** may be expected to show respect by avoiding "put-downs," encouraging peers, communicating respectfully with students having similar and different fitness or skill levels, and to identify and experience diverse cultures' physical habits and activities. **Grades 6-8** may be expected to demonstrate sensitivity and respect for others' feelings when they participate in fitness activities with students having different cultures, skills, abilities, and genders, and to analyze how health behavior is both challenged and enriched by cultural diversity. **Grades 9-12** may be expected to participate with and invite others to physical activities irrespective of different cultural backgrounds, abilities, skills, and limitations, and analyze how developing appreciation of physical, gender, ethnic, and cultural diversity is influenced by sport participation. Higher education students may be expected to invite their family members and friends to participate in physical activities.

## Positive Relationships

Some researchers have found that middle school students perceive close friendships more highly through **positive affect related to physical activity**, and that those perceiving peer acceptance more highly experienced higher **physical self-worth**, which in turn predicts more positive affect. Positive affect also promotes physical activity and challenge preference. Studies have shown that psychosocial outcomes are enhanced through independent contributions from both peer acceptance and friendship. Quality experiences in physical activity have been observed to benefit from the motivation supplied by positive affect, self-perceptions, and relationships with significant others. Multiple studies have found peers critical to such quality experiences with physical activity. Areas of research interest have included how peers influence affect in the physical domain, shape self-perceptions, affect moral attitudes and behaviors, and affect motivation for making choices of physical activity, seeking challenges, and sustaining long-term commitment to physical activity. Studies have found peer relationships and health behavior reciprocally influence each other. Research into sports implies that individuals identifying exclusively as athletes risk more adjustment problems when undergoing injuries or leaving the sport; some researchers suggest peer relationships may influence identity formation.

## Appropriate Vs. Inappropriate PE Practices

To establish a **productive learning environment**, PE teachers systematically plan, develop, and sustain atmospheres of teacher and peer respect and support, emphasizing participation and learning. Sarcasm or insults are unsafe and unsupportive, causing student discomfort, embarrassment, or humiliation. Productive environments support all students' development of positive self-concept, enabling them to try, fail, and try again without fear, teacher or peer criticism, or harassment. Inappropriate environments view more physically fit and skilled students as successful, ignoring or overlooking those who are less fit or skilled. Intrinsic, not extrinsic motivations are stressed, guiding student responsibility for learning and behavior, not fear of punishment. Teachers use and promote exercise for fun, skill development, and health benefits, not punishment. **Classroom management practices** are consistent and fair, not using inconsistent, unclear rules. Teachers immediately address bullying, taunting, and inappropriate student behaviors and comments firmly, not ignoring or overlooking them. They actively teach safety and post and practice emergency plans, not ignoring or permitting unsafe student practices (pushing, shoving, tackling; swinging bats close to others, etc.). They match activities to ability levels, not permitting dodge

- 33 -

ball or drills enabling aggressive behaviors. Updated CPR and AED certifications and regular facility and equipment safety inspections are imperative.

## Promoting Productive Learning Environments

PE teachers should purposefully design situations and activities that teach and help students develop social skills for **cooperation**, **collaboration**, **competition**, and **sportsmanship** rather than leaving these only for "teachable moments" or assuming they are learned incidentally. They must take advantage of strategies including peer teaching, group work, letting students choose equipment, and involving students in making rules. PE class sizes should be similar to other subject classes: teachers should not regularly combine classes with one supervising a doubled class while the other does something else. Teachers must closely monitor students for safety rather than leave classes unsupervised periodically or position themselves without views of all students. They should create environments including and supporting all children regardless of diverse abilities and characteristics, not preferential to skilled athletes. Teachers should include culturally diverse activities, not exclusively teach American team sports, and challenge students of all developmental and ability levels including those with disabilities appropriately, not allowing highly skilled students to dominate. Socialization, support, and encouragement should be equal between genders, without identifying certain activities (e.g., football or dance) with boys or girls; teachers should use gender-neutral language.

## Planning Effective Class Behavior Management

Experienced experts advise PE teachers to get to know every single student as soon as they possibly can as a means of developing **rapport** with students and classes. Teachers should learn some unique fact about each student. Greeting each student by name as he or she arrives to class daily will demonstrate teacher recognition and interest for every individual. Teachers should establish all class routines and procedures, such as for using and returning equipment, bathroom breaks, etc., to be consistent from class to class day to day. PE teachers are advised to develop a set of their written expectations. These should not exceed five in number, as students will not be able to remember or keep track of more. Teachers should enforce these expectations consistently. Expectations should not focus on the negative, i.e., what teachers want students not to do, but on the positive, i.e., what teachers want students to do. They should post copies of these expectations in the locker room or on the bulletin board in their classrooms.

## Effective Behavior Management Techniques

PE teachers should make sure that they prepare gym equipment in **advance**, before classes begin. They should not set up the equipment in the presence of their students. However, they can enlist willing students to help them set up equipment in the mornings before school starts. Another practice for PE teachers to support effective behavior management is putting their agendas on paper and **posting** them on a bulletin board before class. They should hold students accountable for checking the day's agenda and initiating assigned learning experiences. PE teachers should train students always to look at the bulletin board before asking what they are doing that day. Another recommended technique is to use "**high activity roll call taking strategies**" rather than letting students remain inactive while taking attendance. Inactivity encourages misbehavior, and allows students to forget the point of PE class—physical activity. Another technique is to make use of transitions by assigning **time limits**, e.g., giving 10 seconds to get to the basketball court, 30 seconds to get from the gym to the outdoor playing field, etc.

## Keeping Classes Running Smoothly

One component for PE teachers to include in an effective behavior management plan involves how to give students **directions**: teachers should make sure that before telling students *what* to do, they tell them *when* to do it. For example, do not simply say "Each team, pick up a soccer ball" first, or students will stop listening to follow that direction. Instead, say, "When I say 'go,' each team pick up a soccer ball." That way, they will keep students' attention as they will not act until they hear the identified prompt. To keep instructional cues concise, teachers can use the "**rule of threes**" (SPARK PE website), e.g., three players, three passes, three feet, three minutes, three seconds, etc. Also from the SPARK PE website, teachers can use the "**80/20 rule**": teach the class a concept until 80 percent of the students understand it; during the subsequent learning experience, the other 20 percent will figure it out through doing it. Another piece of expert advice for PE teachers is not to talk too much when teaching. PE teachers should use **pair-and-share strategies** and **questioning techniques** to give their students opportunities to talk with one another.

### Expert Recommendations

To **engage** students in their own learning, PE teachers should use approaches like **cooperative learning methods** and **peer assessment** instead of direct instruction. Some experts advise that the teachers should not have to work harder than their students. Another way to prevent behavior problems and delegate effort while teaching responsibility to students is to assign **management and leadership roles** for capable students to perform, such as team captains, referees, equipment managers, squad leaders, warmup leaders, and new student buddies. An additional behavior management method that is effective is to hold students **accountable** for their own behavior through a combination of positive reinforcement for desired behaviors and consequences for undesired ones. In addition to regularly giving ample informal, verbal positive reinforcement for desirable behaviors, the PE teacher should define formal rewards and consequences for students in advance, and enforce them consistently. Experts also advise that when PE teachers discipline students, they should talk to them as if their parents are standing directly behind them.

### Plans for Class Behavior Management

In effective **behavior management plans**, PE teachers should privately and quietly discipline individual students when needed. They should never hold disciplinary talks in front of the other students. When disputes between or among students develop during classes, one strategy that PE teachers can use is to settle them using the "rock, paper, scissors" method. This ensures randomness for objectivity instead of subjective or preferential decisions. When assigning students to groups, PE teachers should consider their individual differences and needs, such as disabilities or special needs, skill levels, English language proficiency, race, gender, etc. To balance groups evenly, teachers should divide their classes into high, middle, and low achievers and then place one from each level into each group. English language learners and special-needs students should be paired with supportive buddies or partners. PE teachers are advised to respect students. Teachers should begin and end class on time, teaching from "bell to bell."

### Applying Effective Behavior Management Plans

To **prevent behavior problems** and **motivate students**, PE teachers should play school-appropriate, current, student-friendly music. Students comply more with clearer expectations. PE teachers should model everything they expect; for example, on rainy days, not running but walking from the gym to the auditorium. To call on students in an equitable manner, PE teachers should set up a tracking system. They should try to alternate calling on female and male students. Over a day or week, depending on student learning experience and class size, PE teachers should ensure each student has a chance to respond. Experts advise PE teachers to enlist students' parents as their allies. They can do this by calling them early in the school year and staying in frequent communication; being sure to talk about students' positive behaviors; using very specific terms and objective descriptions to communicate concerns; focusing not on the student but the behavior; and always allowing time to calm down before contacting parents regarding undesirable behaviors. According to experts, the best behavior management plan is a strong instructional

- 35 -

plan. Thus PE teachers should prepare for each lesson. The more students are engaged in learning activities, the less they will demonstrate maladaptive behaviors.

## Big Five Theory of Personality Traits

In a very popular theory developed by a series of researchers (Fiske, 1949; Norman, 1967; Smith, 1967; Goldberg, 1981; McCrae & Costa, 1987; Costa & McCrae, 1994, etc.), the **Big Five universal personality traits** are extraversion, agreeableness, conscientiousness, neuroticism, and openness. **Extraversion** is characterized by sociability, assertiveness, emotional expressivity, talkativeness, and excitability. **Agreeableness** features affection, kindness, trust, altruism, and similar prosocial behaviors. **Conscientiousness** includes organization, detail-orientation, goal-directed behaviors, good impulse control and thoughtfulness. **Neuroticism** includes anxiety, irritability, moodiness, emotional instability, and sadness. **Openness** has characteristics of broad interests, insight, and imagination. Each trait is a continuum, with individuals demonstrating various degrees of each trait between two extremes, e.g., between extreme extraversion and extreme introversion. Some researchers examining the interaction of personality traits with young adult social relationships have found that, while personality traits predict numbers and qualities of peer relationships, relationships do not reciprocally predict personality traits. Also, major relationship changes do not affect personality traits. Extraversion, agreeableness and conscientiousness affected quality and number of social relationships. Longitudinal study found agreeableness influenced later but not initial peer conflict; and conscientiousness influenced later but not initial family contact. Personality traits are more stable than relationship characteristics.

## Influence of Social Context Factors on Children's Peer Relationships

In studying the peer interactions of children with **attention deficit hyperactivity disorder (ADHD)**, multiple researchers have found peers dislike children with ADHD within hours of first meeting them, across situations and over time; and ADHD plus peer difficulties cumulatively predict **adolescent psychopathology**. These collected findings indicate serious social problems for ADHD populations. One social context factor is **parental influence**. Though disruptive ADHD behaviors cause conflict in parent-child relationships, one lead investigator (Mikami et al, 2010), questioning whether these parenting problems then also worsened children's peer conflicts, found parents indeed more critical of their ADHD children and less likely than other parents to have strong support networks—even after controlling for disruptive child behaviors. While parental warmth toward children, skilled adult-adult interactions, and modeling and coaching of children's peer interactions normally correlate with children's acceptance by peers, both parental criticism and—unexpectedly—praise predicted ADHD children's *poorer* peer interactions (again, after controlling for disruptive behaviors). Possible influences include parental ADHD; peer observations of parent-child interactions; and effects of parent-child relationships on the accuracy of children's self-perceptions of peer competence.

## Social Context Factor of Teacher Influences of Peer Relationships Among Children

Children typically develop likes and dislikes among school peers. Some research has revealed children's observations of **teacher responses** contribute to their **social peer preferences**. Some studies found children with ADHD did not gain better peer acceptance even when they improved their behavior because peers continued rejecting them based on their established negative reputations. But others have found teachers can mitigate these bad reputations by directing **positive attention** to children with ADHD. Multiple researchers concur that children's ADHD behaviors cause many teachers difficulty relating to them. Dislike of children with high levels of ADHD symptoms tends to progress over the school year. However, investigators also find teachers who use instructional practices communicating their belief that all children can learn, and who form positive relationships with all students, can change the association of peer difficulties with ADHD symptoms. Researchers speculate such outcomes may support the possibility that teachers can promote **better peer relationships** through shaping classroom environments. Although studies continue to show peer dislike predicted by children's ADHD symptoms, they also find teacher practices can influence that interaction, making it less invariable.

## Disclosing Uncomfortable Topics in Interpersonal Communication

Communications experts observe that even in healthy relationships, people avoid bringing up some topics. They often do so strategically. Experts point out that constantly expressing every little criticism and stressor can destroy a relationship. Instead, we protect our personal identities and preserve the peace in our relationships by setting **thresholds of privacy**. Researchers studying motivations for **topic avoidance** identify self-protection or protecting the relationship as potential reasons. For example, bringing up a desire to solidify a relatively new relationship risks the partner's rejection. We may avoid broaching other topics to avoid the other's judgmental response. Researchers find that people avoiding topics for self-protection feel less satisfaction than those who do it to protect their relationship. Experts also note that, in romantic relationships, a delicate balance is necessary between avoidance and direct sharing. For example, sharing about past relationships can inform a new partner's understanding of the person, but only to a point; beyond that, too many details offer no benefit. On the other hand, overly repressing feelings and thoughts is found detrimental to health. Studies find habitually avoiding difficult subjects correlates with exacerbation of **irritable bowel syndrome symptoms**; and when families avoid discussing a member's cancer, patient illnesses become worse.

## Main Goals Involved in Interpersonal Conversations

According to communications researchers who have analyzed interpersonal conversations, people frequently strive, consciously or unconsciously, to meet three main goals during serious conversations. (1) **Task goals**. These represent the official purpose or point of the conversation. For example, a conversation with an aging parent may have the purpose of deciding who will make decisions for him/her when s/he is no longer able to make them. (2) **Identity goals**. These are tacit methods of preserving both one's own and another's sense of self. For example, in the preceding example, the family member(s) consider that by bringing up this topic, they are being caring and responsible, and that the aging parent wants to experience continued autonomy despite deteriorating health. (3) **Relationship goals**. These are directed to maintaining interpersonal connections. For example, in the foregoing examples, the parties in the conversation perceive that their open discussion is enabled by their closeness. Conversations with the highest quality entail both (or all) parties' observing these three goals concurrently, which is cognitively very challenging. It requires taking another's perspective, and then composing messages acknowledging that viewpoint while achieving our own goals for the conversation at the same time.

## Relationship Between Interpersonal Communication and Stress

Experts in communications note that research studies show stress is generated by **avoiding discussion** of important subjects, damaging the immune system and personal well-being over time. Conversely, they comment that we are able to achieve some **control** over a problem when we are able to explain it. Therefore, it more often than not benefits us to talk about subjects we find difficult to discuss. Another consideration is that we tend to **expect worse outcomes** of disclosing sensitive information than what really occurs. Research shows that we overestimate how much our negative perceptions coincide with those of our family members or significant others because we project our own beliefs onto them. In reality, it is often both more productive and safer emotionally than we think to bring up a touchy topic. However, another aspect highlighted by communications researchers is that **quality supersedes quantity** in communication. They find when discussing important issues, like serious illness or end-of-life

- 37 -

wishes, it can be more harmful to discuss it in the wrong way than not discuss it at all, and that more is not necessarily better. Some research initiatives in healthcare communications have failed by emphasizing the quantity of communication rather than its quality.

## Effective Interpersonal Communication

Among elements making interpersonal conversations effective, experts in communications and clinical psychology include these: (1) ask yourself "**Why**?" Clarify whether you are sharing to benefit the relationship or yourself. Disclosure for the relationship's benefit supersedes self-interest. (2) Affirm you **deserve to communicate**. Many people are concerned it is not their place to raise certain issues. However, experts point out a close relationship is not close unless each member speaks up sometimes. (3) Use a **less personal approach** first to test another's response. To determine whether to avoid discussing how a topic relates to yourself and/or another, mention a less personal example of it (e.g., "My cousin once had an abortion."). (4) Use **natural openings**. To discuss something naturally, be alert to times when another is willing and able to hear it. As a clinical psychologist puts it, waiting for a door to open is better than breaking down the door. Initiating conversation succeeds more when someone is responsive. (5) Do not raise touchy subjects when **upset**. This is inconvenient, because this is when we most want to talk about them. But experts advise calming down before resuming difficult conversations.

### Elements Recommended for Difficult Subjects

(1) **Aim for productive, quality conversations**. A clinical psychologist says hinting at a subject at ten different times is less productive than one productive talk. However, a communications expert also points out that conversation is more typically a process than a single, conclusive discussion. When people reveal information or feelings in one conversation, this frequently requires additional conversations. (2) **"I" statements**. It is more useful to say "This is how I feel," than "This is how you are." While this advice is common, psychologists caution people not to use it mechanically as a conversational "trick." They should be authentic acknowledgements of our responsibility: when we are hurt, even when it is not our fault, it is still our hurt and our responsibility to find ways of assuaging it. (3) **Take others' points of view**. Empathize to balance honesty; be responsible for your role in a situation. Moreover, be prepared for diverse responses: others can be more sensitive *or* more resilient than we thought. (4) **Stick to the subject**. When others introduce distracting issues, defer discussion. Sometimes neutral third parties (e.g., couples or family counselors) can narrow conversational scope. (5) **Lighten up**: humor can bring perspective and balance to tense situations and ease expressing resentment, anger, sadness, and frustration.

## Discussing Sex in Relationships

Most people's egos are very sensitive to threats regarding their lovemaking abilities. Conversations about **sex** can be particularly difficult for spouses, because rejection from one's lifelong partner hurts most. Experts advise members of couples not to make the assumption that their partners automatically know they are experiencing dissatisfaction. They discourage saying something like "Lately it seems you are tired a lot of the time," and instead saying something like "Lately I have been feeling like I am being ignored, and I want to find out together how we can make our sex life better." Experts also say that after a couple has such a conversation, they should mutually decide on a specific time in the future when they will talk about the subject again and evaluate what progress they have made. Moreover, they should not bring up the subject again or complain about it until the time they have chosen: if the partner perceives such behaviors as nagging, they become self-fulfilling prophecies. The partner thinks, "S/he thinks I can't change, so why should I try?"

## Interpersonal Conversations About Death

Most of us understandably do not want people we love to **die**. Moreover, we do not want loved ones to think we welcome this inevitable life passage, and we often fear this is how they will perceive our talking about death with them. Experts suggest taking advantage of **less personal examples** available about third parties to test loved ones' responses and/or bring up the subject. For example, if a news story reports about an individual in a coma, adult children might use that topic to find out what their aging parents think and feel about end-of-life decisions like DNR (do not resuscitate), living wills, using heroic measures to preserve or prolong life, etc. Communications experts point out that rather than introducing the subject of a living will at Christmas dinner, Easter brunch, or similar family celebrations, it is not as threatening to use relevant third-party examples like news stories to initiate the conversation. A general rule for families is not to wait for an "official Big Conversation," but to start **early** and **regularly**, frequently discussing this important topic.

## Discussing Relationship Status

When people are involved in relationships they have established fairly recently, they frequently have not yet determined how they feel about them. They fear bringing up where the relationship is headed too soon could sabotage its future unnecessarily. This is one reason they avoid talking about **relationship status**, especially early. Another reason is gender differences. Researchers find women want more to **evaluate relationship status**; men tend to allow relationships to unfold **passively** without wanting to talk directly about them. Experts in communications say that in new relationships, partners wanting to assess their status should get information through more **indirect means**. For example, if one asks another, "What are you doing this weekend?" and gets an answer like "I'm incredibly busy," one can assume the other is not very interested; both parties can save face without more pointed questions. When relationships have lasted longer, it is normal to want to know whether they are exclusive. Partners should then more explicitly state their own **rules** so they are not broken, their **expectations** so they are not unmet, and their **questions** so they are not unanswered.

## Signs of Abusive Relationships and Belittling Behaviors

People who want to determine if they are in an **abusive relationship** should consider whether they think or feel the following: they feel afraid of their partner often, they avoid mentioning certain subjects for fear of making their partner angry, they feel they cannot do anything right with their partner, they believe being mistreated is what they deserve, they wonder whether they are the member of the relationship who is crazy, and they feel helpless and/or emotionally numb. To consider whether their partner engages in **belittling behaviors** toward them, they should consider the following: whether their partner yells at them often; whether the partner says or does things to humiliate them; whether the partner insults them or criticizes them regularly; whether the partner treats them so poorly they find it embarrassing for family, friends, or others to witness it; whether the partner dismisses, disparages, or ignores their successes and/or opinions; whether the partner blames them for the partner's abusive behaviors; and whether the partner views and/or treats them as a sexual object or property instead of a human being.

## Behavior of Abusive Partners

Victims in abusive relationships should consider whether their partner behaves in an overly possessive and jealous manner toward them; whether the partner controls what they do or where they go; whether the partner prevents them from seeing their family or friends; whether the partner limits their access to the car, the phone, and/or money; and whether their partner is continually checking up on what they are doing and where they are going. These are all behaviors intended to **control** the other person, and are not normal or healthy. Threats of **violence or violent behaviors** to watch for in a partner include: the partner has a bad temper, and is unpredictable about losing his or her temper; the partner threatens to harm or kill them, or actually does harm them; the partner threatens to hurt their children, actually hurts them, or threatens to take them away; the partner threatens that if they leave, the partner will commit suicide; the partner forces them to engage in sex when they do not want to; or the partner takes away or destroys their personal belongings.

## Domestic Abuse

**Domestic violence** is domestic abuse including physical violence. Physical force that injures or endangers someone is **physical abuse**. Physical battery or assault is a crime: police have the authority and power to protect individuals from physical attacks, whether outside or inside a family or home. **Sexual abuse** is an aggressive, violent act and a type of physical abuse. This includes forced sex, even by a partner with whom one also has consensual sex. Victims of physical and sexual abuse are at greater risk of serious injury and death. Even if incidents seem minor, e.g., being pushed or shoved, they are still abuse, and also can still cause severe injury or death. Even if incidents have only happened once or twice in a relationship, they are still abuse and are likely to continue and escalate. If physical assaults stop when the victim becomes passive, this is not a solution: the victim has given up his/her rights as a partner and a person to independence, self-expression, and decision-making. Even when no physical violence exists, victims may suffer from **verbal and emotional assault and abuse**.

## Emotional and Financial Domestic Abuse

People often associate the idea of domestic abuse with physical battery. However, many partners are victims of **emotional abuse**. Without physical bruises, the victim, abuser, and other people unfortunately overlook or minimize emotional abuse. The intention and result of emotional abuse are to erode the victim's independence, control, and feelings of self-worth. Victims come to feel they have nothing without the abusive partner, or have no way to escape the relationship. Emotional abuse includes **verbal abuse** like blaming, shaming, name-calling, insulting, and yelling. It also includes **controlling behaviors**, **intimidation**, and **isolating** the victim. Threats of punishment, including physical violence, frequently enter into psychological or emotional abuse. Emotional abuse scars are less visible than physical ones, but are equally or more damaging. **Financial or economic abuse** is another way to control the victim. It includes withholding money, checkbooks, credit or debit cards; withholding shelter, food, clothing, medications, or other necessities; making victims account for every cent they spend; rigidly controlling the victim's finances; restricting the victim to an allowance; sabotaging the victim's job by constantly calling there and/or causing the victim to miss work frequently; preventing the victim's working or making career choices; and stealing from or taking the victim's money.

## Choice and Self-Control in Abusive Partners

Some people observe that abusive individuals lose their tempers; apparently have some psychological disorder; and some also abuse substances (though others do not), and, equating their problems with the illness or disease model of substance abuse, mistakenly assume that abusers cannot **control their behavior**. However, experts point out that abusive behaviors and violence are deliberate **choices** that the abusers make to control their victims. Evidence that they can control their behavior includes that they do not abuse everybody in their lives—only those they claim to love who are closest to them; that they choose carefully where and when to abuse, controlling themselves in public but attacking the victim once they are alone; that they can stop the abusive behavior when it is to their benefit, e.g., when their employer calls or the police arrive; and that they frequently aim physical attacks to parts of the victim's body where they are hidden by clothing, so others cannot see them.

## Tactics Employed by Domestic Abusers to Exert Power Over and Manipulate Victims

(1) **Dominance**: abusers, needing to feel in control of victims and relationships, dominate by making decisions for victims and family, giving them orders, and expecting unquestioning compliance. They often treat victims as children, servants, slaves, or possessions. (2) **Humiliation**: to keep victims from leaving, abusers make them feel worthless and that nobody else will want them. To make victims feel inadequate, they insult and shame them publicly and privately, making them feel powerless and destroying their self-esteem. (3) **Isolation**: abusive partners make victims dependent on them by cutting off their contact with others. They may stop victims from visiting with friends and relatives, or even going to school or work. Victims may have to ask permission to see anybody, go anywhere, or do anything. (4) **Threats**: to frighten victims into dropping charges and/or prevent their leaving, abusers typically threaten to: harm or kill victims, children, other family, or pets; commit suicide; report victims to child services; and file false charges against them. (5) **Intimidation**: threatening gestures and looks, property destruction or smashing objects in front of victims, hurting pets, or displaying weapons are tactics signaling violent consequences for noncompliance to frighten victims into submission. (6) **Denial and blame**: abusers minimize or deny abuse or blame it on circumstances or, commonly, the victim. "You made/make me do it" is a frequent accusation used by abusers.

## Warning Signs of Domestic Abuse, Physical Violence, and Isolation

Warning signs of **domestic abuse**: the person agrees with everything the partner does and says; frequently checks in with the partner, reporting what they are doing and where they are; often receives harassing phone calls or texts from the partner; appears anxious or afraid to please the partner; and/or mentions the partner's jealousy, possessiveness, or temper. Warning signs of **physical violence**: the person often misses school, work, or social events without explaining; often has injuries, excusing them as "accidents" or "clumsiness"; and/or wears sunglasses indoors, long sleeves in summer, or other means of hiding injuries. Warning signs of **isolation**: the person never or seldom goes out in public without the partner; is unable to see friends and family; and/or has limited access to the car, money, or credit or debit cards. Psychological warning signs of being abused: someone who used to be confident displays significantly lowered self-esteem. An outgoing person becomes withdrawn; or an individual shows other major personality changes. The person appears anxious; depressed; despondent; or suicidal, verbalizing suicidal ideations or displaying suicidal behaviors.

## Advice for People Who Suspect Somebody They Know is a Victim of Domestic Abuse

Abusers are experts at **manipulating** and **controlling** victims. Victims are drained, frightened, ashamed, depressed, and confused. They need to escape the situation, but frequently have been isolated from others. Those suspecting abuse should be alert to warning signs, offer support to victims for extricating themselves, getting help, and starting the healing process. Some people may hesitate, thinking they could be mistaken; learn the victim does not want to discuss it or have them interfere; or simply be told that it is none of their business. In these cases, experts advise people to **speak up** regardless: expressing concern not only informs a victim somebody cares, it moreover could save that person's life. They should speak with the person privately, identifying signs they have observed and explaining why they are concerned, reassure the individual they will keep all conversation confidential, that they are there whenever s/he is ready to talk, and will help in any way possible. Regarding dos and don'ts, **do** the following: express concern, ask whether something is wrong, listen, validate the person's communications, offer help, and support the individual's decisions. **Don't**: wait for the person to approach you, blame or judge the individual, give advice, pressure the person, or attach conditions to your support.

## Child Abuse

Many things can precipitate child abuse, including stress related to poverty, unemployment, divorce, single parenting, and lack of support. Other causes include parental substance abuse, mental illness, and sociopathic/psychopathic personalities. Child abuse occurs across all socioeconomic levels. **Indications of child abuse** include the following:

- **Physical**: Unexplained bruises and burns, frequent injuries (including fractures), unkempt appearance, and delayed medical treatment. Sexual abuse may result in difficulty sitting or walking, frequent urination, and pain in the genital area.
- **Emotional/Psychological**: Aggressive behavior toward others; shy, withdrawn behavior; fearful of parents and other adults; low self-esteem; poor school performance; marked depression; and anxiety. A child experiencing sexual abuse may refuse to participate in exercises or gym class and may show a precocious interest in sex or sexualized behavior. The child may run away from home, be truant, and show a sudden decline in academic performance. Adolescents who are abused often turn to substance abuse.

## Prevention of Child Abuse and Abduction

Prevention of child abuse and abduction includes a variety of approaches:

- **Parent education**: Includes developmental milestones, positive discipline techniques, age-appropriate behaviors and skills, child safety, and methods to improve parent-child interactions.
- **Support groups**: Parent groups to help members discuss problems and develop coping strategies.
- **Mental health programs**: Support for the child and other family members to help manage symptoms and life challenges.
- **Respite care**: Short-term childcare to allow parents/caregivers to remove themselves from the situation and the stress in order to avoid behaving abusively.
- **Home visiting programs**: Provide guidance for parents/caregivers regarding good health practices, positive parenting, home safety, and community resources.
- **Family resource centers**: Provide education and resources for parents/caregivers, including job training, parenting classes, violence prevention, substance abuse prevention, literacy programs, crisis intervention, respite care, and child care.
- **Law enforcement programs**: Abduction prevention education for parents focusing on how to educate and protect children regarding possible stranger abduction.

## Agencies and Programs Dealing with Child Abuse and Abduction

Agencies and programs that deal with child abuse and abduction include the following:

- **Law enforcement agencies** - They arrest and bring criminal charges against those who abuse and/or abduct children.
- **Government agencies** - State and local child protective services. They investigate charges of child abuse and can remove a child from the home and place in foster care or provide ongoing monitoring of parent(s). They monitor foster children.
- **Children's advocacy centers** - They investigate and collect evidence regarding child abuse and coordinate with law enforcement and child protective services.
- **Nonprofit organizations** - Examples: The International Society for the Prevention of Child Abuse and Neglect, Child Welfare League of America, and National Children's Alliance. These organizations advocate for children, support those working to protect children, and increase public awareness.

- **Professional organizations** - Example: The American Academy of Pediatrics provides guidelines for recognizing, reporting, and dealing with abuse.
- **The National Center for Missing & Exploited Children** - This nonprofit organization established by Congress provides a hotline and tip line, posts pictures and information, raises awareness, and works with law enforcement and families. Serves as a clearinghouse of resources.

## Sexual Harassment, Abuse, and Rape

Sexual harassment can take many forms, including making unwanted personal comments about appearance or lifestyle, pressing the person to date, promoting offensive material (such as showing pornography or telling off-color jokes), making unwanted physical contact (hugging, kissing, touching, standing very close), and behaving inappropriately (leering, catcalling, whistling, bullying). **Sexual abuse** can include all types of harassment as well as inappropriate and unwanted sexual contact. **Rape** involves coerced or violent sexual contact as well as sexual contact with a person who is impaired and unable to give consent (such as a person who is inebriated or under the influence of drugs). **Prevention** requires education about what constitutes harassment, abuse, and rape; prompt response to reports; having support systems in place; bystander intervention; enlisting others to assist; contacting authorities; avoiding alcohol and drugs; and using distraction. Adolescents and adults should have a clear understanding of date rape and the repercussions for both the perpetrator and the victim and should keep social media sites private and avoid tagging people.

### Physical and Emotional/Psychological Effects

Sexual harassment, abuse, and rape may result in similar long-term results:

- **Physical**: The victim may experience vaginal or anal tearing that may result in long-term painful intercourse. Chronic urinary infections may occur. STDs may be transmitted, including HIV/AIDS. Some victims may become pregnant and have to make a difficult decision about aborting or carrying the child and then another decision about keeping the child or placing it for adoption.
- **Emotional/Psychological**: The victim often engages in self-blame and may experience deep guilt. Posttraumatic stress disorder is common with flashbacks, especially with violent encounters. The victim often distrusts others and suffers from unexplained bouts of anger and severe depression. The victim may feel powerless and afraid, feeling as though he or she has lost control of life. Some may become very reclusive, afraid to leave their house or apartment, and become unable to work, resulting in increased stress.

### Agencies, Programs, and Regulations

**Sexual harassment** is covered under **Title VII of the Civil Rights Act** (1964), which prohibits sexual harassment but applies only to employers with 15 or more employees. Complaints are submitted to the Equal Employment Opportunity Commission (EEOC). Employers with fewer employees are covered by various state laws and regulatory agencies. Some nongovernmental agencies have limited programs to assist victims of sexual harassment, including the Legal Advocacy Fund of the American Association of University Women (AAUW). **Sexual abuse and rape** are criminal offenses covered by laws against sexual violence and involve law enforcement agencies, usually the local police, although federal authorities may intervene in sex trafficking and online stalking. Many organizations now have workplace violence prevention programs that include strategies to prevent sexual abuse, stalking, and rape. The National Sexual Assault Hotline refers people to the nearest services. The National Sex Offender Public Website links state, tribal, and territorial sexual offender registries. Numerous organizations provide assistance to victims, including the National Organization for Victim Assistance.

## Communication Skills

### Active Listening

Active listening requires more than passively listening to another individual. **Active listening** includes observing the other individual carefully for nonverbal behaviors, such as posture, eye contact, and facial expression, as well as understanding and reflecting on what the person is saying. The listener should observe carefully for inconsistencies in what the individual is saying or comments that require clarification. **Feedback** is critical to active listening because it shows the speaker that one is paying attention and showing interest and respect. Feedback may be as simple as nodding the head in agreement but should also include asking questions or making comments to show full engagement. Listening with **empathy** is especially important because it helps to build a connection with the speaker. The listener should communicate empathy with words: "You feel (emotion) because (experience)" because the speaker may not be sensitive to what the listener is comprehending.

### Assertiveness

Assertive communication occurs when the individual expresses opinions directly and actions correlate with words. **Assertive communicators** are respectful of others and do not bull, but they are firm and honest about their opinions. They frequently use **"I" statements** to make their point: "I would like. . . ." Communication usually includes **cooperative statements**, such as "What do you think?" and distinguishes between fact and opinion. Assertive communicators often engender trust in others because they are consistent, honest, and open in communicating with others. The assertive communicator feels free to express disagreement and anger but does so in a manner that is nonthreatening and respectful of others' feelings. Assertive communication requires a strong sense of self-worth and the belief that personal opinions have value. Assertive communicators tend to have good **listening skills** because they value the opinions of others and feel comfortable collaborating.

### "I" Messages and Refusal Skills

Using "I" messages is a method of communication in which the speaker focuses on personal feelings rather than characteristics or actions of the listener. For example, if an adolescent stays out late, an **"I" message** would be "I worry that you have been in an accident when you come home late" rather than focusing on the adolescent: "Why are you late?"

**Refusal skills** are those that help people refuse to participate in activities and to say "no" to situations that are dangerous or unwanted, such as drug taking and sexual contact. The person needs to stand up straight, make eye contact, and say "NO" forcefully and support this statement with the appropriate body language and facial expression. The person should avoid making excuses but remain firm and repeat the same message if necessary. Young people may need to practice these techniques in role-playing activities.

### Negotiation Skills

Negotiating may be a formal process (such as negotiating with the administration for increased benefits) or an informal process (such as arriving at a team consensus), depending on the purpose and those involved.

- **Competition** - In this approach, one party wins and the other loses, such as when parties state that their positions are nonnegotiable and are unwilling to compromise. To prevail, one party must remain firm, but this can result in conflict.
- **Accommodation** - One party concedes to the other, but the losing side may gain little or nothing, so this approach should be used when there is a clear benefit to one choice.
- **Avoidance** - When both parties dislike conflict, they may put off negotiating and resolve nothing, and the problems remain.

- **Compromise** - Both parties make concessions to reach a consensus, this can result in decisions that suit no one, compromise is not always the solution.
- **Collaboration** - Both parties receive what they want, a win-win solution, often through creative solutions, but collaboration may be ineffective with highly competitive parties.

## Self-Assessment of Behavioral Risk Factors

Self-assessment of behavioral risk factors begins with identifying risk factors (drinking, sexual activity, dishonesty, drug abuse) that may be an issue and then assessing the **degree of risk**. Although self-reflection may be helpful, in most cases a **self-assessment tool** is the easiest and most effective way to carry out self-assessment. Examples include the student sexual risks scale and suicide risk screening tools. The National Institute on Drug Abuse provides links to a number of evidence-based screening tools that can be used for the assessment of alcohol and drug use for adolescents and adults. Although the results of self-assessment may be enlightening, they do not necessarily lead to **changes** unless the person is motivated to change. If self-assessment indicates behavioral risk, the person should seek help in making changes, such as through a support group or therapist. The person may also enlist family and friends to help in monitoring and assessing change.

## Differentiating Among Safe, Risky, and Harmful Behaviors in Relationships

A **safe** relationship is one in which the individuals have mutual respect and maintain appropriate boundaries. It can be difficult to differentiate between **risky** and **harmful** behaviors in a relationship because risky behaviors are often a precursor to harmful behaviors. The following behaviors are warning signs that the behaviors are not safe:

| Risky behaviors | Harmful behaviors |
|---|---|
| Critical—Public or private criticism, purposefully humiliating the person. Irresponsible/Immature—Constant problems (social, financial) and discord. Noncommunicative—Difficulty expressing feelings and being open with others. Self-centered—thinks only in terms of personal needs. | Aggressive/Abusive—Any type of hitting, shoving, pushing, or physical violence. Controlling/Possessive—Attempts to control another person's life and to isolate the person from others. Volatility—Unpredictable bouts of anger and rage. Manipulative—Pressuring someone to do something or using guilt or threats to get one's way. |

# Living Safely and Reducing Risks

**Medical Emergencies**

Medical emergencies are those in which the person is at severe risk and needs prompt medical attention. For life-threatening **emergencies**, the most appropriate response is to call 9-1-1, but some first-aid procedures may be used if necessary, such as applying pressure to a bleeding wound, while waiting for assistance. In less acute cases (such as severe diarrhea), the person may be transported to an emergency department directly without calling 9-1-1 if he or she appears stable. Medical emergencies include the following:

- Shortness of breath, severe wheezing, difficulty breathing.
- Sudden onset of dizziness and fainting or unexplained weakness.
- Sudden changes in vision.
- Sudden onset of severe pain.
- Chest pain or pressure or pain radiating to neck, shoulders, and arms.
- Severe gastrointestinal problems with vomiting and/or diarrhea.
- Severe uncontrolled hemorrhage.
- Vomiting blood or coughing up blood.
- Difficult speaking or swallowing.
- Threats of suicide.

**Basic First-Aid Procedures in Various Situations**

The following are first-aid procedures in various situations:

- **Anaphylaxis (allergic shock)** - Immediately call 9-1-1. Administer epinephrine (EpiPen) per autoinjector if the person has one. Begin cardiopulmonary resuscitation (CPR) if in respiratory arrest.

**Animal bites**

- *Minor* (if no concern about rabies): Wash with soap and water and apply antibiotic cream/ointment and bandage.
- *Major*: Apply pressure to stop the bleeding with a dry clean bandage, and transport to the emergency department, or call 9-1-1 if severe.
- **Black eye** - Apply cold compress, avoiding pressure on eye. If blood is noted in the eye itself or if vision is impaired, transport to the emergency department.
- **Chemical burns/eye splashes** - Remove contaminated belongings and flush the burn area with a copious amount of tap water for at least 10 minutes. Transport to the emergency department or call 9-1-1 if burns are severe, the patient feels faint, or the burn is more than three inches in diameter. Flush the eyes for at least 20 minutes, and then transport to the emergency department.
- **Cut/Scrapes** - Apply pressure with a clean bandage to stop the bleeding. Rinse with clear water and wash around the wound with soap and water. Apply antibiotic ointment and dressing. If the wound is deep and requires suturing; transport to the emergency department.

## Heat cramps, heat exhaustion, heat stroke

- o *Heat cramps and exhaustion*: Remove the person to the shade, lay flat, and elevate legs; cool by spraying with cold water, and have the person drink cool water.
- o *Heat stroke*: Call 9-1-1. Spray or immerse in cool water and fan; administer CPR if necessary.
- **Hypothermia** - Call 9-1-1. Remove wet clothing, warm gradually with warm compresses to the trunk; give warm drinks. Do not warm too quickly, and do not massage limbs.
- **Insect bites/stings** - Remove stingers, wash with soap and water, and apply a cool compress. Apply cortisone cream to reduce itching. If a severe reaction or bite with a known dangerous insect (such as a scorpion), call 9-1-1. Administer an EpiPen if the person has one for allergies to insects.

## Bleeding

- o *Minor*: Apply pressure with a clean bandage to stop the bleeding and apply dry dressing.
- o *Severe*: Call 9-1-1. Remove any large debris from the wound. Apply pressure with a clean bandage to stop the bleeding but not if debris is imbedded in the wound, and don't apply pressure to an eye. In these cases, simply cover with a clean dressing. Lie the person flat and elevate the feet. Apply a tourniquet for bleeding that is life-threatening only if trained to do so.
- **Snakebites (venomous)** - Call 9-1-1. Position the injury below the level of the heart if possible. Cover the wound with a dry dressing. DO NOT apply ice, cut the skin, or apply a tourniquet. Report a description of the snake to first responders.
- **Spider bite** - Cleanse the bite with soap and water, and apply antibiotic ointment and cool compress. Transport to the emergency department if a poisonous spider, such as a black widow or brown recluse, is suspected.

## Sprains/Fractures/Dislocations

- o *Sprains*: RICE (rest, ice, compress, elevate). Transport to the emergency department if unable to bear weight or use the joint.
- o *Fractures*: Call 9-1-1 or transport to the emergency department. Apply pressure to stop any bleeding, cover with a dry dressing, immobilize the injured limb, and apply an ice pack.
- o *Dislocation*: Transport to the emergency department. Do not attempt to move the joint. Apply an ice compress to the joint.
- **Shock (any cause)** - Call 9-1-1. Lay the person flat, elevate the legs and feet, and keep still. Loosen clothing. Begin CPR if cardiac or respiratory arrest exist.
- **Stroke** - Call 9-1-1. Keep the head elevated.
- **Nosebleeds** - Sit the person upright and pinch nostrils for 5 to 10 minutes. Transport to the emergency department if bleeding follows an accident or if it persists for more than 20 minutes.

## CPR

Hands-only **cardiopulmonary resuscitation** (CPR) is recommended for nonmedical rescuers for unconscious teens or adults who have no pulse or respirations. The rescuer should call 9-1-1 and place the victim supine on a hard surface. To find the correct hand position, run two fingers along the ribs to the center chest, place two fingers over the xiphoid process, and place the palm of the other hand on the sternum directly above the fingers. Then place the other hand on top of the first, fingers linked and elbows locked, to begin **compressions**, which should be done in a rocking movement, using the body to apply pressure. (Note: Use two fingers for infants.) The rate of compressions is at least 100 per minute and at least two inches deep (one-third chest depth for infants and small children). This rate corresponds roughly to the beat of the Bee Gees' song "Staying Alive" (dum, dum, dum, dum, stayin' alive, stayin' alive….). With two trained rescuers, **rescue breathing** may be added at a compression to breathing rate of 30:2.

## Heimlich Maneuver

The universal sign of choking is when a person clutches his or her throat and appears to be choking or gasping for breath. If the person can speak ("Can you speak?") or cough, the **Heimlich maneuver** is not usually necessary. The Heimlich maneuver can be done with the victim sitting, standing, or supine. The Heimlich procedure for children (≥1 year) and adults is as follows:

- Wrap arms around the victim's waist from the back if sitting or standing. Make a fist and place the thumb side against the victim's abdomen slightly above the umbilicus. Grasp this hand with the other and thrust sharply upward to force air out of the lungs.
- Repeat as needed and call 9-1-1 if there is no response.
- If the victim loses consciousness, ease him or her into a supine position on the floor, place hands similarly to CPR but over the abdomen while sitting astride the victim's legs. Repeat upward compressions five times. If no ventilation occurs, attempt to sweep the mouth and ventilate the lungs mouth to mouth. Repeat compressions and ventilations until recovery or emergency personnel arrive.

Indications of **choking** in infants younger than one year include lack of breathing, gasping, cyanosis, and inability to cry. Procedures for the **Heimlich chest thrusts** include the following:

- Position the infant in the prone (face-down) position along the forearm with the infant's head lower than the trunk, being sure to support the head so the airway is not blocked.
- Using the heel of the hand, deliver five forceful upward blows between the shoulder blades.
- Sandwich the child between your two arms, turn the infant into the supine position, and drape him or her over your thigh with the head lower than the trunk and the head supported.
- Using two fingers (as in CPR compressions), give up to five thrusts (about 1.5 inches deep) to the lower third of the sternum.
- Only do a finger sweep and remove any foreign object if the object is visible. Repeat five back blows, five chest thrusts, repeating until the foreign body is ejected or until emergency personnel take over.
- If the infant loses consciousness, begin CPR. If a pulse is noted but spontaneous respirations are absent, continue with ventilation only.

## Health and Safety of Individuals Responding to Medical Emergencies

When responding to a medical emergency, it's important to take measures to **prevent self-injury or infection**. Precautions include the following:

- Assess the **safety risks** of the situation before rendering aid (gunshots, gang activity, fire, fallen electrical wires, severe storm conditions), and do not give aid unless the situation is safe.
- Avoid contact with **body fluids** (blood, urine, feces, semen), and use gloves if available; otherwise, attempt to find some type of barrier (plastic bag, towel) to use to prevent direct contact.
- Use a face mask if possible if in danger of **airborne pathogens**, such as when a person has a severe cough.

- **Standard precautions**: Hand hygiene with soap and water or alcohol scrub should be carried out if possible before touching a person, but this is not always possible in an emergent situation. Hands and any contaminated body parts should be washed with soap and water as soon as possible after contact, especially if contaminated by body fluids.

## American Red Cross Certification Courses in First Aid, CPR, and AED

The American Red Cross states on its website that knowing what to do in the event of an emergency involving respiratory or cardiac problems, or requiring first aid measures, could help save somebody's life. The Red Cross offers course options among hands-on learning of **first aid**, cardiopulmonary resuscitation (**CPR**), and automated external defibrillator (**AED**) use. These courses are all aligned with the *Best Practices for Workplace First Aid Training Programs* issued by the Occupational Safety and Health Administration (OSHA). They are available in both classroom versions, and blended (i.e., combined classroom and online) formats. Depending on the option chosen, courses last from two to five hours. Upon completing a course successfully, people receive a two-year **certification**. The Red Cross offers refresher courses free of charge for all course options, and short classes for renewing current certification. The first aid course, including a pediatric version, teaches people how to respond to common emergencies including cuts, burns, head injuries, neck injuries, back injuries, and other situations requiring first aid. The CPR and AED courses teach how to respond to breathing and heart emergencies, including using AEDs, for adults, children, and infants.

## Practicing Heimlich Maneuver and CPR

For choking, quick response is necessary to prevent unconsciousness, even death. For adults and children (procedures for infants differ), perform the **Heimlich maneuver**: first, remember panicky victims may unintentionally strike out, and protect yourself. Do not perform the Heimlich on someone who is speaking, coughing, or breathing—someone who can do these things is not choking. Stand behind the victim. Wrap your arms around him or her as if hugging. Make a fist with your right hand; put it above the victim's navel. Grasp your right fist with your left hand; thrust in and up forcibly. Repeat thrusting until the victim can breathe. If the victim loses consciousness, begin child **CPR** for children aged 1-8 years, adult CPR above 8 years. Practice universal precautions and use protective equipment if available to avoid contagious or infectious diseases. "Shake and shout" trying to wake the victim. If he or she does not awaken, call 911. If nobody is available, perform CPR for two minutes, then call 911. On children, do two chest compressions per second 30 times; repeat until help arrives. On adults, do chest compressions at least 100 times a minute, 30 times in 18 seconds; repeat until help arrives.

## High School Courses for Emergency Response and First Aid

The American Red Cross offers a course specifically designed for high school and college students. Students who successfully complete this class receive **certification** in first aid, cardiopulmonary resuscitation (CPR), and using automated external defibrillators (AEDs). The course also provides students with a comprehensive array of skills that prepares them for responding to a varied range of **emergencies** that can occur to adults, children, and infants. By learning these skills and applying them in an emergency situation, students might be able to save a life. This course involves 30 hours of instruction with an emphasis on hands-on learning, and awards a two-year certification to students upon its satisfactory completion. The class includes modules that cover first aid techniques, adult and pediatric CPR and AED use, how to manage various injuries, and how to prevent the transmission of different diseases. The American Red Cross website includes a search engine whereby students can enter their city, state, and ZIP code to find and register for classes available in their areas.

## Guidelines for Calling 911

**Emergencies** requiring **911 calls** are defined as any situations that need immediate help from an ambulance, the fire department, or the police. Some examples of such emergencies include medical emergencies needing immediate medical attention, like uncontrollable bleeding, chest pains, allergic reactions, someone not breathing or struggling to breathe, or someone who is unconscious. Automobile accidents, particularly including injuries, are emergencies. Crimes, particularly in progress, are emergencies. Fires are 911 emergencies. Officials recommend if a person is not sure whether a situation is a real emergency or not, he or she should call 911 and let the call-taker help determine this. Callers should be prepared to **answer questions** from the dispatcher like the street address and location of the emergency; the phone number they are calling from; the nature of the emergency; and details, like descriptions of symptoms or injuries in a medical emergency, descriptions of fires in progress, or descriptions of persons who may have committed crimes. Callers should also be prepared to **follow any instructions** given by call-takers, including step-by-step CPR or Heimlich maneuver directions. Callers should not hang up until instructed by the call-taker.

Today **911** can be called using landline and wireless phones. Enabling text messages to 911 is expected in the near future. The National Emergency Number Association (NENA) and 911.gov advise if adults call 911 accidentally, or a child dials 911 with no emergency, callers or parents should briefly explain the mistake, not simply hang up: call-takers may assume there is an emergency and dispatch responders unnecessarily, diverting them from real emergencies. Separate phone numbers exist for non-emergency services. Call-takers can identify emergencies and non-emergencies and direct unsure callers to proper non-emergency numbers. Prank calls to 911 are illegal in most states; local law enforcement agencies address them. Callers should know cross street names, signs, neighboring buildings and other landmarks: 911 centers answering calls may not be those servicing the caller's area. Callers should post their addresses on both mailboxes and houses. Parents should teach young children what 911 is and how to dial from landlines and wireless phones, ensuring they can reach at least one phone in the house. Children must know their name, parents' names, address, and phone number. Parents should teach children to trust 911 call-takers, answer their questions, and not hang up until instructed.

## SHI

The Centers for Disease Control and Prevention (CDC) collaborated with school health experts, administrators and staff, parents, and national non-government health and education agencies to develop the *School Health Index: Self-Assessment & Planning Guide 2012* (**SHI**), an online, confidential, and easy-to-use tool available on the CDC website's SHI page—one PDF for elementary schools and another for middle and high schools—that helps schools identify their health and safety policy and program strength and weaknesses; develop student health-enhancing action plans to incorporate into School Improvement Plans (SIPs); and involve students, teachers, parents, and communities in promoting better health and health-enhancing behaviors. The SHI uses the CDC's research-based guidelines for school health programs as its basis. These guidelines identify policies and practices found most effective for **decreasing health risk behaviors** by students. The SHI covers sexual health topics, including teen pregnancy, HIV and other STD prevention; cross-referential health services, mental health services, and family and community involvement modules; and updated nutritional information aligned with Institute of Medicine recommendations and USDA requirements. The SHI can be customized and used interactively online, and/or downloaded and printed.

## Behavioral Change Theories Applicable to Health Education Programs for Preventing and Controlling Injury

Behavioral change theories applicable to health education injury prevention and control programs include: community organization theory, diffusion of innovations theory, the ecological/social ecological model, the extended parallel processing model, the health belief model, health promotion models, integrated models, the PRECEDE/PROCEED model, the public health model, social-cognitive theory, the theory of reasoned action/planned behavior, and the stages-of-change or transtheoretical model. **Community organization theory** concentrates on community strengths. Main concepts include community capacity, critical consciousness, empowerment, participation, relevance, and issue selection. The federal Health Start program is an example. **Diffusions of innovation theory** focus on processes whereby new ideas are spread through society. Main concepts include social networks, communication channels, innovations, and time to reach members. Examples include collaboration between the Alzheimer's Association and police to augment Alzheimer's patient safety through a community-based initiative, and Australian public hospital prenatal smoking cessation programs. **Ecological/social ecological models** emphasize multilevel approaches to sociological and environmental influences on individual behavior. Applications include road traffic injury prevention, unintentional injury prevention, world violence and health reporting, and needs assessment for community intervention planning.

The **extended parallel processing model of behavior change** is a theory of fear appeal. It describes how people process messages and respond to them to increase their awareness of personal health risk, and how health education program planners can design methods for overcoming health risks. One application of this model has been to prevent noise-induced hearing loss in Appalachian coal miners (Murray-Johnson et al, 2004). The **health belief model** focuses on perceptions of disease threat and the net benefits of behavior change to ascertain whether and why an individual will change his or her behavior. **Health promotion models** have had actual and proposed applications, including to drinking and driving, preventing violence and injuries, increasing bicycle helmet use, prevention of alcohol-related traffic injuries, and improving fire escape behaviors when responding to smoke alarms. **Integrated models**, including the public health model with the social-ecological model and the PRECEDE framework with the Haddon Matrix, have been applied to injury control and health education, epidemiology and disease prevention, interventions in male violence against females, urban violence, and unintentional injury prevention. The **PRECEDE/PROCEED model** includes epidemiological, ecological, environmental, social, behavioral, educational, policy, and administrative assessments; and evaluations of process, implementation, outcomes, and impacts.

## Risks of Drinking and Driving

According to the National Council on Alcoholism and Drug Dependence, Inc. (NCADD), 32 percent of deadly auto crashes are estimated to involve a driver or pedestrian **intoxicated by alcohol**. The influence of alcohol slows reaction time and impairs attention; judgment; the ability to make quick decisions; reactions to environmental changes; and executing precise, difficult maneuvers while driving. Therefore, **driving** is dangerous and can be deadly under the influence of alcohol and other drugs. Though public awareness has increased, many people still drive under the influence. Almost 13,000 individuals die annually in alcohol-related accidents, and hundreds of thousands are injured. These crashes cost over $100 billion to American taxpayers. Yearly arrests for driving while intoxicated number above 1.4 million, representing below one percent of 159 million self-reported instances of drinking and driving. Of those arrested, 780,000 are convicted; two-thirds of those sentenced to prison are repeat offenders. Most deaths are caused by drivers with at least 0.10 **blood alcohol concentration (BAC)**—the common criterion for intoxication. However, even 0.02 BAC impairs driving ability.

# Risks from Smoking Tobacco

More than 480,000 Americans, i.e., around one in five, die annually from **smoking cigarettes**. Smoking causes more mortalities than drinking alcohol, using illegal drugs, auto accidents, gunshots, and human immunodeficiency virus (HIV) *combined.* Compared to all war casualties in US history, smoking cigarettes has killed over 10 times as many citizens. More women die annually from **lung cancer** than breast cancer. Of all lung cancer deaths in women and men, 90 percent are caused by smoking. Eighty percent of **chronic obstructive pulmonary disease (COPD)**, including chronic bronchitis and emphysema) deaths are from smoking. Over the past 50 years, risk of death from smoking has risen in American men and women. Smoking raises death risk from all causes. Smokers are at an estimated two to four times the risk for coronary heart disease and stroke; male smokers have 25 times the risk of lung cancer, and female smokers 25.7 times the risk. COPD deaths are 12-13 times more likely in smokers. Fewer than five cigarettes daily can cause cardiovascular disease. Smoking causes bladder, blood, cervical, colorectal, esophageal, kidney, ureter, laryngeal, liver, oropharyngeal, pancreatic, stomach, tracheal, bronchial, and lung cancer. Smoking causes one of every three cancer deaths in the US.

## Smoking Cigarettes in Addition to Cardiovascular Disease and Cancers

In addition to cardiovascular disease and cancers, smoking cigarettes decreases overall health. Researchers questioning smokers find they self-report **poorer health status**. Smokers are absent from work more often. They require more health care and cost more to themselves, the government, and American taxpayers in healthcare expenses. In addition to the cardiovascular effects of strokes, heart attacks and heart disease—the foremost American killers—plus blood clots, reduced blood flow, blood vessel damage, high blood pressure, multiple cancers, and chronic obstructive lung diseases, smoking can trigger and exacerbate asthma attacks. It damages almost everybody organ. Smoking makes conceiving children more difficult. It also raises risks of miscarriage, premature delivery, stillbirth, low birth weight, sudden infant death syndrome (SIDS), ectopic pregnancy (extrauterine implantation), infant orofacial clefts, and other birth defects. Smoking can lower sperm counts, decreasing fertility. Post-menopausal women smokers have weaker bone density, risking fractures. Smoking damages tooth and gum health and causes tooth loss. Higher risks of eye cataracts and age-related macular degeneration are also associated with smoking. Smoking causes type 2 diabetes, raising risk 30-40 percent, and impedes its treatment. Smoking causes rheumatoid arthritis, other inflammatory conditions, and impairs immune function.

# Benefits of Smoking Cessation

The Centers for Disease Control and Prevention (CDC) reports smoking has been estimated to raise a person's risk of heart disease, including heart attacks, to between double and quadruple those of a nonsmoker's risk; but also has found that risk drops greatly only one year after **quitting smoking**. A stroke or cerebrovascular accident (CVA) happens when either a blood clot blocks blood flow to a part of the brain (an ischemic stroke), or a blood vessel in or near the brain leaks/bursts (a hemorrhagic stroke). Whereas smoking also increases the risk of stroke to two to four times a nonsmoker's risk; two to five years after quitting smoking, that risk can be similar to that of someone who never smoked. Whereas smoking raises an individual's risks for mouth, throat, esophageal, and bladder cancers, these risks decrease by one-half within five years after quitting smoking. While smoking increases a person's risk for lung cancer by 25 times or more, that risk is cut in half by 10 years after the person has quit smoking. Smoking cessation can extend **life expectancy**.

# Cocaine and Crack Cocaine

Cocaine is derived from the coca plant and available in powdered form. It is either injected intravenously or snorted nasally. **Crack cocaine** is produced by processing powdered cocaine, altering its chemical

- 52 -

composition. It is available in the form of "rocks" which are smoked. One distinction is that, while powdered cocaine is typically quite expensive, crack cocaine is comparatively cheap, making it more accessible and hence more dangerous. Either form of cocaine is in the **stimulant** drug class and is extremely addictive. Using any amount of either incurs physical risks, including: elevated heart rate, respiratory rate, body temperature, and blood pressure; respiratory failure; heart attack; stroke; seizures; reduced capacity to resist and fight infections; hepatitis and/or AIDS from sharing needles for injections; and burn injuries from smoking crack. Psychological risks include: hallucinations, including tactile hallucinations of "coke bugs," i.e., the sensation of insects crawling on the skin; paranoid, erratic, and/or violent behavior; loss of appetite; loss of sexual interest; anxiety; depression; confusion; and "cocaine psychosis," i.e., losing interest in family, friends, hobbies, sports, and all other usual activities; and losing touch with reality.

## Methamphetamine

Methamphetamine is a drug in the **stimulant** class. Chemically it is related to the stimulant amphetamine, but it affects the central nervous system more powerfully. Street names for the drug include speed, crank, and meth. It is available in pills for taking orally, or in powder for injecting or snorting. Through a chemical process ("cooking"), it can be crystallized into an even stronger form, called crystal meth, ice, or glass, which is smoked. **Methamphetamine** use produces physiological and psychological effects including: euphoria; insomnia; elevated blood pressure and heart rate; an increase in physical activity; severe anorexia (lack of appetite); irritability; anxiety; confusion; paranoia; violent behavior; tremors; respiratory difficulties; cardiovascular disruptions, which can be fatal; hypothermia; convulsions; and irreversible damage to blood vessels in the brain, causing strokes. In addition, users who inject methamphetamine and share needles with others have the risk of contracting HIV/AIDS.

## Alcohol Abuse and Alcoholism

According to a publication by the US Department of Health and Human Services' Substance Abuse and Mental Health Services Administration (SAMHSA), citing the National Institute on Drug Abuse (NIDA, 2004), a division of the National Institutes of Health (NIH), as its source, **alcohol abuse** is a problematic drinking pattern that causes social problems, health problems, or both. The term **alcoholism**, or alcohol dependence, however, indicates an illness whose symptoms include abnormal behaviors for the purpose of obtaining alcohol, which causes impairment in an individual's control over his or her drinking. Regular, substantial use of alcohol has short-term effects that include impaired judgment, altered emotions and perceptions, impaired coordination, distorted vision and hearing, halitosis, and hangovers. Heavy use of alcohol has long-term effects that include skin problems; vitamin deficiencies; stomach disorders; loss of appetite; sexual impotence; liver damage; loss of memory; and damage to the central nervous system, heart, and cardiovascular system.

## Prescription Drug Abuse

The most commonly abused **prescription drugs** are opiate and opioid painkillers like Vicodin and Oxycontin; anxiolytic and anti-anxiety and sedative medications like Valium and Xanax; hypnotics like Ambien, prescribed for insomnia and anxiety; and stimulants like Ritalin, prescribed for ADHD and some sleep disorders. These are popular for their consciousness-altering effects. Signs of abuse include asking multiple doctors for prescriptions; repeatedly "losing" prescriptions, requiring replacements; forging, selling, and/or stealing prescriptions; abnormally sedated, energetic, or altered behaviors; extreme mood swings; hostility; decreased or increased sleeping; higher-than-prescribed dosing; and reduced decision-making capacity. **Opiates and opioids** cause symptoms including depression, low blood pressure, constipation, lowered respiration, perspiration, incoordination, and confusion. **Anxiolytics** cause confusion, dizziness, drowsiness, unstable gait, rapid involuntary eye movements, and poor judgment.

- 53 -

**Stimulants** cause restlessness, insomnia, irritability, agitation, high blood pressure, heart arrhythmia, weight loss, and impulsivity. Reasons for abuse include to relieve tension or relax; increase alertness; improve concentration, school, or work performance; decrease appetite; get high and feel good; experiment with mental effects; prevent withdrawal once addicted; and/or facilitate socialization and peer acceptance.

Although many patients prescribed pain medications following surgery are afraid they will become addicted to them, this seldom happens when they take them as prescribed. **Addiction** is more likely when potentially addictive drugs are not taken as directed. Some **risk factors** for abusing prescription drugs include: youth, i.e., adolescence or early 20s; some pre-existing psychiatric disorders; current or past addictions to alcohol and other substances; lack of adequate knowledge or information regarding prescription medications; social environments with drug use; peer pressure; and working in healthcare settings or other situations with easier access to prescription drugs. Older adult abuse of prescriptions is an increasing problem: an aging population includes multiple health problems and multiple medications. This creates greater risk for misusing drugs; combining prescriptions with other prescriptions, over-the-counter medications, alcohol, and/or illegal drugs; and addiction. Some serious medical dangers of abusing prescriptions include: memory problems from anxiolytics and sedatives; choking risk; lowered blood pressure; slowed or stopped breathing; coma; and death by overdose from opiates, opioids, anxiolytics, and sedatives. Sudden withdrawal from sedatives and anxiolytics can cause nervous system hyperactivity and seizures. Abusing stimulants can cause paranoia, aggression, tremors, hallucinations, high blood pressure, dangerously high body temperatures, cardiac problems, and seizures.

## Legal and Societal Impacts of Substance Abuse

The National Drug Intelligence Center's National Drug Threat Assessments find millions of people, many aged 18-25, have injected **illegal drugs**. Among adult Americans with AIDS, the CDC reports those contracting it from injecting drugs have lower survival rates than those contracting it from all other forms of transmission. Thousands of Americans die every year from the effects of drug use. **Drug abuse** frequently causes parents to neglect or abuse their children physically and/or emotionally. Children with parents or family members abusing substances are often deprived of shelter, water, food, medical and dental care, and necessary immunizations. Parents manufacturing drugs like methamphetamine pose even higher risks to children for hazardous chemical exposure, neglect, injury, and death. Employee substance abuse causes significant economic impacts on businesses through productivity loss; absenteeism; escalated medical insurance use; workplace accidents; workplace theft; and catastrophic accidents caused by drug impairment in employees like bus drivers, train conductors, air traffic controllers, and airline pilots. Methamphetamine lab operations not only severely strain taxpayer, local, state, and federal government resources, but moreover injure and kill neighbors, police, emergency responders, and children. Meth users seriously increase social services and law enforcement expenses.

## Stage-of-Change Approach to Substance Abuse Treatment

The stages of change are precontemplation, contemplation, preparation, action, and maintenance. In the **action stage**, clinicians should support realistic approaches to change via small steps; acknowledge early-stage change difficulties; engage clients in treatment; emphasize the importance of staying in recovery; help clients use functional analysis to identify high-risk situations, and develop corresponding suitable coping strategies; and help clients find new reinforcers for positive change. In **maintenance**, clinicians should help clients identify and try new, non-substance reinforcers; affirm client self-efficacy and determination; support lifestyle modifications; help clients practice and apply new coping skills to prevent relapse; and maintain supportive contact. Some competing **reinforcers** for clients include: involvement in self-help or 12-step activities and groups; setting goals for educational, employment, nutritional, and fitness improvements; volunteer work to enhance self-efficacy, interact with socially acceptable friends, occupy time, and help others; cultural and spiritual activities; interacting more with significant others and families; learning new hobby skills or improving existing ones; and socializing with non-substance abusers.

## Prevention Strategies for Use and Abuse of Alcohol, Tobacco, and Other Legal and Illegal Drugs

Prevention strategies for the use and abuse of alcohol, tobacco, and other legal and illegal drugs include the following:

- **Enlist the parents/caregivers**: Provide them with information about the signs of use and abuse of alcohol, tobacco, and drugs and guidelines about how to talk to their children about these issues as well as lists of community and Internet resources.
- **Promote self-esteem**: Identify and recognize individuals' talents and skills and encourage them to develop their talents.
- **Develop critical thinking skills**: Focus on problem-solving and values in class discussions and assignments.
- **Educate regarding risks**: Include facts, dangers, and laws related to drug and alcohol use. (However, education alone without skills training has not proven to be effective.)
- **Provide skills training**: Focus on specific skills, such as assertiveness, refusal methods, and methods of withstanding peer pressure.
- **Provide alternatives**: Engage students in activities such as sports, music, and computer clubs. Provide after-school programs/activities for high school students.

## Promoting Individual Responsible Drug/Alcohol Use

Strategies for promoting individual responsible drug/alcohol use include the following:

- **Education**: Include facts about drug/alcohol effects, dangers, and clearance as well as laws related to drugs and alcohol. Outline the effects of mixing drugs with other drugs or alcohol and review safety measures such as the use of designated drivers.
- **Assertiveness training**: Teach the child how to say "no" and how to handle peer pressure to avoid risk-taking behaviors.
- **Designated driver**: One person who uses no drugs or alcohol is designated to drive those using drugs/alcohol to prevent accidents.
- **Sober/Safe ride programs**: Free rides on request for those using drugs/alcohol are available in some communities.
- **Sober friend**: One person is designated to watch over other friends who are using drugs/alcohol to prevent them from risk-taking behavior (such as sexual contact or severe intoxication, or making public displays of risk-taking behavior on social media) and who remains alert to prevent the use of date-rape drugs.

## Intervention and Treatments for Substance Abuse

### Interventions
Interventions substance abuse include the following:

- **Personal intervention**: Friends and/or family may confront the person and explain how the person's substance abuse is affecting them. Interventions are best done with a small group rather than with one individual confronting the abuser; adolescents should generally include adults in the group and not attempt to handle the intervention without assistance. If the drug abuser has overdosed, then 9-1-1 should be called.

- **Tell a responsible adult**: Young people especially are often not prepared to confront others who are participating in substance abuse but should seek help from a parent, counselor, spiritual advisor, or teacher whom they trust and who can help them deal with the problem. Adolescents are often reluctant to divulge others' "secrets," so it's important to have discussions in class about health and safety issues taking precedence over confidentiality.

Treatment

Treatments for substance abuse include the following:

- **Drug rehabilitation**: Addicted and alcoholic substance abusers may require inpatient or outpatient treatment in a drug rehabilitation center. Many programs are covered by insurance, although some may be prohibitively expensive for some students, and others may have waiting lists.
- **Smoking cessation programs**: These include support groups, online programs, and nicotine replacement (such as transdermal patches).
- **Counseling**: Substance abusers often have unresolved problems that require professional intervention, so referral for counseling is often indicated.
- **Detoxification**: This should be carried out under medical supervision because of the potential for life-threatening complications. Adolescents should not attempt detoxification by themselves or under the supervision of friends.
- **Medications**: Methadone or buprenorphine may be used for maintenance after detoxification for drug addicts. Naloxone is administered in emergent conditions for opioid overdose.

**Role of Peer Pressure in Decision Making and Problem Solving Related to Substance Abuse**

Peer pressure is the pressure to conform to the behavior or ideals of a group that is approximately the same age and social class. Most adolescents are introduced to drugs and alcohol by peers, and **peer pressure** to participate in high-risk behavior, such as substance abuse, is very strong because the adolescent wants to be accepted as part of the group. Groups that use drugs or alcohol tend to view others as abnormal, not themselves, so adolescents that refuse to participate may find themselves ostracized. Thus, although an adolescent may be aware of the dangers of drugs and alcohol and doesn't want to participate in use, he or she may feel compelled to do so. **Assertiveness training** and **refusal skills** can help the adolescent to deal with peer pressure, but the reality is that the person may need to align with a **different group of peers** in order to make good decisions about avoiding substance abuse.

**Personal Hygiene**

Good personal hygiene promotes good health by preventing and limiting exposure to bacterial and viral microorganisms. In addition to **physical benefits**, good bodily hygiene also supports good **mental health** by promoting psychological well-being and feeling good about oneself. When people neglect their personal hygiene, they develop body odors, bad breath, damaged and lost teeth, and unkempt hair and clothing. Other people then view them as unhealthy; as a result, they can encounter social and employment discrimination. Some components of good personal hygiene include bathing, nail care, and foot care. Not everybody needs to bathe or shower daily; for some people, this can remove too many body oils, exacerbating dry skin. However, individuals should wash their bodies and hair regularly as often as they find necessary. The skin is continually shedding dead cells, which must be removed. If it accumulates, it can cause health problems. Trimming the fingernails and toenails regularly averts problems like hangnails and infected nailbeds. Keeping the feet clean and dry, and wearing clean flip-flops at public facilities, gyms, health clubs, spas, and around swimming pools prevents contracting athlete's foot and other fungal infections.

## Oral Hygiene, Hand Washing, and Sleep

Ideally, we should brush our teeth after every time we eat. Health professionals recommend brushing and flossing the teeth twice a day at a minimum. **Brushing teeth** removes plaque and reduces mouth bacteria, inhibiting tooth decay. This prevents not only tooth cavities, but also gum disease. **Flossing and gum massage** keep gums healthy and strong. If oral bacteria build up, it can cause gum disease. Gum disease not only causes irreversible bone loss in the jaw; the bacteria can travel from the gums directly to the heart, causing serious heart valve disorders. Unhealthy gums can loosen teeth, causing difficulty chewing, eating, and tooth loss. Most people need dental cleanings and checkups twice yearly, some more often. **Hand washing** prevents bacteria and viruses from spreading. We should wash our hands after using the bathroom; before preparing food and eating; after sneezing or coughing; and after handling garbage. Having alcohol-based hand sanitizing gels on hand is recommended when water is inaccessible. **Sleeping** enough and well must not be overlooked as a component of personal hygiene: insufficient or inadequate sleep impairs the immune system, inviting illness.

## Relationship Between Personal Hygiene and Mental and Emotional Status

Physicians and other experts advise that if a friend or acquaintance is neglecting his or her **personal hygiene**, especially if this is unaccustomed, or has an unkempt appearance, this can be a sign of underlying **depression**. When people are depressed or feeling sad, they tend to neglect taking care of themselves and their bodies. This has multiple sources: depression commonly causes low energy and fatigue, making even routine hygiene practices seem to require too much effort. Depression also lowers self-esteem; people do not feel good enough about themselves to show their bodies and health the self-respect or attention they deserve. Additional depression symptoms are feelings of helplessness, inhibiting motivation to control personal care and health; and hopelessness, removing motivation to take any positive action for self-care. Preoccupation with other concerns can also make people forget hygiene. One should not always assume depression is the cause, however; some people simply lack awareness, particularly if poor hygiene is habitual. Honest yet sensitive conversations about hygiene's importance in disease prevention can help some friends and acquaintances. If not, it is best to encourage their seeing a physician, therapist, or counselor.

## 5th-Grade Lesson Plan in Personal Hygiene Related to Puberty

Traditionally, boys and girls were always separated for classes in health, hygiene, and sexuality. Today, health educators may teach general lessons on **personal hygiene** with whole classes, and then divide the sexes for **gender-specific lessons**, e.g., on nocturnal emissions for boys and toxic shock syndrome associated with tampon use for girls. Teachers can discuss with classes the importance of personal hygiene during adolescence, such as staying healthy, feeling better about themselves, not offending others, avoiding being made fun of, fitting in better, enhancing peer acceptance, projecting the best possible self, etc. A learning activity that 5th-graders will find fun as well as informative is to assign students to find pictures in provided magazines that illustrate good hygiene practices, including pictures of showering or bathing, soaps and body washes, deodorants, hair products, dental hygiene products, skin care products, and clean clothing. With teacher-provided construction paper and aluminum foil, have students create "mirrors" and paste or tape their good hygiene images onto them, reinforcing the concept that caring for our personal hygiene "reflects" our best selves to others.

## Information Related to Pubertal Changes for Preadolescent and Adolescent Students

Teachers can inform preadolescent and adolescent students that around 80 percent of them do or will experience **acne**, which is caused primarily by hormonal changes, not uncleanliness, and usually minimally influenced by diet. They can explain how sebaceous skin glands secrete increased oil called **sebum** in response to elevated hormone levels, and how pimples, whiteheads, and blackheads come from pores blocked by that sebum. They should warn students not to squeeze or pick eruptions, which can cause permanent scars; and reassure them that nearly all acne can be successfully treated. They may discuss gentle, regular washing; avoidance of heavy or oil-based moisturizers, benzoyl peroxide treatments like Proactiv+® and other over-the-counter medications; or, in more severe cases, consulting a dermatologist. Teachers can advise students that puberty's hormonal changes can make hair oily, requiring more frequent washing; and that these changes also increase perspiration and perspiration odor, requiring regular bathing, changing clothes, and using antiperspirant and/or deodorant which they may not have done or needed as children. Discussions should include how **oral hygiene** becomes more challenging as fresh breath gains importance and many teens wear braces. Teachers should discuss **genital hygiene** with separate female and male classes.

## Decreasing Tobacco Use

WHO recognizes tobacco as "the most widely available harmful product on the market." Therefore, it negotiated the first international, legally binding treaty, the **WHO Framework Convention on Tobacco Control (FCTC)**, providing protocols and guidelines for evidence-based interventions to decrease tobacco supply and consumption. Raising tobacco prices and taxes is a documented cost-effective method that substantially increases quitting and decreases starting smoking, particularly among poor and young people. With proper implementation, enforcing smoke-free public place and workplace laws obtains high compliance levels: fewer youths start smoking; smokers are supported in quitting or reducing smoking; and smoke-free policies prevent perpetuating addiction at earlier stages, especially in youth. Informing and educating the public is another cost-effective measure. Studies in multiple countries find graphic health warnings on cigarette and tobacco packaging and creative media campaigns succeed in powerfully decreasing consumer demand, despite opposition from wealthy tobacco companies and health officials' comparatively limited resources. Another cost-effective measure is providing smoking cessation assistance, combining pharmaceutical and behavioral therapies, through primary medical care and public health providers. Though a minority of the global population has received these measures, research finds them affordable in all world nations.

## Role of Physical Activity in Preventing and Reducing Health Risks

Studies demonstrate regular **physical activity (PA)** lowers risks of heart disease, strokes, diabetes, colon cancer, and breast cancer. Thirty to 60 minutes daily of PA decreases breast and colon cancer risks significantly; 150 minutes weekly of PA commonly reduces cardiovascular disease and diabetes risks. The World Health Organization (WHO) finds media promotion of combined PA and healthy diet very cost-effective, inexpensive, and feasible. **Schools** should include physical education with trained teachers and parental involvement in supportive environments. Successful **workplace** strategies include furnishing fitness spaces and signs encouraging staircase use; engaging employees in planning and implementing fitness programs; engaging families via festivals, newsletters, self-learning programs, etc.; and supplying self-monitoring and individual behavior change strategies. Effective **community** interventions include group PA classes and programs; community development campaigns concentrating on shared goals like reducing cardiovascular disease risk; and lifestyle modification advice regarding diet and physical activity, which research has proven to prevent diabetes with effectiveness similar to pharmacological therapy in people with impaired glucose tolerance.

## Measures Found Globally to Decrease Harmful Alcohol Consumption

To be effective, strategies for prevention of cardiovascular disease, cirrhosis of the liver, and certain cancers secondary to **harmful alcohol consumption** must change both amounts and patterns of use. Based on evidence from research in Brazil, China, Mexico, Russia, Vietnam, and other countries, the World Health Organization (WHO) recommends these interventions to reduce harmful alcohol use: raising alcoholic beverage taxes; government monopolies of retail alcohol sales where applicable; restricting

- 58 -

sales times and outlet density; regulating alcoholic beverage availability and minimum legal purchasing age; comprehensive advertising bans and/or effective marketing regulations limiting exposure to alcoholic drink advertising and marketing; measures to counter drinking and driving including lower (a half-gram per liter) driver blood alcohol concentration limits, zero tolerance or limits lowered further for younger drivers, sobriety checkpoints, and random breath testing; brief interventions for harmful and hazardous drinking, and treatment for alcohol abuse disorders. Isolated classroom and public education, mass media campaigns, and consumer warning messages and labels have not been found effective by research; however, informational and educational campaigns supporting the aforementioned effective measures can enhance their public acceptance.

## Healthy Diet Components for Preventing and Reducing Health Risks

To prevent and reduce risks of cardiovascular disease, diabetes, and some cancers, healthy diets should balance calorie intake and expenditure for healthy weight maintenance; limit intake from total fats to 30 percent; eliminate trans fats, and substitute unsaturated fats for saturated; limit consumption of free sugars; increase consumption of vegetables, legumes, fruits, whole grains, and nuts; make all salt iodized; and limit sodium intake from all sources. Although studies find multiple nutritional interventions more cost-effective with greater potential health gains than individual interventions, the World Health Organization (WHO) also identifies **salt reduction** for preventing noncommunicable diseases. A major cause of death is high blood pressure, frequently caused or exacerbated by excess dietary sodium. About 75 percent of salt intake in North America and Europe comes from sodium added to manufactured meals and foods. Most sodium consumed in many Asian and African countries is from soy sauce and salt added at home during cooking and eating. WHO estimates decreasing salt to recommended levels could prevent up to 2.5 million deaths annually. Finland, France, Ireland, Japan, and the United Kingdom have successfully implemented salt reduction initiatives, preventing thousands of premature deaths and saving billions in healthcare and other expenses annually.

## Life Choices to Prevent Chronic Diseases and Health Conditions, and Contrasting Health Risk Behaviors

Regular **aerobic exercise** or **physical activity** can prevent cardiovascular disease. Weight-bearing exercise strengthens bones, preventing osteoporosis which leads to fractures. Exercising, limiting sodium intake, not smoking, eating diets low in saturated and trans fats and high in fiber, and losing or controlling weight all reduce risks for strokes and heart disease by strengthening the heart and blood vessels and reducing blood pressure, cholesterol and arterial plaque. **Not smoking** also prevents lung cancer and other respiratory, oral, and digestive system cancers. **Eating vegetables and fruits** accesses antioxidants protecting against many cancers, and fibers protecting against colorectal cancers, as does eating whole grains. Binge drinking kills many Americans, most of whom are not alcohol-dependent; hence **avoiding binge drinking** prevents deaths. According to the CDC, more than half of adults do not get recommended levels of aerobic or muscle-strengthening exercise or physical activity. Most Americans consume **excessive sodium**, risking hypertension. Almost half have other major heart-disease risk factors, i.e., uncontrolled hypertension and/or high LDL cholesterol. Over one-third of adults reported (2011) eating fruit less than once daily, almost one-fourth vegetables less than once daily; over one-third of teens ate fruit and vegetables less than once daily. Nearly 20 percent of adults smoked in 2012.

## Treatment for Many Types of Cancer

Whether they involve localized solid tumors or diffuse conditions like leukemia and other cancers of the blood, all **cancer** is, by definition, an uncontrolled growth of abnormal cells. Therefore, treatment typically involves removing and/or killing the cancerous cells, growths, or masses. One treatment is **surgically removing** cancerous tissue. Some inoperable cancers would require removing needed healthy

- 59 -

tissue, as with sarcoidosis wrapped around the spinal cord, or aggressive tumors having invaded too much of vital organs. In some cases, an entire organ may be surgically replaced by **donor transplantation**. Surgical removal of a cancerous growth is often followed by **radiation treatment**—exposure to radioactive elements—to eliminate any remaining cancer cells and/or prevent new regrowth. Side-effects include burns or other damages to the treatment site. Another treatment method to kill cancer cells is **chemotherapy**. Various drugs, administered orally or intravenously, are toxic to cancer growths. Unfortunately, most treatments toxic enough to kill cancer cells are also toxic to the patient. Chemotherapy side effects include severe nausea, vomiting, debilitating fatigue, hair loss, skin damage, and osteoporosis. Some treatment protocols combine methods, e.g., surgery followed by radiation and chemotherapy, radiation to shrink a tumor followed by surgery, etc.

## Health Education Program for Managing Chronic Diseases and Health Conditions

Stanford University's School of Medicine Patient Education Research Center offers a chronic disease self-management program called the **Better Choices, Better Health® Workshop**. Facilitated by two trained leaders, one or both non-health professionals with their own chronic diseases, this workshop is held in hospitals, libraries, senior centers, churches, and other community settings. Weekly classes are two-and-a-half hours each for six weeks. The workshop covers subjects including techniques for coping with pain, fatigue, frustration, and isolation; exercises appropriate for preserving and enhancing endurance, strength, and flexibility; using medications appropriately; nutrition; decision-making; effective communication with health professionals, family, and friends; and how to evaluate new treatments. Participants are given the accompanying *Relaxation for Mind and Body* audio CD and *Living a Healthy Life with Chronic Conditions, 4th edition* book. Sessions involve high participation levels, mutual success, and support. This course was developed based on federally- and state-funded research. Researchers included Stanford psychologist Albert Bandura, originator of self-efficacy, i.e., self-confidence for mastering new skills or influencing one's health. Bandura and colleagues deemed **self-management skills instruction** instrumental in managing chronic disease; program evaluation yielded positive outcomes. Stanford offers healthcare organization representatives program training four to five times yearly.

## HIV/AIDS

The **human immunodeficiency virus** (HIV) impairs or destroys an infected individual's immune system, raising infection risk and ruining infection defenses. As HIV advances, its final stage is **AIDS**, acquired immune deficiency syndrome. The World Health Organization (WHO) estimated that by the end of 2013, 35 million humans were living with HIV. Of these, 23.4-26.2 million lived in sub-Saharan Africa. Global health community efforts include research and development of new medications to address symptoms for people already infected, as well as preventing new infections; outreach and education to stop HIV spread; and supporting children and families who have lost parents to AIDS deaths. **Anti-retroviral therapy (ART) drugs** have enabled many HIV patients to survive 15+ years before developing AIDS symptoms. WHO estimated 12.9 million people were receiving these by the end of 2013, 11.7 million of them in low-income and middle-income nations. The most successful global health effort, this program has been significantly helped by the **President's Emergency Plan for AIDS Relief (PEPFAR)**. Additionally, the US Department of Health and Human Services (HHS), National Institutes of Health (NIH) offices, Gates Foundation, and Centers for Disease Control and Prevention (CDC) are all actively involved in global HIV/AIDS research, researcher training, coordination, and vaccine development.

## Cystic Fibrosis

In cystic fibrosis (**CF**), a defective gene produces a protein causing the body to secrete mucus that is much thicker and stickier than normal. This mucus clogs up the lungs, resulting in infections that can cause or threaten death. It also blocks the pancreas from delivering enzymes that help break down and absorb necessary nutrients from foods. Over 75 percent of CF patients are diagnosed by age 2. Today, almost half of CF patients are aged 18 or more. Around 1,000 new CF cases are diagnosed annually. Symptoms include shortness of breath; wheezing; chronic persistent coughing, including phlegm-productive coughs; slow weight gain and inadequate growth despite good appetite; frequently developing lung infections; difficult, bulky, greasy, and/or frequent bowel movements; and skin with an extremely salty taste. Most children with CF died before entering elementary school during the 1950s. Today, significant progress in the understanding and treatment of CF has dramatically improved longevity and life quality in CF patients. Many now live into middle adulthood or older; life expectancy has doubled in the past three decades. The **Cystic Fibrosis Foundation**, whose support has enabled almost all available CF treatment medications, views research for a cure as "promising."

## Sickle Cell Anemia

Anemia means the blood has fewer **red blood cells (RBC)** than normal. RBCs, which transport oxygen in **hemoglobin** (an iron-rich protein) through the bloodstream and remove the waste product carbon dioxide, are produced in the bone marrow, normally living about four months. **Sickle cell** is one genetic type of anemia, inherited when both parents have the gene. When one parent has this gene but the other's is normal, children inherit sickle cell trait; they do not have the disease, but pass the sickle hemoglobin gene to their children. In America, sickle cell anemia is commonest in African-Americans (around one in 500). It also affects Hispanic-Americans (around one in 36,000); and people of Caribbean, Mediterranean, Indian, and Saudi Arabian descent. Normal RBCs are disc-shaped and travel easily through blood vessels. Sickle cells are crescent-shaped, sticky, and stiff, impeding blood flow. This causes organ damage, pain, and increased risk of infections. Some patients have chronic fatigue and/or pain. A few patients may receive future cures through stem cell transplants, but no widespread cure currently exists. Symptoms and complications are managed through treatments. Improved care and treatments enable some patients to live into their 40s, 50s, or older.

## Tay-Sachs Disease

Tay-Sachs disease is a rare genetic disorder, inherited through an **autosomal recessive pattern**; i.e., both parents carry copies of a mutated gene and are usually asymptomatic, but pass these to their children. **Tay-Sachs** is rare overall, and more common among Eastern/Central European Jewish, certain Quebec French-Canadian, Old-Order Pennsylvania Dutch/Amish, and Louisiana Cajun populations. The genetic defect prevents an enzyme from breaking down a toxic substance, which builds up in the brain and spinal cord, progressively destroying neurons. The commonest form appears in infancy, typically around 3-6 months. A typical sign is a "cherry-red spot" eye abnormality, detectable through eye examination. Babies' motor muscles weaken; development slows; they lose motor skills like turning over, sitting up, and crawling; and develop exaggerated startle reactions to loud sounds. As it progresses, this disease causes seizures, loss of vision and hearing, intellectual impairment, and paralysis. Most children with the commoner infantile form of Tay-Sachs disease typically only survive until early childhood. Later-onset forms of the disease are extremely rare, typically with milder, highly variable symptoms including muscular weakness, poor coordination, other motor symptoms, speech difficulties, and mental illness.

## Type 2 Diabetes

Historically, type 1 diabetes, which has a greater genetic component, was called "juvenile diabetes" because symptoms appeared during childhood, contrasting with type 2 "adult-onset diabetes." However, these terms were abandoned as more cases of **type 2 diabetes** are occurring in childhood and adolescence—evidence of the contributions of **lifestyle factors** including obesity, poor nutrition, and physical inactivity. When people consume large amounts of refined carbohydrates (simple sugars and starches processed to remove all fibers) with no fiber slowing digestion, these enter the bloodstream

- 61 -

rapidly, causing a sudden spike in blood sugar, experienced by some as an energy rush. However, with quick metabolism and the pancreas' secretion of extra insulin to neutralize excessive blood sugar, sugars exit as fast as they entered, causing a precipitous blood-sugar drop, or "crash," with fatigue, sleepiness, irritability, depression and cycle-perpetuating cravings for more sugar or starch. Moreover, **metabolic syndrome** eventually develops—insulin resistance to the pancreas' attempts to neutralize repeated artificial blood sugar elevation. In type 1 diabetes, the pancreas fails to produce insulin; in type 2, the body becomes immune to insulin, causing chronically high, unstable blood sugar. Blindness, limb loss, shock, coma, and death are a few of many sequelae from uncontrolled diabetes.

## Chronic, Noncommunicable Diseases

According to the World Health Organization (WHO, 2013), over 36 million people die annually from **noncommunicable diseases (NCDs)**, with almost 80 percent (29 million) in low-income and middle-income nations. Of these, over 9 million are before age 60. Of these premature deaths, 90 percent are in low-income and middle-income nations. Roughly 80 percent of all NCD deaths are due to four disease types: **cardiovascular diseases**, e.g., strokes and heart attacks, which cause the majority (17.3 million yearly); **cancers** (7.6 million yearly); **respiratory diseases** like asthma and chronic obstructive pulmonary disease (COPD) (4.2 million yearly); and **diabetes** (1.3 million yearly). These four disease groups have four **risk factors** in common: tobacco use, physical inactivity, harmful alcohol use, and poor nutrition. WHO projects the greatest increases in NCD mortality by 2020 will be in African countries, where NCDs are also predicted to surpass maternal and infant mortality from childbirth and nutritional and communicable diseases combined as the most common killers by 2030. Behavioral risk factors for NCDs that can be modified are tobacco use, physical inactivity, unhealthy diets, and harmful alcohol consumption.

## Measures Taken by WHO to Prevent NCDs

WHO's *Action Plan of the global strategy for the prevention and control of noncommunicable diseases* gives member states and international partners steps for preventing and addressing NCDs in world nations. WHO is also working to reduce **NCD risk factors**, including: implementing anti-tobacco measures identified in the WHO Framework Convention on Tobacco Control in world nations to decrease public tobacco exposure; helping world communities lower rates of death and disease from physical inactivity and unhealthy diets through the WHO *Global strategy on diet, physical activity and health aims to promote and protect health;* identifying action areas with priority and recommending measures of protection against the harmful consumption of alcohol through the WHO *Global strategy to reduce the harmful use of alcohol;* responding to the United Nations Political Declaration on NCDs by developing a comprehensive framework for global NCD prevention, monitoring, and control, which includes a group of global voluntary targets and a list of indicators; and responding to the World Health Assembly's resolution (WHA 64.11) by developing a 2013-2020 **Global NCD Action Plan** with comprehensive guidance for implementing the United Nations High-Level Meeting's political commitments. WHA endorsed this plan, urging member state, Director-General and Secretariat implementation and future WHA progress reports.

## Disease Etiology

Etiology is defined in medicine as the study of origins or causes of diseases or pathological conditions. Early writings attributed diseases to various unproven "causes" including spells, curses, and imbalances in bodily humors. Ancient Greek physicians Galen and Hippocrates often associated disease with unidentified components in the air, influencing miasmatic perspectives on disease etiology of Medieval European physicians. Ancient Roman scholar Marcus Terentius Varro suggested **microorganisms** caused diseases in his book *On Agriculture* in the 1st century BCE. German physician Robert Koch (1843-1910), modern bacteriology founder, discovered scientific evidence of microorganisms causing the infectious diseases anthrax, cholera, and tuberculosis. As in all experimental science, in **epidemiology**, statistical correlation between/among variables does not prove causation. Sir Austin Bradford-Hill, the epidemiologist who proved causal relationship between tobacco smoking and lung cancer, defined criteria for showing causation. American epidemiologist Alfred Evans proposed the **Unified Concept of Causation**, synthesizing previous thinking. **Etiology** can contribute to causal chains including independent co-factors and promoters. For example, stress, once believed to cause peptic ulcer disease, was belatedly identified as a promoter, with excess stomach acid a prerequisite and *Helicobacter pylori* infection the primary etiology.

Relationships Among and Within Disease Etiologies

Certain diseases, e.g., hepatitis or diabetes, can be diagnosed according to their symptoms. However, these diseases can also develop from **different etiologies**, and can co-exist with, result from, or result in various other conditions. For instance, type 1 diabetes includes a strong genetic component in its etiology, though it also appears to involve complex interactions of genetic and environmental influences; whereas type 2 diabetes more often appears to result from environmental (i.e., lifestyle) influences to a greater extent. Hepatitis (liver inflammation) has separate etiologies: hepatitis A, B, and C are each caused by distinct viruses; autoimmune hepatitis is not infectious, but caused by the patient's own immune system attacking the liver. On the other hand, several different diseases can also result from one **single etiology**. For example, the Epstein-Barr virus can cause the infectious disease mononucleosis, or either of two types of cancer—Burkitt's lymphoma or nasopharyngeal carcinoma—under different conditions.

**Influenza**

Influenza (flu) is an infectious viral respiratory illness. Its symptoms can range from mild to fatal. Young children, seniors, and people with some health conditions have greatest risk for serious complications. Annual **vaccination** is the best way to prevent it. The US Department of Health and Human Services' (HHS) Office of Global Affairs, International Influenza Unit (IIU) is an international partnership to enhance global flu identification and response, coordinated by HHS personnel and Operation Divisions including National Institutes of Health (NIH); Centers for Disease Control and Infection (CDC); Food and Drug Administration (FDA); Office of the Assistant Secretary for Preparedness and Response, Biomedical Advanced Research and Development Authority (ASPR/BARDA); the US Departments of State (DOS), Defense (DOD), Agriculture (USDA), Commerce, and Treasury; the US Agency for International Development (USAID); foreign governments; the international World Health Organization (WHO), World Bank, International Partnership on Avian and Pandemic Influenza (IPAPI), Global Health Security Action Group (GHSAG), UN System Influenza Coordination (UNSIC), Pan-American Health Organization (PAHO); and nonprofits like PATH and the Gates Foundation. **Influenza pandemics**—world outbreaks—occur when a new virus with little or no human immunity emerges. There were three in the 20th century and one so far in the 21st.

**Relationship Between Communicable Diseases and Emergency and Disaster Conditions**

According to the World Health Organization (WHO), **natural disasters** and **war conditions** can break water and sewer pipes and sewage treatment mechanisms, and disrupt electricity for pumping water. This can lead to **waterborne** and **vector-borne diseases**. When disaster or war survivors live in crowded temporary arrangements with inadequate personal hygiene and laundry facilities and poor ventilation, personal contact can spread highly contagious diseases into **epidemics**. Disaster victims are also more susceptible to communicable diseases as unsanitary living conditions, stress, fatigue, and malnutrition lower their resistance. An additional disease transmission factor is how long refugees live in temporary shelters: mass settlement for extended times can cause epidemic outbreaks. Famine relief camps particularly involve many people already weakened, potentially ill, and staying there for long durations. Storms, floods, earthquakes, mudslides, etc. can both contaminate water supplies with sewage and waste and create standing water where insect disease vectors breed. **Communicable disease control** requires adequate shelter, sanitation, clean water, vector control, health workers trained in early diagnosis and treatment, and immunization which combine to produce healthy environments.

Preparing for and Preventing Communicable Disease Outbreaks

Research by the World Health Organization (WHO) has identified the five commonest **causes of mortality** related to emergency and disaster conditions: malaria (in certain areas), malnutrition, diarrhea, measles, and acute respiratory infections. While not a communicable disease, **malnutrition** is made significantly worse by communicable diseases; the others, all communicable diseases, are related directly to environmental health conditions. When conditions preceding disasters are **unsanitary,** as in large cities with dense populations in developing nations, disease problems following disasters are more likely. Therefore, advance measures to alleviate poverty, raise awareness, improve organization, and establish sanitary and health services offer greater community protection in the event of disaster. **Preparedness** includes training outreach and health personnel to identify and manage specific disease threats; stocking equipment and supplies locally for environmental health; diagnosis and treatment for potential disease outbreaks; applying protocols for information management practices regarding particular diseases; raising local awareness of communicable diseases and the importance of early health facility referral; strengthening health-surveillance systems; promoting hygiene; and providing adequate clean water supplies, suitable shelter, sanitation facilities, and advance vaccination campaigns.

Public Health Surveillance

Public health surveillance involves collecting, analyzing, and distributing health information for the purpose of taking prompt and appropriate action. As reported by Doctors Without Borders, during emergency and disaster situations, affected populations are more susceptible to diseases; the instability of the circumstances causes sudden changes in health; and to take effective action quickly, health workers must share quantitative data with a variety of partners. The World Health Organization (WHO) emphasizes the importance of designating certain health personnel to conduct public health surveillance. Hospital staff, temporary relief center workers, and community and neighborhood health personnel must be vigilant for unusual numbers of malaria cases, food poisoning, other toxicity, encephalitis, meningitis, cholera, plague, typhus, typhoid fever, paratyphoid fever, and other ailments or diseases. Workers should take patient histories, identify contacts, and isolate disease sources. **Public health surveillance** can be conducted to some degree even in large-scale population movement's worst circumstances. Health workers can extend existing reporting systems to area-wide surveillance systems addressing sanitation- and water-related epidemics and other high-priority diseases. **Active population movement pattern surveillance** affords data for predicting future settlement patterns, general disease surveillance, and emergency intervention planning.

**Advising Students About Ways Unprotected Sex Can Cause Unwanted Pregnancy, and Pregnancy Prevention**

Some teens may not know how **pregnancy** occurs; others may believe it can only happen when a male ejaculates inside a female's vagina. However, a few drops of pre-ejaculate released before and during sex, which can be almost undetectable, also contains sperm. Though the probability of conception from this small amount is lower, it is still possible. Though less common, conception can also result from semen on the vulva without penetration. Males cannot control pre-ejaculate release; therefore, they should be advised to put on a condom *before*, and wear it continuously during, sex. Though the point is not to encourage sex among immature students, educators can inform those harboring misunderstandings that kissing, body rubbing, masturbating, and oral and anal sex cannot cause pregnancy without vaginal or vulvar contact with sperm; and that abstaining from sex, or using both a condom and birth control continuously during sex, are the ways of preventing pregnancy. Teen couples contemplating sex should

- 64 -

discuss birth control with each other and a parent or trusted adult, and see a physician, nurse, or healthcare provider.

## Information to Give Students About STDs

Over half of Americans contract an **STD** during their lives. Practicing **safer sex** can include using condoms, having strictly monogamous sex, and engaging in sexual activities that do not transmit STDs. Vaginal and anal intercourse are high-risk activities. Without condoms, they are likely to transmit chancroid, chlamydia, cytomegalovirus (CMV), genital warts, gonorrhea, hepatitis B, herpes, HIV, human papilloma virus (HPV), molluscum contagiosum virus, pelvic inflammatory disease (PID), pubic lice ("crabs"), scabies, syphilis, and trichomoniasis. Unprotected oral sex is high-risk for transmitting CMV, gonorrhea, hepatitis B, herpes, syphilis, and HPV. Skin-to-skin contact without intercourse is risky for transmitting CMV, herpes, HPV, molluscum contagiosum, pubic lice, and scabies. Many STDs are often asymptomatic.

## Rape

An estimated 80-90 percent of **rapes** go unreported. Recent trends project one-third of American women will be assaulted sexually in life. Typical assailants usually choose women of their race, and at least casually know victims almost half the time from living or working near them. Over one-third of rapes involve alcohol. Over half happen in victims' homes, via break-ins or entry by false pretenses. Expressed via sex, rape is primarily violent, not sexual. Prostitutes and prisoners with reduced credibility, those with limited language or disabilities who cannot call for help, and those facing discrimination are more vulnerable. **Prevention** includes locking doors and windows in homes and cars; checking car backseats before entering; parking in well-lit, open areas; not jogging or walking in isolated or secluded areas at night or when alone; displaying confidence, security, awareness, and strength in surroundings; sitting near drivers or in the front in public transportation; avoiding proximity to young male groups; self-defense training; carrying personal alarms or whistles; screaming loudly or blowing whistles if assaulted; actively resisting attacks and not being passive; and not hitchhiking. PTSD is a common complication. Over half of rape victims have difficulty re-establishing existing relationships or establishing new ones. Victims should avoid urinating, changing clothes, bathing, or douching pre-ER to preserve evidence; should be allowed to interview dressed, not hospital-gowned; and not left alone unless desired. **Treatment** includes examining for and addressing STDs, pregnancy, and physical injury; and providing emotional support.

## Development of Female Reproductive System

Because females do not have a Y-chromosome, during embryonic and fetal development they are not affected by **testosterone** to develop male reproductive organs. Without testosterone stimulation, reproductive organs develop into ovaries, a uterus, and other female organs. Most internal female organs are formed by the end of the first trimester. Immature eggs (ova) form in the ovaries in utero; all of a female's eggs are produced before birth. Female infants are born with all **reproductive organs** formed, but immature and not functional. These do not grow much in childhood, but rapidly mature and grow during puberty. Girls typically start **puberty** one or two years before boys; and take around four years to complete, whereas boys take around six years. The primary female sex hormone is **estrogen**. In the brain, the hypothalamus stimulates the pituitary gland to secrete **luteinizing hormone (LH)** and **follicle-stimulating hormone (FSH)**, which stimulate the ovary to produce estrogen. (The same hormones stimulate the testes' testosterone production in males.) Estrogen stimulates uterus and breast growth; pubic hair growth; bone development; the adolescent growth spurt, which begins and ends earlier than in males; and menarche (menstrual cycle onset).

## Growth and Development of Human Male Reproductive System

While a male fetus develops in utero, the **testes** begin to develop. Around two months before birth, the testes begin descending into the scrotal sacs outside of the main body cavity, allowing slightly lower temperatures aiding sperm production. The testes additionally produce hormones enabling development of secondary male sex characteristics. **Puberty** activates an increase in brain hormones, triggering the pituitary gland's increased production and release into the bloodstream of **luteinizing hormone (LH)** and **follicle-stimulating hormone (FSH)**. In the bloodstream, LH stimulates testes cells to produce and release **testosterone**, which enlarges and develops the penis and other sex organs, promotes skeletal and muscular growth, and deepens the voice. Testosterone and FSH stimulate **sperm production** in seminiferous tubules within the testes. Each sperm cell takes 65-75 days to form; about 300 million are produced daily, stored in the epididymis, wherefrom the vas deferens carries sperm through the prostate gland below the bladder to the urethra. The male urethra releases both sperm and urine. The prostate gland and seminal vesicles—accessory sex glands—produce specialized fluids, mixing with sperm during transport, creating **semen** which exits from the urethra through the penis during ejaculation.

## Influence of Media Messages on Adolescent Sexuality

Researchers find that, although any age group can be influenced by sexual media content, teens can be especially vulnerable to **media messages**. Adolescence is a developmental time when individuals are forming their sexual attitudes, behaviors, and gender roles. Teenagers have recently developed the ability to think abstractly and critically; however, their **cognitive skills** are still not completely developed for critical analysis of media messages and decision-making that takes into account future potential consequences. This places them at higher risk for **media influence**. Researchers have found (Gruber, 2000) that teens viewed an average of 143 instances of sexual behavior on TV weekly during prime time. Activities between unmarried partners were depicted three to four times more often than between spouses. Network and cable TV channels show movies, an estimated 80 percent of which include sexual content. Researchers analysis of music videos estimated that 60 percent included sexual impulses and feelings. Sexual TV messages are found to be nearly always presented in positive terms, with scarce treatment of negative consequences or risks of unprotected sex. High school students have reported substantial access to and viewing of TV and video. Over 80 percent of teens report peer discovery about sex from entertainment media.

## Research Findings About Adolescent Sexual Attitudes and Behaviors

Various studies find teens' sexual attitudes influenced by variables including their parents' attitudes regarding teen sex, religiosity, the media, bonding in school relationships, and adolescents' perceptions of social norms among their peers. According to some experts, such research demonstrates the necessity of considering the wide range of **sexual attitudes** teenagers consider. Warning of **negative consequences** is insufficient; adults must provide **information** enabling teens to weigh positive and negative aspects of both engaging in and abstaining from sex to make their own best decisions as they mature and develop physically, intellectually, emotionally, and socially. While many models of teen risk behaviors emphasize perceptions of possible consequences in decision-making, studies also find positive motivations for having sex. Some investigators found teens valued sexual goals and expectations of intimacy, then social status, then pleasure in that order; but then expected sex to result in pleasure, then intimacy, then social status in that order. Male adolescents valued pleasure more; females valued intimacy more. The National Adolescent and Young Adult Health Information Center (NAHIC, 2007) found almost half of high school students reported having sex. CDC's Youth Risk Behavior Surveillance (YRBS, 2008) found sexual intercourse most prevalent in black, then Hispanic, then white, then Asian teens.

## Significant Aspects of the Stages of Pregnancy

In the **first trimester**, a zygote transforms into an implanted embryo; organs, hair follicles, nail beds, muscles, white blood cells, and vocal cords form; and the baby starts moving around week eight. While pregnancy does not show externally, mothers awash in **pregnancy hormones** feel many symptoms. However, every woman and pregnancy are different; no two necessarily have the same symptoms, but most diminish further into pregnancy (though others develop). During the **second trimester**, babies grow hair; begin sucking and swallowing; and their eyes and ears reposition. They have fingerprints and can hiccup and yawn by week 18. Their limbs are coordinated and their senses develop by week 21. Weight gain, capillary formation, and opening eyes occur by six months. By seven months, fetal weight doubles to two pounds. Babies perceive light and dark, taste what mothers eat, and hear their voices by week 31. Transparent skin becomes opaque by week 32; length may increase an inch during week 33. Weight reaches around six pounds by week 36; waxy vernix and hairy lanugo shed in week 38. By week 40, fetal weight is 6-9 pounds, length 19-22 inches; babies dream, blink, and regulate their body temperatures.

## Human Labor and Childbirth

In late pregnancy, symptoms can mask labor signs, or some contractions can be false labor. If contractions persist, become stronger, last longer, and occur closer together, this usually indicates **labor**. The "411" method is one way to judge: contractions 4 minutes apart, lasting 1 minute each, continuing for at least 1 hour. Labor's **first stage** is typically the longest, marked by contractions and gradual cervical dilation. The first stage has three phases: the **early phase**, usually comfortable, with contractions 20 minutes apart progressing to 5 minutes apart. The second, **active phase** generally involves 1-minute contractions every 4-5 minutes. The third, **transition phase** is among the shortest (1-2 hours) but hardest. Contractions are 2-3 minutes apart; some women shake and may vomit. This phase ends with complete dilation. Some women temporarily cease contractions but feel no need to push. Labor's **second stage** involves a need to push. It can last 3+ hours, but often less. Contractions spread out again to around every 4 minutes. This stage culminates in **childbirth**. Then the mother must push out the **placenta**; nursing the newborn aids uterine contractions to expel it. The fourth labor stage is **postpartum**.

## Contraception Methods

Some young (or uninformed older) people assume **condoms** worn by males are sufficient for **contraception**. However, condoms can break, leak, or slip off during or following intercourse. Ideally, foam, gel, or other spermicide should accompany condoms. Female contraception includes IUDs, diaphragms, and birth control pills. **IUDs** are typically inserted by physicians and worn continuously. They can periodically require removal and replacement. While effective, they can have undesirable side-effects for some women including irritation, inflammation, cramping, spotting, tissue damage, etc. **Diaphragms** are typically self-inserted by women before intercourse, often with spermicidal gel applied to the surface, and removed afterward. They are also effective, but some women have difficulty inserting them properly and/or cannot tolerate their presence. They can also sometimes shift position, impeding contraception. **Birth control pills** are very effective, though a very small percentage of women using them might still get pregnant. Oral hormones cause some women undesirable side effects like weight gain and symptoms resembling pregnancy. Lower-dose pills have fewer side effects; different dosages affect individual women differently. More extreme measures include **tubal ligation** (reversible but not always) and **hysterectomy** (irreversible) for women, and **vasectomy** (reversible but not always) for men.

# HIV/AIDS

The first known case of **human immunodeficiency virus/acquired immunodeficiency syndrome (HIV/AIDS)** occurred in 1951 in the Congo, but the first U.S. case occurred in 1981. Dr. Robert Gallo of the National Cancer Institute identified the cause in 1984. The first cases were in the gay population, resulting in the disease being initially labeled a "gay disease," although it later became clear that it was not limited to gays. AIDS resulted in the deaths of millions of people worldwide before the first Food and Drug Administration (FDA)-approved treatment was available in 1995. By 2002, home testing kits were available. Currently, although males having sex with males are most at risk and African American have the highest rate of racial groups, HIV/AIDS affects all populations, races, and socioeconomic groups with about 50,000 new infections in the United States each year. About 25% of cases are female, and 25% are older than age 50. Modes of transmission include oral, anal, and vaginal sex as well as the sharing of needles and contact with infected blood, semen, vaginal fluids, and breast milk.

## Prevention and Treatment

Treatment for HIV/AIDS should begin with **diagnosis** and includes medication management, mental health counseling, and supportive and social care as needed. The first step after diagnosis is to undergo a number of **laboratory tests** to determine the viral load and CD4 count (measures the CD4 T lymphocytes to determine the strength of the immune system). Although **antiretroviral therapy (ART)** does not cure HIV/AIDS, it can slow the progression. Six classes of drugs are currently used to treat HIV with initial treatment usually involving three drugs from at least two different drug classes. Several drug regimens are available, depending on the patient's condition, drug resistance, and comorbid diseases. **HIV/AIDS prevention** includes universal testing, needle exchange programs, sex education, consistent and correct use of latex condoms, substance abuse prevention, and treatment programs. Individuals should understand that risk increases with multiple sexual partners, and males having sex with males are particularly at risk.

## Conflict in Relationships

Many people try to avoid **conflict** at all costs because they find it unpleasant and feel threatened by **confrontation**. However, conflict is normal and integral to healthy relationships. Its source is differences between and among people, whether major or minor. No two (or more) people can agree about everything 100 percent of the time. Anytime that people disagree, conflict results. Though some disagreements seem unimportant, any conflict that evokes strong emotions indicates some deep personal need at its core—e.g., to be valued or respected, to be closer or more intimate, or to feel safety or security. As one example, young children need to explore and take risks to learn and develop normally, while parents need to protect children's safety, and this can present a child-parent conflict. Conflicts in **personal relationships** can cause discord and even end them when members do not understand each other's different needs. Conflicts in **workplaces** can ruin deals, lower profits, and end jobs. Acknowledging needs that conflict, and a willingness to examine them in understanding, compassionate environments enable team-building and creative problem-solving. Both avoiding and mismanaging conflict can damage relationships, but positive and respectful conflict management can improve them.

## Characteristics of Conflict People Need to Know in Order to Resolve Them

According to experts, a **conflict** is not simply a disagreement, but a situation wherein both or either party perceives a real or imagined **threat**. Because such perceived threats are to people's survival and well-being, conflicts continue; ignoring them does not make them go away. **Confronting** and **resolving** conflicts stop them from going on indefinitely, or until the relationship ends. People do not necessarily (or usually) respond to conflicts based on objectively considering the facts, they react to them based on their personal values, beliefs, cultural backgrounds, and life experiences. Hence individual reactions to conflict are according to individual perceptions of the situation. Conflicts naturally provoke strong feelings. Therefore, people who cannot manage their emotions under stress or who are uncomfortable with them will be unable to succeed at resolving conflicts. Another characteristic of conflicts is that they present opportunities for **growth**. When members of a relationship succeed at resolving interpersonal conflict, they build **trust** between themselves. They gain direct experience that their relationship can withstand disagreements and challenges. This proof enables them to feel more secure about their relationship's existence and future.

## Unhealthy vs. Healthy Ways of Responding to, Managing, and Resolving Conflict

When conflict inevitably arises, one **unhealthy** reaction is being unable to recognize and respond to things that are most important to the other person. A **healthier** response is being able to identify and address things that matter most to another. Emotional reactions that are resentful, angry, explosive, or designed to hurt the other person's feelings are unhealthy. Healthier responses involve staying calm, not becoming defensive, and showing respect for the other person. When one person reacts to conflict by rejecting the other, withdrawing his/her affection, isolating himself/herself, saying or doing things to shame the other, or showing or expressing fears of being abandoned, these are unhealthy reactions. Healthier responses are being willing to forgive the other person; forget undesirable reactions, words and deeds; and progress beyond the conflict without retaining anger or resentment. Being unable to see the other person's viewpoint or make any compromises is unhealthy; being able to compromise instead of punishing the other person is healthier. Fearing and avoiding conflict due to expected negative outcomes is unhealthy; believing in the mutual benefit of confronting conflict head-on is healthier.

## Effects of Stress

Excessive stress and/or not coping effectively with stress impede the ability to understand other people's nonverbal communications. **Stress** interferes with people's ability to hear what another person is really saying, to be aware of and in touch with their own emotions, and to connect with their deepest personal needs. Moreover, being affected by stress makes a person much less able to **communicate** his or her own needs clearly. These abilities are all required for positively resolving conflict, so when stress interferes with them, it interferes with conflict resolution. Some people become so habituated to stress that they lose recognition of it. Some ways to identify if it is a problem in life are to observe whether conflict preoccupies their attention and time, whether they cannot feel movement in their chests or stomachs while breathing, and/or whether they often feel tightness or tension in certain body parts. Excessive stress limits how many emotions one can attend to, preventing understanding and thus communicating one's needs. Hence stress interferes with **emotional awareness**, which interferes with communicating problems and resolving conflicts.

## Relationship Patterns in Murray Bowen's Family Systems Theory

### Marital Conflict

Bowen's concept of the nuclear family emotional system consists of four basic relationship patterns that determine where family problems develop. Clinical symptoms or problems typically emerge during times of intensified and protracted tension in a family. Stress levels, family adaptations to stress, and family connections with extended family and social support networks determine tension levels. In the **marital conflict pattern**, spouses project their increasing anxiety into the marital relationship. Each partner becomes preoccupied with the other's shortcomings, tries to control him or her, and resists being controlled. For example, a couple with a young child conceives a second child. The wife becomes anxious about meeting two children's needs. The husband questions his wife's ability to cope in order to avoid facing his own anxieties. After the second child's birth, the husband, observing his wife's stress, helps out more at home and is more controlling of her. He starts to feel neglected and disappointed in his wife's inadequate coping. The wife, who used to drink but quit while pregnant, resumes drinking.

- 69 -

## Dysfunction in One Spouse

In Bowen theory, the relationship pattern of **dysfunction in one spouse** involves one partner pressuring the other to behave in certain ways, and the other acceding to that pressure. While both partners accommodate for maintaining harmony, eventually one does more than the other. Both are comfortable with this interaction for some time; however, if family tensions increase, the subordinate partner gives up enough self-control, yielding to the dominant partner to become significantly more anxious. Combined with other factors, this **anxiety** contributes to a psychiatric, social, or medical problem. For example, a couple with one young child has a second child. In the relationship pattern of marital conflict, the husband projects his own anxiety into criticizing his wife's coping abilities, taking on more household duties, and controlling her while the wife addresses her anxiety by drinking. The husband accuses her of selfishness and lack of effort. She agrees with but resents his criticism, feeling more dependent on him. Feeling increasingly unable to cope and make decisions, she escalates her drinking. He calls her an alcoholic. The wife becomes increasingly under-functional, the husband increasingly over-functional, functioning for her—all in an effort to avoid direct conflict and maintain harmony.

## Impairment of One or More Children

In the pattern of impairment of a child or children, parents project their own anxieties onto their child/children. They view the child **unrealistically**—either negatively or idealistically. The child **reciprocates** excessive parental focus by focusing excessively on the parents, overreacting to parental expectations, needs, and attitudes. This undermines the child's differentiation of self from family, increasing his or her susceptibility to either internalizing or acting out family tensions. **Anxiety** can disrupt the child's social relationships, school progress, and health. For example, a couple with one young child has another baby. Anxieties over the added stress of raising another child cause marital conflict and a dysfunctional relationship, developing into greater dysfunction in one spouse or parent. This causes emotional distance between spouses, who focus anxiously on the older child. She reacts by regressing, making immature demands of the parents, especially her mother. The mother externalizes her anxiety onto the child, worrying the new baby will displace her, acceding increasingly to her demands. The father avoids conflict with his wife by supporting her focus on the child, relieving her by giving the child attention when he gets home from work. Parents and child unwittingly conspire in seeing and creating **dysfunction in the child**.

## Emotional Distance

In Bowen's family systems theory, the four basic relationship patterns are marital conflict, spousal dysfunction, child impairment, and emotional distance. Whichever pattern predominates will dictate which family members will manifest familial tensions by developing psychological, social, or medical symptoms. The pattern of **emotional distance** consistently occurs in relation to the other three patterns. When interactions between family members become too intense, they develop emotional distance to decrease intensity. However, the drawbacks of emotional distance are that distanced members can become overly isolated, and can lose intimacy in their relationship. For example, when a couple with one child has another baby, they first project their anxieties onto each other and experience marital conflict. They then withdraw from one another emotionally to reduce the intensity of the conflict. They react to the emotional distance between them by externalizing their anxieties onto the first child, worrying she will feel left out with the new baby. The child reacts to the obsessive parental emotional over-involvement with her, reciprocating their emotional focus and overreacting to real or imagined parental withdrawal— creating impairment of a child. Thus, emotional distance **interacts** with the other patterns.

### Influence of Socioeconomic and Health Variables on Parent-Adult Child Relationships

Some sociological researchers investigating relationships of parents in their mid-50s to mid-70s with their adult children found **intergenerational exchanges** were characterized by strong **reciprocity** in both the United States and Great Britain. Contrary to stereotypical views of elderly adults becoming "burdens" on adult children, researchers have seen instead that married parents who gave help and support to at least one adult child were twice as likely to receive support from another adult child as parents who did not provide such support. Investigations showed when researchers controlled for various other parent and child variables, parents who owned homes, had higher incomes, and were married or widowed were more likely to help adult children than divorced parents. Conversely, parents with homes and higher incomes were less likely to receive help from adult children. Parental disability and advanced age **correlated positively** with adult children's responding to parent needs. Investigators inferred socioeconomic variations in support exchange balances between parents and adult children. Researchers predicted in 2005 that demographic trends would likely increase adult children's demands for support from older parents in the future.

## Talking About Procreation with Children

Many parents feel squeamish about "The Talk" or discussing "the birds and bees" with their maturing children. This is not just discomfort over an intimate topic; parents frequently fear that discussing sex with preadolescent and adolescent children is akin to giving them **permission** to engage in it. However, research studies find the opposite is true: teens are more prone to sexual behaviors when their parents have *not* talked about sex with them. When uninformed of possible **consequences**, they are more likely to act, not knowing of any disadvantages; they may experiment to get knowledge their parents have not imparted; and/or sexual behavior may be a reaction against parental avoidance and lack of openness. Communications researchers say sex is a continuing, two-way conversation that starts when very young children see pregnant women and ask questions. They advise parents to use Socratic questions, e.g., "What do you think the right time is for having sex?" and sharing their own thoughts after children do. **Open, receptive attitudes** are critical: if children bring up sex and perceive avoidant or shocked parental reactions, they will stop approaching parents, shutting down this vital conversation.

## Roles and Responsibilities of Effective Parenting

### Responsibilities

Effective parenting includes ensuring the safety and well-being of one's children by providing adequate shelter and food as well as the following:

- **Helping the child build self-esteem**: Encouraging the child to become self-sufficient and demonstrate skills.
- **Providing positive reinforcement**: Recognizing and rewarding the child for doing something right rather than focusing on negatives.
- **Setting limits**: Establishing reasonable rules and discipline.
- **Providing consistent discipline**: Following through by providing consequences.
- **Spending quality time with the child**: Engaging one on one with the child. Scheduling activities and time together and being available when the child wants to talk or interact.
- **Providing a good role model**: Modeling the type of behavior that is expected of the child.
- **Communicating with the child**: Being open, honest, and willing to listen and stating expectations directly.
- **Exhibiting flexibility in the parenting role**: Recognizing that children have different needs at different times in their lives and allowing the child to have increasing autonomy with age.
- Providing unconditional love and support: Being nurturing and kind.

## Discipline

Parents use a number of different approaches to discipline adolescents:

| Strategy | Parent action |
|---|---|
| Behavior modification | Uses positive reinforcement to encourage appropriate behavior and ignores inappropriate behavior. |
| Consequences | Inappropriate behavior results in a consequence, such as losing privileges or a specified punishment. |
| Corporal punishment | Spanks or otherwise inflicts pain on the adolescent to force appropriate behavior but may have serious negative impacts on self-esteem of adolescent and, in some cases, may cause injury. |
| Scolding | Uses harsh, often loud, language to express unhappiness with an adolescent's behavior. |
| Time-out | Uses a specified period of time-out away from activities or time-out from phone, Internet, or other desired activity. |
| Reasoning | Discusses problem behavior and the reason that it is not appropriate. |

## Promoting Good Behavior

Discipline entails more than punishing or correcting inappropriate behavior. A good parent also uses strategies to **promote good behavior**. Strategies include the following:

- Being realistic about what the adolescent can do and understand, depending on the child's age and maturity level.
- Modeling appropriate behavior.
- Discussing appropriate behavior in new situations, such as before a family event or an outing.
- Attending to inappropriate behavior immediately, including discussion of more appropriate actions.
- Reprimanding the adolescent for bad behavior and not for being a bad person.
- Anticipating circumstances that may encourage inappropriate behavior, such as when the adolescent is stressed or tired.
- Providing reminders to help the adolescent control his/her own behavior.
- Providing rationale for appropriate behavior in accordance to the adolescent's ability to understand.
- Helping the adolescent to understand that different situations require different standards of behavior and language, such as partying with friends as opposed to attending a wedding.

# Consumer and Safety Skills

### Aspects of Decision-Making to Consider for Instructing Adolescents

The life stage of **adolescence** brings greater pressures on teenagers to solve more difficult problems and make harder decisions about matters like risk behaviors, sexuality, school involvement, and career choices. Thus, **decision-making** during adolescence can powerfully affect adult futures. Awareness of the possible impacts of their decisions informs teen motivation to learn effective **decision-making skills**. Such skills incorporate identifying available options and their potential consequences, evaluating the relative desirability or undesirability of each consequence, estimating each consequence's probability, and using a "decision rule" to choose among options. Decision-making models (e.g., Wilson & Kirby, 1984) require the skills of defining a necessary decision, gathering information for self-education and thinking of alternatives, considering options and choosing one, making a plan to execute the decision, and evaluating the decision and its results. Such models enable planned, goal-directed decision-making. Researchers have noted both cognitive elements of decision-making, and other aspects beyond cognition, as important in **adolescent risk-taking**.

### Research-Based Conclusions About How Adolescents Make Decisions

Various studies have identified variables that determine how prepared each individual adolescent is to make **effective decisions**, including intelligence, age, gender, race or ethnicity, social class, temperament, family dynamics and structure, cultural and social environment, and religiosity. Additionally, adolescent perceptions of and attitudes toward risk, perspectives regarding time, and compliance and conformity relative to parents and peers influence decision making abilities. Both contextual and developmental variables affect how teens ascribe subjective value to consequences, and how they use information, for decision-making. The **teen dilemma** is a need to make critical decisions having lifelong consequences, yet lacking ample life experience to inform those decisions. Studies have found positive results from **intervention programs** to improve adolescent decision-making skills, including decreased antisocial, socially disordered, and self-destructive behavior and increased prosocial, positive behavior; reduced tobacco use; more responsible sexual behavior in parenting and pregnant teens; higher school retention levels; and greater economic self-sufficiency. Some researchers consider decision-making ability to be one component of risk behavior. They emphasize assessing teen decision-making and planning skills for identifying intervention need areas, and teaching future orientation for considering long-term as well as short-term consequences and goals. Transferring acquired cognitive decision-making skills effectively requires opportunities for practicing real-life decision-making.

### Assertiveness

Assertiveness can be defined as expressing our personal rights, feelings, needs and wants honestly, directly, clearly, and appropriately, and insisting that others recognize these, while still always respecting the beliefs, thoughts, and feelings of other people. While not being **assertive** may ultimately be a result of having low self-esteem, **non-assertiveness** may be functionally defined as using **inefficient communication skills**. Assertiveness, in contrast, is viewed as a balanced response in that it is neither aggressive nor passive. Some people confuse assertiveness with aggression. However, aggressiveness is not balanced in that it involves such behaviors as telling people to do things instead of asking them; ignoring others; being inconsiderate of others' feelings; unnecessarily rushing others; verbally insulting, blaming, or attacking others; or being pushy in general. Aggression discourages assertive responses and invites passivity or mutual aggression. Passive responses include saying "yes" when wanting to say "no"; agreeing outwardly when disagreeing inwardly; deferring one's wishes to others'; and not communicating or asserting one's feelings, thoughts, needs, or wants—often motivated by needing to please others and be liked. Passivity avoids and cedes responsibility and decision-making to others.

<u>Assertive Communication</u>

In **empathic assertion**, first acknowledge how the other person feels, then express what you need. For example, "I understand you are having trouble working together, but we need to finish this by Friday. Let's make a plan together." When needs are not met after repeated requests, **escalating assertion** involves increasing firmness, including informing others of consequences for continued noncompliance. Requesting more time is an assertiveness technique to use when caught off-guard, need to compose your thoughts, don't know what you want yet, or are too emotional to respond immediately. Changing verbs can make responses more assertive: substitute "won't" for "can't," "need" for "want," "I choose to" for "I have to," and "could" for "should." Another technique is the "broken record": when someone tries alternately to intimidate, bully, force, wheedle, cajole, beg, or bribe you to do something you cannot, repeat the same "no" message, e.g., "I cannot take on any more work right now." Whether the other person says "I'll pay you for helping me," "This is seriously important," "I'll be in big trouble if you don't help," "Please do a personal favor", etc., repeating the message will eventually make the point clear. This should not be used to manipulate others, but to protect yourself from exploitation.

**Character Education**

Academic underachievement, failure in school, antisocial behaviors, aggressive behaviors, drug use, premature sexual activity, and criminal activities are all social problems among students that researchers have found can be prevented by high-quality, comprehensive **character education programs**. Even though such programs are designed for the purpose of promoting young people's development of good character and their overall positive development, they are also found to be just as effective for preventing specific negative behaviors as other, more specific programs designed specially to prevent those behaviors. Character education not only **reduces youth risk** for engaging in detrimental behaviors, it also has positive effects of helping students develop **proactive attitudes and skills**, personally and socially, that enable their living productive, satisfying lives and participating in society as effective, active citizens. Researchers think this may make effective character education programs more cost-effective in terms of policy to augment learning—as well as promote prosocial behaviors and prevent problems—than implementing numbers of separate specific school-based behavioral prevention programs.

<u>Definitions of Character and Character Education</u>

While some people recognize following rules, avoiding criminal acts, completing school, and becoming productively employed as criteria for having character, experts say these are not enough. They define **character** as encompassing a wider range of attitudes, motivations, skills, and behaviors. These include wanting to do one's best; caring about others' welfare; being committed to contributing to the community and society; critical thinking and moral reasoning skills; emotional intelligence and interpersonal skills enabling effective interactions in various situations; and responsibility, honesty, and confronting injustice by defending moral principles. Experts interpret these qualities to mean character equals a person's realizing positive intellectual, emotional, social, and ethical development to be the best person s/he can be. They also point out that good character is not only personal, but also social, e.g., supporting respect, equality, and justice for all people as part of democratic living. This sometimes includes breaking rules predicated on conscience rather than constant conformation to the status quo. **Character education** is defined as purposefully using all aspects of school—e.g., curriculum content, instructional processes, disciplinary management, co-curricular activity management, relationship quality, and the full learning environment's ethos—to create learning environments enabling all students' optimal character development.

## Comprehensive Approach to Character Education

The Character Education Partnership (CEP), has identified the following 11 general principles (Lickona, Schaps, and Lewis, 2003) that serve to articulate **character education** in terms of a comprehensive approach. (1) Comprehensively defining character as encompassing thought, emotion, and behavior. (2) Applying a proactive, intentional, effective, comprehensive approach. (3) Furthering core ethical values as the foundations of good character. (4) Establishing caring learning communities in schools. (5) Cultivating internal student motivation to be good persons and to learn. (6) Giving opportunities for students to act morally. (7) Engaging school personnel as professional members of moral learning communities. (8) Supplying students with a challenging, relevant curriculum that assists all of them in succeeding. (9) Cultivating long-term support for character education and shared moral leadership. (10) Engaging students' families and members of the community as partners in character education. (11) Informing the endeavor of character education by evaluating the character of the students, employees, and the school itself.

## Health-Related Decision-Making Skills Needed to Make Positive Health Choices

Individuals need a number of health-related decision-making skills to make positive health choices and to express health information and concepts. Education to improve **health-related decision making** should begin in elementary school so students entering high school have a good base and understand when assistance is needed, what healthy and unhealthy options are, and what outcomes may result from poor choices. The high school student should have the knowledge to understand health information and the skills to identify barriers (such as peer pressure) to good decision making, to understand when to use a problem-solving approach, to justify reaching a decision in collaboration with others or independently, to recognize alternative solutions to health-related problems/issues, to defend the choices they make, and to assess the outcomes of their decisions. Students can participate in role-playing and problem-solving exercises to improve these skills.

## Influences on Health Decisions and Behaviors

Many factors influence health decisions and behaviors, including the following:

- **Beliefs**: Beliefs about health are often culture-bound and may influence behavior. Some cultures, for example, believe that illness is a punishment or it means that life is out of balance, whereas others believe in karma. Some cultures believe that it is shameful to have a mental disorder and may deny problems or refuse treatment.
- **Knowledge**: People are often better able to make decisions if they are armed with factual knowledge and can use critical thinking skills. Lack of knowledge may lead to confusion about the best health decisions and reliance on anecdotal advice.
- **Attitudes**: Despite knowledge, some people (especially adolescents) may feel that they are invincible and that problems that arise for others, such as from drinking alcohol, will not occur with themselves. Some may have difficulty accepting cause-and-effect relationships, and some may feel resentful of those in authority, such as parents, and purposefully make poor decisions.
- **Peers**: Friends and other peers often have a profound influence on health decisions and behaviors because of the strong desire to be accepted. This influence can be negative or positive, depending on the relationship.
- **Family**: The influence that parents or caregivers have varies according to the relationship. If the relationship is poor, then the influence may be minimal. Older siblings often exert a strong influence, either negative or positive, on younger siblings who look up to the older sibling and try to emulate that person.

- **Role models**: People that adolescents look up to—often sports figures, actors, or singers—may have some influence on behaviors, sometimes in ways that are negative, but positive role models who are actually in the person's life, such as a teacher, can have a more direct positive influence if the adolescent sees the person as a model for success.

## Seeking Advice and Guidance in Making Decisions About Personal Health

Adolescents are often unprepared to make decisions about personal health because of a lack of knowledge and experience. They may be uncertain about decisions or unaware of resources and may need **assistance**. If their relationships with their family members are positive, then those family members can provide valuable **guidance** because they know the individual well and may understand the implications of health decisions. However, they may also be biased toward certain decisions. Healthcare professionals may provide the best advice, especially if the adolescent is concerned about confidentiality. The healthcare professional has the expertise to know what options are available and whether referral is needed, and the adolescent may feel more comfortable asking him or her for help. For example, an adolescent may want to use birth control but is unwilling to or afraid to ask family members.

## Teaching Responsible Decision-Making to Students

A health educator teaching a responsible decision-making model to middle and high school students can begin with an overhead projection and student worksheets with term definitions. They discuss definitions with students: **empowerment** is feeling control over one's decisions and behavior, resulting in inspiration. Teachers tell students they must take responsibility for their decisions to achieve empowerment; decision-making styles determine responsibility. They explain that teens with **inactive decision-making styles** cannot or do not make choices; they lack control, accountability, and the ensuing self-confidence and empowerment. They explain that teens with **reactive decision-making styles** let others make decisions for them; needing others to like them and being easily influenced by others also impede self-confidence and empowerment. They then identify **proactive decision-making styles** as those involving analyzing a necessary decision, identifying and evaluating potential actions, choosing one action, and taking responsibility for the consequences of taking that action. Teachers can then introduce students to a model for **responsible decision-making** as a guide for making proactive decisions.

A model for responsible decision-making is meant to make sure that student decisions result in actions that show good character; that follow guidelines which parents, guardians or other responsible adults have established for them; that demonstrate self-respect and respect for others; and that protect safety, obey the laws, and promote health. A health educator can teach students in grades 6-12 the following seven steps included in a **responsible decision-making model**: (1) Describe the situation requiring you to make a decision. (2) List all of the decisions you could potentially make. (3) Share this list of potential decisions with an adult you trust. (4) Evaluate what the consequences of each of the decisions could be. (5) Determine which of the potential decisions you identified is the most appropriate and responsible one. (6) Take action on the decision that you have chosen. (7) Evaluate the outcomes of the decision that you have made.

When instructing middle and high school students, a health educator can help them define **peer pressure** as the influences that individuals exert on others of similar status or age to engage in certain behaviors or decisions. S/he can explain that peer pressure may be positive or negative. The class can then discuss **resistance skills**, defined as skills enabling individuals to leave situations or say no to actions. A model for using resistance skills includes the following steps: (1) The student says "no" in an assertive manner to individual(s) attempting to exert peer pressure. (2) The student tells the other(s) his/her reasons for saying no. (3) The student uses nonverbal communication that matches his/her verbal communication— e.g., eye contact, facial expressions, body postures, and gestures consistent with what s/he is saying. (4)

The student avoids getting into situations with peers that will involve pressure from them to make detrimental decisions. (5) The student resists peer pressure to engage in illegal actions. (6) The student works to exert influences on his/her peers to make responsible decisions.

## Elements That Influence Adolescent Decision-Making

Adolescent decision-making is influenced by both **external variables**, like relationships with parents and friends; and **internal variables**, like personal self-concept and locus of control. Teen decision-making is influenced by **motivational variables**, e.g., personal values, beliefs, attitudes, goals, and emotional states. **Developmental variables** including cognitive (intellectual) development, affective (emotional) development, and social development are additional influences. Coping ability also affects decision-making ability. Because critical decisions that teens make occur in changing social contexts, they must develop abilities for evaluating decisions and adjusting and adapting them as needed. Due to society's constraints, teens must learn to identify and cope with options that are relatively more and less available to them. They must learn to apply different decision-making styles to different decision types, like career decisions as opposed to stressful or emotionally sensitive circumstances. Educators can advise teens that any single decision may be viewed as a series of choices rather than a one-time occurrence. Teens do not decide in isolation; decisions are influenced by feedback. Because current decisions influence future ones, decision-making sets precedents. Decision-making is not a linear process but a complex one; as teenagers mature and gain experience, their decision-making skills develop.

## Resisting Pressure from Others

Children and teens often have more life experience being cared for, controlled, and told what to do, and relatively less experience being on their own, making independent choices, and taking initiative. Adults should tell them that being **pressured** is not good for them and is not right. Many children and teens (and even adults) have difficulty resisting pressure. **Motivations** include because they want to be liked, don't want to alienate friends, are afraid others will reject them, do not want others to make fun of them, do not want to hurt other people's feelings, are afraid others will perceive refusal as rejection, are not sure what they actually want, or do not know how to extricate themselves from the situation. Children and teens must know they have the right to say no, not to give any reason, and to walk away from any situation involving pressure. Some brief tips to support **resisting pressure** and **refusing** include standing up straight, making eye contact with the other person, stating one's feelings clearly, not making excuses, and standing up for oneself.

### Refusal Strategies for Children and Adolescents

Children and teens (and adults as well) can find it hard to **resist pressure** that other people exert on them through their words. It is normal for most of us not to want to hurt other people's feelings or feel responsible for bad feelings in others. However, children and teens especially must be reminded how important it is for them to stand up for themselves in order to prevent others from verbally pressuring them into doing unsafe or unwanted things. Some strategies recommended by experts to help young people refuse to use alcohol, or to do other things that they know are not in their best interests and that they do not wish to do, include the "Dos and Don'ts." **Dos**: do say no assertively. Do abstain from drinking alcohol. Do propose some alternate activity. Do stand up for others being pressured who do not want to drink. Do walk away from the situation. Do look for something else to do with other friends. **Don'ts**: don't go to a party without being prepared to resist alcohol use. Don't be afraid to say "no." Don't mumble. Don't say "no" in an overly aggressive way. Don't behave like a "know-it-all" when refusing.

## Teaching Responsible Decision-Making to Students

<u>Questions Students Can Ask Themselves in the Fourth Step for Evaluating the Potential Consequences</u>

The steps in the **responsible decision-making model** are describing the situation wherein they need to make a decision, listing the decisions they could potentially make, sharing their list with a parent or other responsible adult, evaluating each decision's potential consequences, deciding which decision is the most suitable and responsible, acting on the chosen decision, and evaluating the outcomes of that decision. When evaluating **potential consequences** of each decision, students can ask themselves the following six questions. (1) Will making this decision lead to taking actions that are lawful or legal? (2) Will making this decision lead to taking actions protecting my and others' safety? (3) Will making this decision lead to taking actions that agree with the guidelines and advice that my parents and other responsible adults have given me? (4) Will making this decision lead to taking actions that demonstrate my respect for myself and for other people? (5) Will making this decision lead to taking actions that are demonstrations of good character?

<u>Steps Related to the Responsible Decision-Making Model in the Event of an Incorrect or Poor Decision</u>

As they learn to make decisions responsibly, students are bound to make mistakes as with all new learning. Teens may experience anxiety over responsibility for poor decisions with unwelcome consequences. Paralyzed by doubt and indecision, they may avoid taking responsibility and action. In the same way that many teens fear being judged, rejected, disliked, or even viewed as different, they also fear **doing the wrong thing**. In addition to peer pressure and desiring acceptance, fear of misusing new responsibilities can motivate inaction to avoid unintentionally doing harm and experiencing guilt. Health educators can offer four steps to take after a bad or otherwise **wrong decision**: (1) Admit it; take responsibility, not trying to hide the mistake, blame others, or make excuses. (2) Immediately consider things done based on the decision; avoid perpetuating actions misguided by a wrong choice. (3) Parents and guardians are responsible for decision-making guidance: inform them of the decision and discuss corrective actions. (4) Apologizing is not always adequate: make restitution for any harm, damage, or loss by paying, replacing something, volunteering time, and/or similar appropriate effort as applies.

## Steps for Students to Take for Setting Health Goals for Themselves

(1) Students write long-term and short-term **health goals** in brief sentences starting with "I will…" Educators may suggest potential goals. **Long-term goals** can require a month, year, or even lifetime to attain and may be broken down to more achievable **short-term goals**. For example, a student's long-term goal could be "I will run a mile daily," with the preceding short-term goal being "I will run a quarter-mile daily." (2) Make **action plans**, i.e., detailed descriptions of steps for attaining goals, and have teachers review them for realism. Some teachers and students may establish health behavior contracts as action plans. (3) Identify potential **obstacles** to realizing the action plan. Prioritize these; brainstorm how to address high-priority ones. (4) Establish **timelines** with specific dates for reaching health goals. Consider whether these are realistic in light of other responsibilities. (5) Use a chart, graph, journal, or diary to **track progress**. Keeping records makes goals and progress concrete, supporting accountability. (6) Develop a **support system**. List people to give advice and encouragement, join a support group, form a club, and/or enlist friends. Avoid people who could sabotage health goals. (7) If needed, **revise** timelines and/or action plans, allowing additional time and/or requesting help. (8) Give yourself healthy **rewards** for meeting health goals.

## Health Equity Terms and Issues Related to US Demographic Disparities

The **Healthy People 2020** government initiative informs its focus on eliminating health disparities, attaining health equity, and improving American health with these 2008 US Census Bureau statistics: over 100 million people, approximately 33 percent, belonged to racial or ethnic minorities. Of these, 154 million, i.e., 51 percent, were women. Another 36 million, around 12 percent, not living in nursing homes or other residential care facilities, had disabilities. Yet another 70.5 million, or 23 percent, were estimated to live in rural areas; 233.5 million, or 77 percent, lived in urban areas. HealthyPeople.gov also cites 2002 data that four percent of the American population 18-44 years old was estimated to identify as gay, lesbian, bisexual, or transgender. The initiative defines **health disparity** as a specific health difference associated with environmental, economic, and/or social disadvantages. In the past, endeavors toward health equity and away from disparities mainly concentrated on healthcare services and illnesses or diseases. But current Healthy People 2020 experts point out that good health does not equal absence of illness. They define **individual and population health determinants** as interrelationships among genetics, biology, physical environment, socioeconomic status, individual behavior, literacy levels, discrimination, racism, legislative policies, health, and health services.

## Factors That Influence American Health and Federal Health Initiatives

All American citizens experience numerous **influences on their health status**. These include whether the following **factors** are available, and whether people have access to them: unpolluted air and clean water; safe, adequate housing; reliable, affordable public transportation; nutritious food; high-quality educations; health insurance coverage; and culturally sensitive healthcare providers. The Healthy People federal initiative (www.HealthyPeople.gov) has historically set goals focusing on changing **health disparities** over the past 20 years. In the Healthy People 2000 program, the goal was to decrease health disparities for American citizens. The Healthy People 2010 program augmented its goal to eliminate health disparities rather than just decrease them. The Healthy People 2020 program additionally extended the goal, not only to eliminate health disparities, but also to establish **health equity** and improve all Americans' health. This initiative plans, from 2014-2024, to track the rates of diseases, mortality, chronic conditions, behaviors, and other factors relative to race, ethnicity, gender, sexual identity, sexual orientation, disability status, special healthcare needs, urban and rural geographic locations, and other demographic factors. Through such research, the Healthy People staff members hope to achieve their health equity and improvement goals.

## Resources for Coordinated School Health Approaches

Basic information on **coordinated school health approaches** include: "School Health 101 Packets" from the National School Boards Association; *Guidelines for a Coordinated Approach to School Health: Addressing the Physical, Social, and Emotional Health Needs of the School Community* from the Connecticut State Department of Education; *Guidelines for Coordinating School Health Programs* from the Maine Departments of Education and Health and Human Services; the Comprehensive Health Education Network (CHEN) listserv, a mailing list of national, state, and local school health professionals; a PDF, "Building a Healthier Future through School Health Programs" from the CDC's *Promising Practices in Chronic Disease Prevention and Control;* and an "at a glance" webpage, "School Health Programs: Improving the Health of Our Nation's Youth." All of these are on the CDC website's page of Coordinated School Health Publications and Resources. This page also offers links and PDF documents on the relationship between school and student health and academic achievement. For school health assessment and planning, it includes links to the School Health Index (SHI) Self-Assessment and Planning Guide, and to Curriculum Analysis Tools for Health Education and Physical Education.

## Resources for Collaboration and Partnership, Evaluation, and Parent and Family Involvement

The Centers for Disease Control and Prevention (CDC) website's page on Coordinated School Health Publications and Resources includes links to PDF documents on **collaboration and partnership**, including a primer for professionals serving children and youth and a guide to community-school health councils, a link to the National Association of Chronic Disease Directors page about how health departments function and how schools can partner with them, and a link to the American Cancer Society's

- 79 -

PDF on community-school health councils. Regarding **evaluation** of coordinated school health approaches, the CDC website includes a page, "Evaluations of Innovative Programs," including an overview of its Division of Adolescent and School Health's (DASH) assistance with evaluating programs, a list of links to applied evaluation projects, information on eligibility, characteristics of initiatives subject to applied evaluations, and a contact link for the CDC Evaluation Research Team. Regarding **parent and family involvement**, CDC's web page on Coordinated School Health Publications and Resources offers a PDF, *Parent Engagement: Strategies for Involving Parents in School Health.*

Resources Pertaining to Policy, Professional Associations, and Promising Practices

Addressing **policy** related to coordinated school health approaches, the Centers for Disease Control and Prevention (CDC) website page of Coordinated School Health Publications and Resources includes download links to PDF documents of an Executive Summary; *A CDC Review of School Laws and Policies Concerning Child and Adolescent Health;* and a link to the National Association of State Boards of Education resource, the State School Health Policy Database, which includes compiled laws and policies from all 50 states covering over 40 school health subjects, e.g., school health councils, school health coordinators, and coordination. This page offers external links to these **professional associations**: American Association for Health Education; American Dietetic Association; School Nutrition Association; National Association for Sport and Physical Education (NASPE); National Association of School Nurses; American School Counselor Association; National Association of School Psychologists; School Social Work Association of America; and the Health Educator, School Health Coordinators, and Mental Health Professionals Sections of the American School Health Association. Under "**Promising Practices**," this page includes links to National Association of County and City Health Officials, "Building Healthier Schools"; National School Boards Association's database of successful school district health policies and practices; and partnership program and school nutrition success stories.

**Effective Communication with Students, Parents, and the Community**

Forming and sustaining partnerships depend on **effective communication** among schools, students, parents, and community. Also, schools are responsible for assisting parents in understanding learning language. School health educators should consider whether and how they communicate student progress to parents in relevant, positive ways; whether and how they clarify what teachers and parents must discuss; whether they have established a language of learning that teachers and parents share for exploring student learning successes, challenges, and development; how schools can collaborate with parents and communities to develop shared educational expectations; how parents with language barriers and/or busy work schedules communicate with the school; and how the school communicates with business and industry partners. Possible **strategies** include: home-school liaisons to teach parents educational language, current classroom characteristics, and how to talk with teachers and children about school experiences. Parent/community and parent-teacher meetings, newsletters, websites, web conferencing, emails, text messages, and assemblies are communication channels and tools to utilize. School-year transition calendars highlighting specific times and activities critical to parent and community engagement can also help. Educators should know and share how to access information in diverse forms and languages. Sharing consistent and ongoing high expectations of students and professional teacher development in communicating with parents are additional strategies.

There are several things that school health educators should consider for open, genuine **consultative communication**. They should encourage honest, open dialogues. To empower parents for effective consulting participation, their schools should offer support and training to build parental leadership capacities. When schools make informal and/or formal decisions, policy reviews and new policies regarding curriculum, assessment, and reporting, they should invite interested community members to consult. They can apply strategies such as flexible consulting with a representative cross-section of students, parents, and community members, rather than only those who are most assertive; make sure they broadly disseminate information in a variety of formats about opportunities to consult; offer opportunities for skill development and/or training to teachers and parents; develop solutions to aid teachers in balancing issues of workloads and time to facilitate their engagement in decision-making consultation; and encourage students to participate in decision-making processes and participate actively in the school council and/or parent and citizen groups.

## Indications of Effective Communication

Effective communication achieving strong engagement is indicated when educators acknowledge **parents** as their children's first educators; engage them as partners in children's learning; and encourage their close, sincere interest in the school's work. Educators communicate information to parents about current student learning status, progress over time, and how they can support their further learning. Language used by students, parents, and school personnel in both informal and formal settings reflects caring, respectful relationships. Schools have established continuing, regular methods for determining what parents require for engaging with their children's learning. Parents are able to identify the school's primary expectations for student attendance, homework, and behavior. Teachers and administrators applying diverse communication styles appropriately to parental availability, work conditions, cultural backgrounds, etc., also indicates effective communication, which produces strong engagement. Another indication is that school administrators and teachers connect with every student's parents regularly. Additionally, a school that has mechanisms established for building relationships with pertinent community members indicates effective communication for strong engagement.

## FERPA

"FERPA" stands for the **Family Educational Rights and Privacy Act**. According to the US Departments of Health and Human Services and of Education (2008), any educational agency or institution that receives federal funding under any program administered by the Department of Education is subject to FERPA regulations protecting the privacy of **student educational records**. This federal funding specification includes all public school districts and schools, as well as most public and private post-secondary schools, including medical and other professional schools. Elementary and secondary religious and private schools not receiving such funding are not subject to FERPA. "Education records" refers to records directly related to a student, and maintained by an educational institution, agency, or a party acting on its behalf. These include elementary and secondary student health records, immunization records, and records kept by public school nurses. Special education student records kept by public schools, including records of services these students receive under the Individuals with Disabilities Education Act (IDEA), are also included in the FERPA definition of "education records."

## HIPAA

HIPAA is the **Health Insurance Portability and Accountability Act** (1996). Among its purposes are to protect the security and privacy of individually identifiable health information and improve the effectiveness and efficiency of the healthcare system by setting national requirements and standards for electronic healthcare transactions. Provisions related to these purposes issued by the US Department of Health and Human Services are called **HIPAA Administrative Simplification Rules**, including a **Privacy Rule**. "Covered entities" subject to these rules include health insurance plans; healthcare clearinghouses; and healthcare providers, e.g., doctors, dentists, other practitioners, hospitals, other medical and health service providers, and any other organizations or persons that provide, are paid for, or bill for healthcare in their normal courses of business, and electronically transmit health information associated with covered transactions. HIPAA's Privacy Rule requires covered entities to protect the privacy of individuals' health records and other information by limiting disclosure without patient permission; and ensures patient rights to examine, get copies, and request corrections of their health records. Schools providing student healthcare with related electronic transactions are "covered entities." However, when school health records are defined as "education records" or "treatment records" under FERPA, they are not subject to the HIPAA Privacy Rule.

## Mandated Reporting of Child Maltreatment

According to the US Department of Health and Human Services Administration on Children, Youth and Families (ACYF) Child Welfare Information Gateway, Children's Bureau (www.childwelfare.gov), as of 2012, 48 states, D.C., American Samoa, Guam, the Northern Mariana Islands, Puerto Rico, and the Virgin Islands designate professions legally required to **report child maltreatment**. These mandated reporters typically are often in contact with children. Such professionals include teachers, principals, administrators, and other school employees; physicians, nurses, and other healthcare employees; social workers; therapists, counselors, psychologists, psychiatrists, and other mental health professionals; child care providers; coroners and medical examiners; and law enforcement officers. Additional professions often mandated to report include clergy in 27 states and Guam; probation and parole officers in 17 states; substance abuse counselors in 14 states; commercial film processors in 12 states, Guam, and Puerto Rico; directors, employees, and volunteers at camps and day camps, youth and recreation centers and other places providing organized activities for children in 11 states; court-appointed special advocates in 10 states; domestic violence workers in seven states and D.C.; humane and animal control officers in seven states and D.C.; and faculty, administrators, other employees and volunteers at public and private colleges, universities, and technical and vocational schools in four states.

## Prevalence of Health Quackery in Advertising

Advertising has long promised results "too good to be true," such as instant miracle cures for cancer, "smart" drugs ensuring longevity, or things that "magically" make arthritis pain "disappear." **Quackery** is the activity of selling unproven remedies. While quacks have existed for many years, today they have more venues than ever before—in addition to word of mouth, newspapers, magazines, and direct mail, TV and radio have been added, and then the Internet. Not only do websites abound selling a variety of health scams, but most of us are also familiar with seeing ads all over our computer screens as we view our email or surf the web. According to government research, the majority of **healthcare scam** victims are above age 65; fraudsters target vulnerable older people. Unproven remedies not only waste consumers' money, they can also prevent them from getting genuine, effective medical treatment. Some, beyond being useless, can be harmful. They also offer false hope, preying on people's pain and fear. Two of the most common fraudulent remedy categories advertised are for arthritis relief and anti-aging claims.

## Access to Healthcare

Access to quality, comprehensive healthcare is critical to increasing health and life quality for all. **Healthcare access** involves three steps: (1) acquiring healthcare system entry, (2) accessing locations providing needed services, (3) finding providers that patients can communicate with and trust. Healthcare access has impacts on overall physical, mental, and social health; disease and disability prevention; health condition identification and treatment; life quality; life expectancy; and preventable deaths. **Impacts** on individuals and society are caused by healthcare access disparities; access limitations impede individuals' abilities to realize their full potentials, diminishing their quality of life. **Service obstacles** include lack of insurance coverage, lack of available services and providers, and expenses; the consequences of these obstacles include lack of preventive services, delayed care, unmet health needs, and hospitalizations which could have been avoided. People without health insurance coverage are less likely to get healthcare, more likely to have poor health status, and more likely to die sooner.

According to the Healthy People 2020 initiative (www.HealthyPeople.gov), an important factor in healthcare access is **primary care providers (PCPs)** as ongoing, regular, usual health-care sources. PCPs are significant for good patient-provider relationships and communication, higher patient trust, and greater probabilities of receiving needed care. Preventive services include primary prevention, like detecting early symptoms and signs to prevent illness; and secondary prevention, such as identifying illness earlier when more treatable. **Emergency medical services (EMS)** constitute another crucial healthcare area, including basic and advanced life support. In recent years, complicated emergency care system problems have developed. HealthyPeople.gov identifies all citizens' access to pre-hospital, rapid-response EMS as an important population health improvement goal. Time waiting in ERs and provider offices, and time between identification and receipt of tests and treatments, are measures of **healthcare system timeliness**. Delays increase patient attrition, decrease patient satisfaction, and cause clinically significant care delays. More non-emergency patients attending ERs, and fewer total ERs, cause delays. Fewer PCPs and medical students interested in primary care are workforce concerns. Emerging issues include meeting needs for many more newly-insured Americans; measuring and increasing access to safe, quality preventive, emergency, long-term, and palliative services; and decreasing disparities and measuring access for elders and minorities.

## Electronic Personal Health Records

Electronic personal health records eliminate problems with paper records like disorganization, losing and misplacing individual papers, and not having papers available when needed. Unlike hospital, physician practice, or health insurance company electronic medical records, **personal health records** are accessible to **patients**. Though electronic adoption has been slow relative to technological capability, more physician practices, hospitals, and insurance companies are providing records accessible over the Internet via computer, tablet, and smartphone. According to the Mayo Clinic (2014), patients should add information including their PCP name and phone number; drug and other allergies; current medications and dosages; chronic health conditions, e.g., hypertension; major surgeries and their dates; any advance directives or living will; immunization history; and family history. They may also want to include prevention activities, e.g., blood pressure, cholesterol levels, dietary and exercise habits, screening test results; and health goals, e.g., losing weight or smoking cessation. Benefits are not only organization, but emergency life-saving; health assessment and tracking; doctor visit preparation; health management between doctor visits; and timely scheduling of wellness, prevention and screening services, vaccinations, and appointments.

## Mobile Healthcare and Medical Applications

The mobile applications industry estimates that by 2015, 500 million people in the world will be using healthcare apps on their smartphones; and by 2018, half of all smartphone and tablet users, who number over 3.4 billion, will have downloaded **mobile health apps**. Consumers, patients, and healthcare professionals are included among these users. The US Food and Drug Administration (FDA), which oversees safety and effectiveness in medical devices, includes mobile medical apps among those devices, and encourages mobile medical app development that will give consumers and healthcare professionals valuable health information and improve healthcare. Consumers can use mobile apps like **MyFitnessPal** to monitor and manage how many calories they eat and burn to manage their own wellness. The National Institutes of Health provides **LactMed**, an app that gives nursing mothers information about how various medications affect their breast milk and their nursing infants. Healthcare professionals can use apps like **Radiation Emergency Medical Management (REMM)**, which offers guidance for diagnosis and treatment of radiation injuries. Other mobile medical apps can diagnose heart arrhythmias or cancer. And some can serve as command centers for insulin-dependent diabetes patients' glucose meter use and measurements.

- 83 -

## Student Access to Valid Healthcare Information, Products, and Services

**Students** should first identify health information, products, and services they need, contacting healthcare providers for information and product recommendations; then find identified information, services, and products. Students researching reports on health topics can find free, reliable **information** from websites including CDC, American Heart Association, American Cancer Society, American Medical Association, and American Association for Health Education; print and online medical journals, public libraries; professional health organization-produced TV programs and videos; school counselors; and healthcare professionals. They can obtain **health products** from healthcare providers, pharmacies, and supermarkets; and parental help accessing prescription and over-the-counter medications. To evaluate information, students should consider source reliability, qualifications of information providers, information's currency, reputable healthcare professional evaluations, whether information's purpose is to inform or sell, whether it educates or only appeals to emotions, how to acquire additional information, and whether claims are realistic. Before paying for products or services, they should consider whether they need them; understand how to use them and what they do; if they are safe, high-quality, and worth their price; consumer agency reviews; and what to do if dissatisfied. The Food and Drug Administration (FDA), Federal Trade Commission (FTC), Consumer Product Safety Commission (CPSC), and US Postal Service for mail-order products and services can help with complaints.

## Community Health Services Offered by the American Red Cross

The American Red Cross is a national nonprofit health agency with many local community chapters. It offers **training** in swimming safety for lifeguards, physical education teachers, and others; in first aid techniques, cardiopulmonary resuscitation (CPR), automated external defibrillator (AED) use, how to control bleeding, what to do in the event of seizures, what to do if someone is choking, and other training for dealing with emergencies until medical personnel arrive. Training is also provided to prepare individuals who want to become instructors in American Red Cross first aid, CPR, and AED courses. The Red Cross also offers Babysitter's Training to teach 11-15-year-olds the confidence and skills they need for safely and responsibly caring for infants and children. The training includes caregiving skills like feeding, diapering, playtime, and bedtime routines; and how to address illnesses, household accidents, injuries, and other child emergencies.

## Community Health Centers

The US Department of Health and Human Services (HHS) supports community-based health centers nationwide through its **Health Resources and Services Administration (HRSA)**. These centers are patient-directed organizations designed to serve populations with limited healthcare access. They provide quality, comprehensive, and culturally competent primary healthcare services to vulnerable populations and medically underserved communities. HRSA defines **medically underserved** populations and areas as having insufficient primary care providers, high poverty rates, high infant mortality rates, and/or large elderly populations. It defines **Health Professional Shortage Areas** as geographical (service areas and counties), demographic (low-income populations), or institutional (federally qualified health centers and other public facilities or comprehensive health centers) having shortages of primary medical, dental, or mental health care providers. Health centers serve such high-need communities; are governed by community boards, with 51 percent or more being patients representing the population served; provide comprehensive primary healthcare and support services (translation, transportation, education, etc.) promoting healthcare access; and provide services to all patients, adjusting fees based on ability to pay. Public and private non-profit health centers meeting Medicare and Medicaid criteria are grant-supported, non-grant-supported, identified by HRSA and Medicare and Medicaid-certified, or outpatient health facilities and programs run by tribal organizations under the Indian Self-Determination Act or Indian Health Care Improvement Act.

## Mass Media Campaigns for Promoting Health Messages

Mass media campaigns can deliver health-promoting messages to large numbers of people. By raising their awareness and communicating educational information through social media, they can enforce positive health behaviors to achieve large-scale **positive health changes**. Messages can be communicated in **print and digital media**. Another avenue is **radio**, found more cost-effective than TV by health organizations because it not only costs less, but moreover it reaches people at work and in cars as well as at home. Also, research in America found radio listeners surprisingly accurate in their memories of broadcast details months later. This retention supports radio's educational potential. In other countries, particularly developing ones, TV and electricity are unavailable in rural villages; however, battery-operated radios are common. Public health, rural development, health education, nutritional education, family planning, and awareness of correct breastfeeding practices have been promoted respectively in Swaziland, India, Nicaragua, the Philippines, and Trinidad and Tobago. **Puppet shows** appeal to younger students and can introduce hygiene, nutrition, and other health topics. Puppetry is an important cultural tradition in Cambodia, and is often used to teach critical health concepts to all ages. UNAIDS advocates mass media TV and radio campaigns for AIDS awareness, education, and destigmatization.

## Food Product Labels

The FDA, under the Federal Food, Drug, and Cosmetic Act, regulates **product labeling**. Labels on food products contain information specific to the product, but the same type of information is contained for all food products:

- **Serving size, servings per container, and calories**: The calories are based on the serving size, so if there are three servings and the calorie count is 150, then the entire product has 450 calories. The calorie count also indicates the number of calories derived from fat.
- **Nutrients**: This includes the amount of fat, carbohydrates, and protein per serving as well as cholesterol, sodium, sugar, and fiber. The amounts are indicated in grams or milligrams but also as a percentage of the daily recommended value. Grams of dietary fiber can be subtracted from the total carbohydrate grams because fiber is carbohydrate that is not digested.
- **Vitamins and minerals**: These are listed as a percentage of daily recommended value per serving.
- **Footnote**: This explains how the percentages displayed are based on a 2,000-calorie diet.

## Roles of Governmental and Nongovernmental Agencies in Providing Reliable Health Information

The National Institutes of Health (NIH) is the primary health-related **U.S. governmental agency** that is involved in health research and health education. The NIH supports numerous individual institutes, including the National Cancer Institute, National Eye Institute, National Institute on Aging, National Institute on Alcohol Abuse and Alcoholism, National Institute on Drug Abuse, and National Institute of Mental Health. The Centers for Disease Control and Prevention (CDC), another governmental agency, provides current information on numerous topics including health conditions, healthy living, travelers' health, and emergency preparedness. The government sponsors numerous prevention centers. **Nongovernmental professional organizations**, such as the American Medical Association, and numerous prevention centers, such as the Child Abuse Prevention Center, carry out or support independent research and publish the results of this research. The Prevention Research Centers are 26 academic research centers in public institutions, such as medical schools, that carry out preventive research and influence public health policy.

## Federal Employees and Departments Responsible for Infectious Disease Control

The **Secretary of the US Department of Health and Human Services** is legally responsible to prevent introduction, transmission, and spreading of communicable diseases in the US. The **Division of Global Migration and Quarantine** is delegated the authority for meeting this responsibility via activities that include operating quarantine stations at entry ports; establishing standards for medical examinations of people coming to the US; and administering foreign and interstate quarantine regulations of the international and interstate movements of people, animals, and cargo. These activities are legally founded in Titles 8 and 42 of the US Code, and pertinent supporting regulations. The US federal government is authorized for isolation and quarantine through the US Constitution's Commerce Clause. US Code 42, Section 264 – Regulations to control communicable diseases, authorizes the **Surgeon General** to make and enforce regulations including inspection, fumigation, disinfection, sanitation, pest extermination, and destruction of articles or animals contaminated or infected with sources of dangerous infections to humans. Individuals may not be apprehended, detained, conditionally released, or examined under this regulation except for preventing introduction, transmission, and spread of communicable diseases. Amendments include executive orders for public health authority evaluation, and a revised list of quarantinable communicable diseases.

## Federal and State Regulations Concerning Immunizations

There are no federal-level **immunization laws** in the US; however, certain vaccinations are required for children to enter **public schools** in all 50 states, varying by state. Children are required to be vaccinated for some or all of the following diseases to enter public schools: diphtheria, measles, mumps, pertussis, poliomyelitis, rubella, and tetanus. Because each state has its own requirements, the US Centers for Disease Control and Prevention (CDC) provides a database of state immunization laws, with results from a legislative review of laws in all 50 states requiring vaccination status assessment and vaccine administration for patients, residents, and healthcare workers. The CDC conducted this review in 2005, collecting data on laws for hospitals, individual provider practices, ambulatory care facilities, facilities for the developmentally disabled, and correctional facilities. The CDC also provides data on requirements for school entry by disease and by state. This includes a tool with state vaccination requirements for school and childcare, state exemptions, and links to state websites; a tool listing diseases preventable by vaccines; and state mandates for immunizations required in prenatal, daycare, childcare, kindergarten, elementary, secondary, K-12, college and university, and long-term care facilities.

## Medical and Health Myths

For many years, some people believed that drinking milk caused certain individuals' bodies to secrete more mucus. Even some doctors believed this, considering it a type of lactose intolerance that is not necessarily concentrated in the digestive system. Physician authors (Carroll and Vreeman, 2009) report that in a study of over 300 patients, almost two-thirds of them believed in such a relationship between milk and phlegm. However, in an experiment with volunteers who had cold viruses, some drank a lot of milk and were found to have no more nasal secretions, congestion, or coughing than those who did not drink as much milk. Another popular **misconception** is the idea that one can develop arthritis from repeatedly cracking one's knuckles. Scientists find no correlation between cracking the knuckles having arthritis, although one study found it could affect soft tissue around the knuckle joint. It can also decrease hand grip strength and increase hand swelling. However, people who crack their knuckles were not found likelier to develop osteoarthritis.

## Occupational Positions in the Healthcare Field

**Physicians** diagnose and treat illnesses; perform, order, and interpret diagnostic tests and procedures; prescribe medications; perform surgeries; specialize in specific patient populations and diseases and treatments; and counsel patients. **Physician assistants (PAs)** assist with surgical procedures rather than performing surgeries; counsel patients under physician direction; prescribe medication in most US states; diagnose and treat illnesses; and perform, order, and interpret diagnostic tests and procedures. **Registered nurses (RNs)** treat patients, administer medications, execute physician orders, and advise and educate patients. **Medical assistants** obtain medical histories and vital signs; draw blood; collect laboratory specimens; prepare patients for examination; assist physicians during examinations; and perform administrative duties like filing charts, scheduling appointments, answering phones, and medical coding and billing. **Surgical technologists** prepare patients for surgery, organize operating room instruments and equipment, and assist physicians during surgical operations and procedures. **Pharmacists** fill prescriptions; compound medications; educate patients about medications; advise physicians and other clinical personnel about drug selection and dosages; and conduct drug experiments, tests, and research. **Clinical psychologists** evaluate and treat mental and emotional disorders. There are many more professions.

## Educational Requirements for Different Healthcare Professions

**Physicians** must complete undergraduate degrees plus 4 years of medical school, 3-8 years of residency or internship, and pass a national licensure test. **Physician assistants** must complete a 2-4-year PA certification program and pass a national licensure test. **RNs** must complete a bachelor's/associate's degree or diploma and pass a national licensure test. **Medical assistants** must attain a 1-year diploma or certificate or a 2-year associate's degree, and in some US states pass a national certification test. **Surgical technologists** must receive a 9-month diploma/certificate or 2-year associate's degree and pass a national certification test. **Pharmacists** must complete a 6-8-year Doctor of Pharmacy degree and pass a national licensure test. **Clinical psychologists** must complete a doctoral (Ph.D. or Psy.D.) degree and pass a national licensure test. **Audiologists and speech-language therapists** must each complete Master's degrees and pass national licensure tests; in some US states, audiologists must pass an additional licensure test for dispensing hearing aids.

## Examples of Health Organizations Using Community and School Events to Deliver Health Education

Healthcare system leaders recognize the importance of **prevention** and **early detection** to sustaining health and reducing illness. For example, physicians and health teams at the leading nonprofit comprehensive healthcare system **WellStar** demonstrate their belief in prevention and early detection by providing screenings, health fairs, and educational opportunities in a diverse range of settings to help people improve individual and family health and well-being. They produce community events free of charge or low in cost. Throughout communities, health fairs feature medical screenings, community education, and basic preventive medicine through interactive educational events. Some health fairs have particular themes, e.g., weight loss and fitness, diabetes, or heart health. Well*Screen Events offer affordable, convenient screenings for early detection of diabetes, prostate conditions, thyroid disorders, high cholesterol, and other medical issues. Multiple WellStar facilities and other locations like senior centers, religious organizations, and YMCAs host **screening events** throughout the year. WellStar also offers educational events and classes for schools, community groups, local businesses, and religious organizations; and the nationally recognized Safe Sitter babysitter education program for ages 11-13, teaching personal safety, behavior management, injury prevention, first aid, CPR, choking care, and business and ethical aspects of babysitting.

## Planning School Health Fairs as a Means of Health Education Advocacy

Fuel Up to Play 60 (© 2013), a program of Play 60, the NFL Movement for an Active Generation supported by the National Dairy Council, offers these tips to educators and parents: work with the school nurse and other health professionals to produce a list of potential **health fair presenters**. Invite community members to set up tables with physical activity and healthy eating information, give presentations, and even just attend to learn more. Guests could include local chefs, health news broadcasters or other local celebrities, and local pediatricians and hospital staff. Plan space and time for an event, including events such as family contests, races, and other fun activities; space for presentations; and healthy picnic foods to eat. Form a team and decide the best place, day, and time with the principal. Indoor and outdoor activities combined enable greater attendee movement to derive the most from the event. Collaborate with **school nutrition professionals** to choose healthy foods, and **physical educators** to choose and organize fun physical activities. Enlist student and parent volunteers to manage activity stations. Contact local organizations and businesses for donations of tables, food, equipment, prizes, etc. Invite the donors.

## Health Educators Serving as Liaisons between School Personnel, Students, Parents, and Communities

Many health educator activities connect different education stakeholders. For example, when they identify and request resources from school administrators for meeting learning goals and objectives they have developed, they are acting as **liaisons** between students and administrators. When they develop processes to **integrate health education** into other programs across the curriculum, they liaise with school administrators, curriculum coordinators, other school subject teachers, and students. By training others to implement health education, they liaise between trainees and students. When developing and conducting research, they liaise between the school and the research community. They are liaisons between support providers and students when requesting program support; and liaisons among all stakeholders when promoting their collaboration. As resource persons, they are liaisons communicating health information from resources to stakeholders, between existing resources and trainees when providing training, and between other trainers and trainees when they implement training programs and sessions. As consultants, they may liaise between or among different personnel whom they provide consultative assistance. As advocates, they are liaisons between students and parents and families to promote healthy home practices and parental school involvement in health education, and between policymakers and schools and communities when advocating health promotion policies.

### Skills and Abilities

Health educator skills for assessing community as well as individual needs enable them to **liaison** between the school and the community to **promote school and community health**. Their skills for planning health education programs mean they can interact with other educators, school administrators, curriculum coordinators, etc. Skills for coordinating health education programs naturally require them to liaison among different school personnel, as do skills for managing health education programs and personnel. Coalition-building skills mean they can liaise among the diverse stakeholders they recruit to form coalitions for health promotion, advocacy, and health education advocacy. Skills for making referrals make them liaisons between students and parents and various agencies and service providers to whom they refer them. Skills for developing mass media and social marketing campaigns enable them to liaison between media representatives and the public. Abilities for mobilizing and organizing communities make them liaisons among various community members, and school and community. Abilities to encourage healthy behaviors, and to manage controversial health content and issues, enable them to liaise between parents and students.

# GSHS

The **Global School Health-based Student Health Survey** (GSHS), developed in a joint effort by the World Health Organization (WHO), the United Nations organizations UNAIDS, UNESCO, and UNICEF with technical assistance from the Centers for Disease Control and Prevention (CDC), is a school-based survey of **health behaviors and health-protective factors** in students 13-17 years old in over 120 countries. Over 450,000 students had participated through 2013. The data gleaned from this survey is intended to assist world nations in setting priorities, developing programs, and advocating for youth and school health policies and programs; help nations, international agencies, and others compare the prevalence of protective factors and health behaviors across different countries; and determine trends in protective factor and health behavior prevalence according to each nation to utilize for evaluating youth health advocacy and school health. GSHS core questionnaire modules cover hygiene and diet; alcohol, drug, and tobacco use; physical activity; mental health; protective factors; sexual behaviors; unintentional injury; and violence. WHO and CDC offer technical support and continuing capacity-building via training, materials, data analysis, and software. Country reports, data, documentation, bibliography, and fact sheets are available online.

## Promoting Student Participation in School-/Community-Based Efforts to Address High-Risk Behaviors Associated with Substance Abuse

Promoting student participation in school-/community-based efforts to address high-risk behaviors associated with substance abuse often begins by recruiting **student leaders** to participate and lead these efforts because students look to their peers for guidance. **Sports coaches** are also often role models and can influence athletes to participate, and athletes often are admired by other students, who may follow their lead. The leaders of school clubs, such as the honor society or chess club, should also be recruited because they can positively influence club members. The school can also include **families** in prevention methods through such programs as Family Matters, in which parents receive booklets and telephone guidance by the health educator. Programs for adolescents that have proven successful include Life Skills Training (focuses on decision making, problem solving, and critical thinking); Lions Quest Skills for Adolescence (focuses on civic responsibility, social skills, and resisting peer pressure); ALERT Plus (Adolescent Learning Experiences Resistance Training), a 9–10th-grade extension of the middle school program; and the Project Toward No Drug Abuse (an interactive classroom project that focuses on motivation, life skills, and decision making).

## Health-Related Careers and Educational Requirements

Health-related careers:

- **Physicians** - Requires a bachelor's degree, four years of medical school, internship, and residency and licensure.
- **Nurses (RNs, LVN, APNs)** - Registered nurses (RNs) require two- to five-year training programs (ASN, BSN) and licensure as well as additional training for advance practice nurses (APNs). Licensed vocational nurses (LVNs) require an 18-month to 2-year training period, licensure, and work under RN supervision.
- **Nutritionists** - Requires bachelor's or master's degree.
- **Certified nurse assistant (aide)** - Requires six to eight weeks of training. Work under the supervision of RNs and LVNs.
- **Physician assistant** - Requires a two-year master degree program. PAs carry out many of the tasks of physicians.

- 89 -

- **Technicians** - Technicians include x-ray technicians, laboratory technicians, ultrasound technicians, dental hygienists, pharmacy technicians, emergency medical technicians, echocardiogram technicians, and phlebotomists. Training varies but is often approximately for two years, whereas those that require one skill, such as phlebotomists, may be trained in a matter of weeks. Some require licensure.
- **Medical assistant** - Programs vary from one to two years and include a certificate and/or associate's degree.

## WHO's World Health Surveys

The World Health Organization (WHO) began the **World Health Surveys (WHS)** in 2002-2004, partnering with 70 world nations to gather information about adult health populations and health systems through cross-sectional survey studies. More than 300,000 people aged 18 years and older participated in the studies, yielding a very large sample size. The WHS extended the results of WHO's 2000-2001 Multi-country Survey Study. The purpose of the WHS was to use a valid, reliable survey instrument to reinforce national capacities for monitoring **health systems** and **critical health outcomes**. WHO used statistical probability to select nationally representative samples from countries chosen to represent all of the world's regions. They adjusted the weights of sampling according to population distribution, and corrected for non-response following stratification. The surveys covered household data including household members, health insurance coverage, health expenditures, and permanent wealth or income indicators. On the individual level, the survey information included sociodemographic data, descriptions of health states, valuations of health states, health risk factors, chronic health conditions, healthcare use, mortality, social capital, and responsiveness of healthcare systems.

## EPA Source for Reducing, Reusing, and Recycling to Help the Environment

The **US Environmental Protection Agency** (EPA) website offers information on how to reduce, reuse, and donate products to protect the environment and save natural resources and money; how to donate and recycle used electronics; how to compost and reduce wasted food; how to reduce, reuse, and recycle at home, school, work, in the community, and on the go on its wastes website; resources for educators and students including publications, games, and activities; and information on the basics, benefits, and how-to of recycling. **Recycling** reduces waste going to incinerators and landfills; conserves water, wood, minerals and other natural resources; saves energy; reduces greenhouse gas emissions involved in world climate change; sustains the environment for posterity; and creates new, well-paid jobs in American manufacturing and recycling industries. Recycling steps are: (1) collection and processing, (2) manufacturing, and (3) purchasing products made from recycled materials. Recycled product contents include: aluminum cans, car bumpers, carpeting, cereal boxes, comic books, egg cartons, glass containers, laundry detergent bottles, motor oil, nails, newspapers, paper towels, steel products, and garbage bags. EPA also provides instructions on recycling paper, batteries, plastics including plastic ID codes, glass, oil, household hazardous waste, tires, compact fluorescent light bulbs, etc.

## Conserving Energy for Sustainable Living and Prevention of Severe Global Disruptions from Greenhouse Gas Emissions

In 2009, America produced one-fifth of the world's $CO_2$ emissions, approximately 6 billion metric tons annually—7 billion projected by 2030. **Buildings** produce the most, 38 percent from private homes, shopping malls, warehouses, and offices, primarily from using electricity; average new American houses are 45 percent larger than 30 years ago. Walmart, maintaining thousands of buildings, has significantly conserved energy by using natural light in shopping areas, radiant floors, high-efficiency refrigeration, evaporative cooling units, etc.; one pilot supercenter consumed 45 percent less power than comparable stores. Oak Ridge National Laboratory researchers say 200 million tons of $CO_2$ could be reduced annually through smart design and retrofitting, but find this unlikely without financial incentives, appliance standards, and new building codes. For example, commercial building owners are unmotivated because tenants pay power bills. Development increases traveling distance, making **transportation** the second-biggest source. **Industry** is third. Dow saved $7 billion from 1995-2009 by reducing energy intensity, reducing $CO_2$ emissions 20 percent; DuPont and 3M have also profited through energy-efficiency. Other developed nations surpass America with solar and wind power, bicycling, fuel-efficient cars, and carbon-neutral houses. Experts advocate developing $CO_2$-burial and elimination technologies, slowing deforestation, and replacing fossil fuels with renewable energy faster to reduce global emissions 80-100 percent by 2050.

## Causes and Effects of Environmental Problems

### Air Pollution

Air pollution is primarily caused by the use of fossil fuels, such as oil, gas, natural gas, and coal; these fuels release carbon monoxide, hydrocarbons, and other pollutants into the atmosphere when they are burned. **Motor vehicles** are the primary polluters, but industrial emissions from factories and manufacturing plants also are implicated because many depend on fossil fuels as well, and some release various chemicals used in or resulting from the manufacturing process. Air pollution can also result from **agricultural chemicals** (such as crop spraying) and **household chemicals** (such as fumigants). Air pollution can reduce visibility in some cases, but it may also be invisible, so people may be unaware that the air is polluted. Air pollution is considered to be one of the causes of **global warming**. Air pollution can also have a serious impact on **health** by impairing lung function and resulting in an increased incidence of cancer and respiratory diseases, such as asthma and chronic obstructive pulmonary disease.

### Water Pollution

Water pollution occurs when pollutants flow into surface water sources, such as rivers, lakes, reservoirs, and oceans. Contamination of **surface water** can result from sewage, oil spills, industrial wastes, and chemical runoffs (fertilizers, weed killers). In areas with air pollution, surface water may become contaminated through atmospheric deposition (rain, snow). **Drinking water**, even from clean water sources, can become contaminated through erosion of lead pipes or lead solder used with other types of pipes that are part of the delivery system. **Groundwater** can also become polluted as pollutants, such as noxious chemicals from fertilizers and weed killers, are leached through the ground and enter underground water. Water pollution not only kills fish and wildlife, but it can harm wetlands and coral reefs. Water pollution has been implicated in waterborne diseases (such as typhoid fever), neurological impairment, and cancer. Children exposed to polluted water may suffer developmental disorders and mental retardation.

### Hazardous Waste

Hazardous waste is waste that poses a threat to the health of individuals or to the environment. The Environmental Protection Agency (EPA) classifies hazardous wastes according to the following characteristics:

- **Ignitable**: Liquids and nonliquids that can ignite and cause fires.
- **Corrosive**: Based on pH or the ability to corrode steel.
- **Reactive**: Wastes that are unstable, may react with water, or result in toxic gases. They may also explode.
- **Toxic**: Wastes that are harmful if ingested or absorbed.

Wastes may also be classified as **listed wastes**. These include wastes from manufacturing and industrial processes. **Hazardous wastes** are often produced in manufacturing, nuclear power plants (nuclear wastes), and healthcare facilities (needles, materials contaminated with body fluids). **Nuclear wastes** are classified as mixed waste because they contain a radioactive component as well as a hazardous component. Hazardous wastes can result in disease (such as from needle punctures), injury (from fire and explosions), and death (from toxic exposure, disease).

## Noise Pollution and Overcrowding

Noise pollution is increasingly a problem in the urban environment where individuals are almost constantly surrounded by transportation noises, people, alarms, sirens, dogs barking, and everyday noise from walking, eating, and interacting. Noise is often an issue in the work environment because of the equipment used, especially in manufacturing. **Noise pollution** may also result from inadequate urban planning, social events, and construction. The results of noise pollution can be hearing impairment (especially if exposed to high decibels), stress, fatigue, insomnia, and high blood pressure. Animals exposed to noise pollution may become aggressive, disoriented, or hard of hearing. Wildlife that use mating calls or echolocation may not reproduce or migrate. **Overcrowding,** too many people in a space, is often associated with noise pollution and can occur in individual homes, such as with four or five families sharing one apartment, or in an urban area, such as when a large population is impacted by a severe housing shortage. Overcrowding can result in disease epidemics, mental health problems, and academic problems.

## Strategies for Reducing Environmental Hazards and Promoting Health

### Water Purification and Emission Control

Water purification is the process that removes contaminants, such as biological matter, chemicals, gases, and debris, from water in order to make it safe for drinking or other purposes. Boiling water does not always remove all contaminants—nor does the use of activated charcoal filters. **Drinking water** is typically not made sterile, whereas water for **medical purposes** should be sterile. Steps to purification include pumping the water from the source, screening to remove debris, pH adjustment, coagulation/flocculation, sedimentation, filtering, and disinfection.

**Emission control** is the system used to reduce emissions that result in air pollution from both mobile sources (such as motor vehicles) and point sources (power plants, manufacturing plants). **Toxic emission pollutants** include carbon monoxide, hydrocarbons, sulfur oxide, organic compounds, nitrogen dioxide, smoke, and soot. Emissions are regulated by the EPA as well as some state regulation agencies. Motor vehicles use catalytic converters to convert carbon monoxide, hydrocarbons, and nitrous oxide to harmless gases.

### Waste Management

Waste management is the process by which waste products are collected, transported, and disposed of or recycled. **Municipal waste management** usually involves weekly collection with separate containers sometimes provided for garden waste, recyclables, and garbage, although garbage is mixed by the consumer and then separated at a facility in some waste management plants. Waste management is regulated by the EPA through the **Resource Conservation and Recovery Act**, which regulates the handling and disposal of hazardous and nonhazardous waste. Because **hazardous waste** can result in disease, injury, or death, special handling is required. Hazardous waste cannot be disposed of with regular trash or in drains or the sewer system. In schools, chemistry labs often have hazardous wastes to dispose of, such as corrosive liquids, heavy-metal solutions, and organic solvents. The art department and the school nurse may also have hazardous wastes, such as used paints, pigments, dyes, needles, and dressings contaminated with body fluids.

- 92 -

## Improving Community and Environmental Health

Individuals can contribute to improving community and environmental health through the following actions:

- **Advocacy**: This include identifying public health problems within the community and/or environment, researching the problems and possible solutions, and taking steps to educate the public and those in positions of power to help reduce or eliminate the problems by influencing political and social policy. A primary goal of advocacy is to increase public awareness in order to generate support for change.
- **Volunteerism**: This involves providing services in the community without financial gain or coercion, such as volunteering to clean up the environment or volunteering in a local hospital or school. Many nonprofit agencies and governmental agencies welcome volunteers or have volunteer programs. Volunteerism is a required part of service learning for students in some areas, but students can often be mobilized to volunteer for causes that interest them, and an educator can provide a good role model through volunteerism.

# Motor Skills and Movement Activities

## Reaching and Grasping

Even before birth, fetuses display **arm and hand movements**—waving arms, making isolated finger movements, and using coordinated arm-hand movements like moving their thumbs to their mouths. Outside the womb, without the buoyancy of amniotic fluid, newborns must contend with gravity. Beginning with jerky extensions and flapping of the arms, they develop successful **reaching** for objects by 4-5 months. Detailed motion analysis reveals that infants initially problem-solve by moving their hands to targets individually. More sedentary babies must transcend gravity to raise their arms, while more active babies must damp inertia to control spontaneous, continuous arm-flapping. Both only open their hands into fitting shapes after touching objects. By around 8 months, babies can adjust their hand shapes prior to object contact, informing themselves visually about object shapes, sizes, and orientations. While visual information about object properties and locations is critical to adaptive planning of arm and hand movements, babies can **reach and grasp** as successfully in the dark as in light, so they need not see their arms or hands to guide them—likely because kinesthetics and proprioception work for body parts but not separate objects.

## Using Hand-Held Tools

After babies have mastered the **motor actions** involved in reaching and grasping objects, they can apply their skills to achieve rewarding results. They learn to differentiate **textures**: they will bang hard objects against hard surfaces because this makes noise, but will not repeat banging soft objects against soft surfaces as it makes no noise. Infants are observed to test different combinations of objects and surfaces to determine which is noisiest. At 9 months, babies typically can bang on surfaces with spoons, but they take several months longer to develop the **fine motor control** for using spoons in the complex operation of scooping and bringing food to their mouths. Cognitive developmental psychologist Jean Piaget first described how older babies differentiate their reaching and grasping skills into instrumental actions to attain their goals. For example, around 8 months, babies reach and pull a cloth to move a toy on the cloth closer. Older babies lean forward, holding sticks, to extend their reach for objects. Toddlers rake in out-of-reach objects using canes as tools. They demonstrate comprehension of the tool-target relationship by turning the canes functionally.

## Walking Development

Newborns may already have **inter-limb coordination**, as demonstrated by their crawling, swimming, and stepping reflexes. After developing the locomotion skills of crawling, babies go through several transitional upright stages of pulling up, balancing while standing, and sideways cruising while holding onto furniture for support. These transitional stages culminate in independent walking. From babies' first steps, to toddling, to eventual adult-like walking around elementary school ages, children evidence dramatic **gait changes**. When babies first begin to walk, their feet are spaced widely apart, with their toes pointed outward. They hold their legs nearly straight, not bending their knees. They typically bend their elbows upward, with the palms of their hands facing the ceiling. They either set each foot down all at once or walk on their toes, instead of rolling the foot from heel to toe as adults do. As their bodies and brains mature, their body proportions change, their balance improves and they gain additional experience, their gait patterns gradually change until by around seven years old, they walk the way adults walk.

- 94 -

## Maturational Considerations

Despite common PE class **segregation** of males from females, some experts find it appropriate to allow adolescents of both genders to participate **together** in physical activities without body contact that require agility and lower-body strength. Some examples of these include running, ultimate Frisbee, and capture the flag. For activities that need more upper-body strength, PE teachers and coaches should base their assignment of teams on the skill levels of the individual students to prevent them from injuring themselves and one another. Experts also point out the importance of evenly matching sports teams on the basis of levels of maturation and skills. That way, deficits in individual student skill levels are not as obvious, and all students have fun participating. Some examples of suitable activities include individual and/or partners' tennis, badminton, and competitive team activities like flag football. It is important for PE teachers and coaches to monitor student physical activities, and adjust them as needed to assure all students have competitive, positive, and enjoyable experiences.

## Perceptual Exploration

Infants need visual information about the characteristics and locations of objects to reach and grasp, as evidenced by their intercepting moving objects, moving their opposite hand to the right place before object arrival. Researchers have observed a basic motor development need is coordination of **perceptual exploring** and **manual skills**. Newborns not only bring hands to mouths; when stretching arms out, they also turn their heads to maintain their arm view. As they grow, older babies bring not only fingers, but also objects to their mouths. They coordinate among visual, tactile, and oral exploration; looking at; reaching; grasping; touching; turning; and mouthing objects. Babies also must use balance control, even for simple reaching actions: extending one arm out from the base of support displaces the center of gravity, requiring counterbalancing through opposition. When infants' abdominal and back muscles are not yet strong enough to support them in sitting positions, they use their hands to achieve a "tripod" (three-point) balance. Once they sit independently around 5-6 months, this frees their hands to reach, grasp, and manipulate smaller objects. Within several more months, they can coordinate leaning with reaching to avoid tipping over.

## Contribution of Perception

The process of absorbing, organizing, and interpreting sensory input—i.e., **perception**—is multisensory: information from all of the senses contributes to a child's motor behaviors in response to the input received. For example, when infants see a face and hear a voice, they turn their heads. From natural newborn waving and kicking, babies adapt to their environments by developing control over reaching for things; locomotion, i.e., learning to crawl, then walk, then run, etc.; and eventually learning complex skills for sports participation. **Developing infant motor behaviors** include control over eye movements to gaze at people and things, and control over head movements. As motor competence develops, babies use perceptual information to choose which motor actions to perform. Reciprocally, they get most of this perceptual information through motor movements of their eyes, arms, hands, and legs. According to how slippery, rigid, or sloped a surface is, they will adjust their crawling or walking. Changes in size, weight, muscular strength, and body fat from infancy to toddlerhood present perceptual-motor challenges as they practice various actions.

## Kinesthesis and Equilibrium

**Kinesthesis** is the sense of the body parts' positions and movements. Muscles, tendons, and joints contain receptors enabling kinesthesis. We are able to know where all of our body parts are at any time, and in what manner and direction they are moving, through kinesthesis. **Equilibrium** is our sense of balance. This gives us information regarding where our bodies are in space. For example, we can distinguish whether we are standing up, sitting, or lying down; in an ascending or descending elevator; or riding a roller coaster through our sense of equilibrium. The vestibular system in the inner ear is the sensory system that provides equilibrium. Specifically, the three semicircular canals contain fluid. Whenever our heads move, this fluid moves along with the head. The fluid's movement stimulates hair cells/cilia in the semicircular canals. These receptors send impulses to the brain via nerves. The brain interprets these impulses to understand the movement, giving us feedback about it. Our brains interpret the combined feedback from kinesthesis and equilibrium for orienting ourselves in space.

## Perceptual and Motor Behaviors

While research has long observed that the **developmental domains** are interrelated, recent research further reinforces the depth of **interdependence** among developmental domains, processes, and factors. Some researchers point out that cognition, perception, and motor behavior transpire in the context of culture, social relationships, experience, and emotion, affecting overall brain function and mental and physical health. Others also find **perception and motor actions** are not independent, but interdependent processes; they characterize these as parts of an action system. Very early strong motivation in infants to pay attention, obtain information, explore, and engage their physical and social environments is evidence that cognitive, perceptual, motor, emotional, and social domains of development are interrelated, demonstrated by visual tracking, head-turning, and reaching. One investigator has observed that infants do not reach for desired objects because of brain programming; rather, they match their movements to their goals and the specific tasks involved. As some define it, behavior equals movement. Psychology is the study of human behavior; perception and motor behaviors inform psychological development. Some researchers find excellent opportunities for studying infants' social cognition by observing how they use social information to guide motor behavior in unfamiliar or physically challenging situations.

## Promoting Motor Learning for Sports

Researchers into education have examined whether learning **specific** academic subjects could expand students' **general** attentional and learning skills. Many have concluded the nature of learning is more specific, in that the mind functions in a very detailed manner by adapting to the particular information it experiences. They additionally find that improving any individual mental process seldom improves any other individual one. These conclusions have been applied to the subject of motor learning. Experimental studies have demonstrated that movement is very closely related to sensory stimuli. This indicates that specificity in physical training is necessary for attaining successful outcomes in motor learning. Prevailing scientific evidence shows that, for students to acquire motor skills, the most important factor in practice is practicing the actual target skill itself, rather than related skills or other skills. For functional sport motor skills to become permanent behavior changes, the stimuli presented must duplicate the energy systems and movements used in a designated sport activity. Therefore, researchers conclude actually performing a sport itself is the best training for learning the motor skills involved in that sport.

## Training an Athletic Skill

A common consideration in teaching new athletic skills is whether to teach a skill as a **whole**, or to break it down into its component pieces and teach those **individually**. Although task analysis has proven valuable for some purposes to education, to acquire specific sport skills, whole training has been found superior to part training for motor learning. For example, in volleyball, to teach spiking the ball, the parts would consist of approach footwork, arm work, jumping, contacting the ball, and recovery. The whole of spiking would be all these elements together. A part of spiking would be contacting the ball alone, or jumping alone, etc. Investigators reviewing the literature could not find even one study showing better results from teaching individual parts of such sport skills, or teaching individual skill parts in progressive sequence. Much additional research corroborates the concept that volleyball and other athletic skills

- 96 -

demanding high levels of inter-limb coordination are learned best through teaching and practicing the whole skill rather than the parts, or even progressive parts.

## Teaching Methods vs Experience Levels

By studying **sports training methods** as they are informed by **principles of motor learning**, researchers have found that, while educators must structure learning environments according to their particular students' skill levels and information-processing abilities, the training methods they use should nevertheless be constant across students. Neuroscience informs that beginners are more limited in their ability to process information. Additionally, motor learning principles dictate a positive correspondence between the relative complexity of the regulatory stimuli educators use and of students' experience, and vice versa. The balance is such that, without enough novelty, motor learning will not take place, while too much novelty will overwhelm student processing capacities. Teachers can control the learning environment to accommodate beginners' lower processing abilities. For example, when teaching volleyball to 3rd-graders, they can limit the content by using a smaller court, fewer players, a lighter ball, and/or a lower net. As students gain playing skills, teachers can introduce more new stimuli, enabling student motor behaviors to progress in complexity.

## Significance of Posture

In both classical and contemporary theories of motor development, the role played by **posture** is central. In classical theories, which attributed motor skills development to neuromuscular maturation, the gradually increasing erectness of babies' postures as they progressed in overcoming the effects of gravity was demonstration of the growth of control over actions in their cerebral cortices. In contemporary theories involving dynamic systems approaches and perception-action relationships, posture is equally important as action's biomechanical basis. Not only locomotor skills, but manual skills and even raising and turning the head all depend on having a **stable postural base**. Sitting up, crawling, walking, and every other developmental milestone in posture necessitates learning about new perception-action systems. In learning control over a new postural system, the first step is co-contraction of large muscle groups. This enables focusing attention on the movement's goal-directed aspects by freeing more resources. But movements initiated by co-contraction are energy-inefficient and jerky. With enough practice, babies learn to activate muscles in sequence and take advantage of the forces of inertia and gravity, allowing much lesser exertion of muscular force.

## Influences of Maturation and Experience

While historically, scientists believed that genetically determined growth and development—i.e., **maturation**—was responsible for motor skill development, more recent research has uncovered evidence that the motor development process is not simply passive in nature, but is also **active**, as when babies engage in movement and physically explore their environments. As they develop physical abilities through growth and acquire motor skills through independent learning, maturation and experience and their interaction all influence motor development. Earlier motor skills like crawling and walking are more strongly influenced by **maturation**, though experience also clearly plays a part, as evidenced by babies' learning through experience in early attempts, errors, failures, repetitions, and eventual success. Later, more sophisticated motor skills like playing basketball or juggling are even more influenced by **experience**, instruction, and social factors as well as genetic predispositions. While early motor skill development follows similar sequences and timing across different cultures, cultural differences do influence the rates at which motor skills develop. For example, babies sit, stand, and walk later in cultures where mothers carry them more, and earlier in cultures where parents train them early in these skills.

## Promoting Psychomotor Learning

Some instructional methods PE teachers can use to promote student psychomotor learning include the **task/reciprocal method**. In this technique, the teacher uses stations to integrate the students' learning of specific tasks into the learning setup. Another is the **command/direct method**. In this style, teacher-centered task instruction is utilized: The PE teacher gives students clear explanations of the learning goals, explains the skills to be learned, and then demonstrates these skills for the students. The PE teacher then gives the students time to practice the new skills. During their practice, the PE teacher monitors their progress frequently and regularly. Another instructional method PE teachers can use to promote psychomotor learning is the **contingency/contract approach**. In this type of instruction, the PE teacher offers specified rewards to students, which are contingent upon their completing the indicated tasks. This behavioral method reinforces psychomotor behaviors, i.e., increases the probability of students' repeating them, by rewarding the behaviors.

## Development of Children's Motor Skills

- **Muscle tone** during contraction and at rest varies among children. Hypotonia is low muscle tone, causing floppiness, weakness, and poor balance; hypertonia is high muscle tone, causing stiffness and difficult movement. Children with Down syndrome may have hypotonia, while those with cerebral palsy often have hypertonia.
- **Strength** is relative force of muscular contractions against resistance. Children with weak muscles may have difficulty achieving motor development milestones.
- **Endurance** enables children to sustain exertion over time, entailing multiple factors including muscle tone, strength, cardiovascular and pulmonary function, and motivation. Children with low endurance may be able to step up one stair but not climb a whole flight.
- **Balance** while stationary and while moving results from vestibular equilibrium interacting with sensory information, including sight, proprioception, muscle tone, and strength.
- **Motor planning** coordinates systems controlling perception, movement intensity, speed, and sequencing in the complex and frequently intuitive process of executing steps in physical activities.
- **Sensory integration** is interpreting environmental sensory input correctly and responding with appropriate motor activity. Children's response thresholds vary along a continuum among ranges of understimulation, average stimulation, and overstimulation.

## Effects of Experience on Motor Patterns

Neurophysiological studies have found the brain has **plasticity**; i.e., both its structures and functions can be modified by various influences, such as behavioral training and other new learning. **Neuroplasticity** affords great promise for improving abilities in people with neurological damage or deficits, and those wanting to enhance their cognitive processing skills. Furthermore, some researchers have found specific **motor experiences** determine the place and character of plasticity in the corticospinal system. For example, training in motor skills stimulates generation of new synapses, enhances synaptic potential, and restructures movement representations in the motor cortex. Training in endurance generates formation of new blood vessels in the motor cortex, but does not change number of synapses or organization of motor maps. Strength training changes activation of spinal motor neurons and generates new synapses in the spinal cord, but does not change motor map organization. All three types of training modify spinal reflexes that rely on each task's specific behavioral requirements. These findings show acquiring skilled movements causes neural circuits in the motor cortex to be reorganized to support producing and refining skilled movement sequences.

## Helping Students Acquire Motor Skills

PE teachers not only need to know the process of motor development thoroughly, they moreover need to understand the **principles** whereby their students learn and transfer new information to progress in learning motor skills and refining them. **Instruction and practice** are critical: without these, the extent of children's motor skills development is determined only by their natural talents and abilities. But when PE teachers give students structured, frequent practice, their motor skills development improves. In motor skills development, **student self-assessment** is a tool that can have powerful impact. When PE teachers require students to assess their own abilities and skills, students are encouraged to reflect about their current levels of skill; they become more motivated to advance these levels, and assume control over their development processes. **Observational learning** is a key principle of PE because students learn motor skills more easily by observing their correct performance demonstrated by teachers than they can by trying to follow verbal directions. It is easier to reproduce physical movements we see than imagine and produce them from what we hear.

## Principle of Feedback

**Input** from teachers and coaches is vital for students to learn motor skills. Student motivation and interest are enhanced by **positive feedback**, while student recognition and correction of errors are enhanced by **negative feedback**. When students learn motor skills, these are temporarily saved in short-term memory. Positive feedback supports transfer to permanent, long-term memory. It not only encourages, but also helps students remember all aspects of their performance. Negative feedback is not only corrective, but also motivational: when students and athletes do not improve their technique over time, they lose motivation. Students receive **internal feedback** through kinesthesia and proprioception. When they produce movements, they receive sensations and information from their muscles, joints, and vestibular (balance) systems. They receive verbal and visual **external feedback** from teachers and coaches. External feedback that improves internal feedback by enabling students and athletes to establish kinesthetic references for correct movements and techniques is called **augmented feedback**. Extrinsic feedback includes knowledge of performance, and information about performance and technique. Studies find feedback timing equally important as feedback content. Positive feedback is crucial to beginners for successfully learning skills. Beginners may be bored by negative feedback, but corrections and results are very important to advanced students and athletes.

## PE Techniques and Strategies

For students to develop greater **spatial awareness and coordination**, they need both maturity and plenty of practice. In their lessons, PE teachers should concentrate on activities that require vision, hearing, and/or touch; that are sequential in nature; and that children enjoy performing. It is very beneficial to students for PE teachers to discuss the specific steps for performing fundamental skills with them. For example, running; hitting and catching a ball; dribbling a basketball, making a basket; and setting a volleyball are all skills and activities that PE teachers can break down into incremental steps and teach them one step at a time. Instructional strategies that are recommended include first introducing a skill to students; having the students practice the skill using a variety of equipment and in a variety of settings; modifying games to incorporate practice of the requisite skills; implementing lead-up games containing these practice modifications; and then, after enough practice, giving students the opportunity to use the skills they have learned and practiced in the contexts of real games.

## Spatial Awareness

**Spatial awareness** involves consciousness of and decisions about changes in objects' positions within three-dimensional space. The sequence of developing spatial awareness has two phases:

- recognizing object locations in space **relative to one's own body**; and
- locating multiple objects in space relative to each other, **independently of one's body**.

PE teachers can apply the concept of spatial awareness to class activities by instructing students to move toward and away from, behind and in front of, over and under, next to, inside, and outside various objects. They can provide hoops, balls, boxes, etc. as objects in various sizes and shapes. These activities develop spatial awareness, particularly in younger children or students with spatial awareness deficits. PE teachers can assess student body awareness by observing them play Simon Says; asking them to touch their body parts; make straight, twisted, and round shapes with their bodies; and fit them into variously-sized spaces. They can enhance body awareness by having children touch one body part to another, twist their necks, nod heads, wiggle noses, open mouths, close eyes, shrug shoulders, bend elbows, clap hands, snap fingers, bend knees, stamp feet, and wiggle toes.

## Define Effort Awareness.

**Effort awareness** refers to an individual's knowledge of time, force, and balance and how these are related to physical movements and athletic activities. According to the findings of research studies, movement concepts are interrelated and interactive with the concepts of space, direction, and speed. When students understand these concepts, they will be able to move so as to avoid collisions with other people and/or objects, and they will have self-confidence in their ability to move effectively. In order to understand a sport and perform it successfully, a student or athlete must incorporate the movement concepts of vision, space, direction, and speed. For example, when a student plays basketball or soccer, s/he has to determine what the appropriate amount or distance of personal space is among players. In addition, these movement concepts are all connected with one another. For example, a student playing a sport has to coordinate speed and direction in order to change or maintain his or her pathway without losing speed. This consists of the abilities to perform ably within space and to change one's motion.

## Develop Body and Spatial Awareness

To help students develop **body awareness**, PE teachers can instruct them to touch or point to their various body parts, form their bodies into different shapes, and to fit their bodies into differently sized and shaped spaces. These can both assess and develop body awareness. To assess and develop **spatial awareness**, PE teachers can provide differently sized and shaped objects like boxes, balls, hoops, etc. and have students move around, over, under, into, out of, in front of, in back of, and toward and away from them. To help students develop understanding of force, PE teachers can place targets at varying distances and have students throw beanbags, balls, or other objects at the targets. They can prompt students to notice how much force they must use to reach nearer vs. farther targets, and discuss use of relatively too much and too little force. Another exercise is to have spotters (carefully) positioned behind each student, and have students forcefully throw or otherwise propel wind-resistant objects like swim fins away from them to observe how this forces their bodies backward. This can also be done in swimming pools.

## Concepts of Direction and Level

PE teachers can help students develop their understanding of the **spatial concept of direction** by instructing them to move to the left, to the right, forward, backward, up, down, and diagonally in space. They can prompt students to be aware of their own kinesthetic feedback that tells them in which directions they are moving. Activities that develop **rotation skills** also help children's awareness and

- 100 -

control of the directions in which they are turning. Locomotor "car" activities for children that involve taking turns walking in pairs, one behind the other with hands on the front child's shoulders, can include having the front child "steer," changing walking directions. This develops the front child's skill in controlling **direction**, and the back child's skill in following directional changes. Rotation activities for middle childhood using equipment can involve exploring moving in various directions. Students learning to fall sideways should practice doing this in both directions. PE teachers can direct students to notice the high, middle, or low levels of their bodies or body parts during movements. When teaching how to land safely from falls by rolling sideways, PE teachers can have students practice with falling from different levels.

## Pathway, Energy, Time, Speed, and Force

PE teachers can help students develop understanding and control of **pathways of movement through space** by having them walk and run in a circle, a zigzag pattern, a serpentine pattern, etc. They can also help students develop concepts of **planes in space** by having them move along circular, vertical, or horizontal pathways. To help students understand different types of **energy** required in different activities, they can have them perform short-term, high-intensity activities like lifting weights and sprinting, and explain these use fast-twitch/type II/"white" muscle fibers; and longer-duration, lower-intensity activities like distance running and bicycling, and explain these use slow-twitch/type I/"red" muscle fibers. The latter require more aerobic/oxygen-using energy whereas the former do not use oxygen and cannot be repeated once muscles fatigue until rested and replenished. PE teachers can have students run or perform other movements at different speeds to understand the roles of **time** and **speed** in movement, and have them practice increasing and decreasing the rates of their movements to gain control over speed. They can teach students how force, time, and speed interact during running as they must modify their stance time and peak force/impact time to change running speeds.

## Measuring Torque

**Torque** is the rotational version of force. In other words, torque represents how much a given force can make something or someone rotate or turn. **Large torque** is strong rotation; **small torque** is weak rotation. In the US/English system, the unit of torque measurement is the foot-pound; in the SI system, it is the Newton-meter (Nm). With torque represented as T, force as F, and the perpendicular (right-angle) distance from the force's action line as $^{\perp}$d, the formula for measuring torque is T=F$^{\perp}$d. A practical example to illustrate how torque operates is to imagine two skaters on ice. One skater has longer arms and the other has shorter arms. Each skater's body is equal to a rotational axis. If both skaters extend their arms horizontally and a third person pushes on each skater's arm, this will cause the skaters to rotate. Each skater's arm length equals the quantity $^{\perp}$d, i.e., distance between the axis (skater's body) and force. Equal force will make the longer-armed skater rotate faster because the longer arm creates greater torque.

## Biomechanical Summation of Forces

**Summation of forces** is to attain maximal force with any movement that uses multiple muscles in a manner that enables generating the maximum force possible. Thus the total amount of force is a sum of the total individual muscles when these are added together. The **general principle of the order of use** is that larger, stronger muscle groups in the center of the body initiate power, and smaller muscles in the extremities are used for coordination and finer movements. The largest, heaviest body parts are slowest and move first; smaller body parts are faster and move last. Force is both simultaneous and sequential. To attain maximal force, use as many body parts as possible. **Sequential force**, e.g., of body, then arm, then forearm, must be well-timed: if these follow too early or late in the sequence, they are ineffective. For example, the summation events in kicking a football are: body weight is transferred forward with the

- 101 -

abdominals leading, the hip moves forward, the leg trailing, abdominals and quadriceps move the thigh forward, quadriceps and calf muscles straighten the lower leg, and calf muscles snap the foot.

## Center of Gravity

The **center of gravity** is the point at which a single force, of magnitude mg, meaning the weight of the system or body, would have to be applied to a rigid system or body in order to achieve an exact balance of the rotational and translational effects of the gravitational forces that act on the parts of the system or body. Put another way, the center of gravity is the point at which the weight of a system or body can be considered as acting. Although there is a minuscule difference between the center of gravity and the **center of mass**, they can be considered as the same for all practical applications. Therefore, center of mass is considered a synonym for center of gravity; however, center of pressure is not a synonym. In terms of the human body, its center of gravity is not fixed at any certain location in the anatomy. The location of the human body's center of gravity changes in accordance with the positions of the various body parts. The symbols used for center of gravity are C of G or COG.

## Kinetics and Running.

Most sports require running speed—to outrun opponents in races, as a running start to develop enough takeoff velocity for jumping distance or height, to get to a base before being tagged, to evade tacklers, etc. Although speed-walkers can attain high speeds via an unusual gait that drops the hip with each step, running typically has faster speeds than walking. **Kinetics** is the part of biomechanics involving the study of movement and the forces that produce movement. The definition of **running** is a gait that includes an aerial phase when no body parts contact the ground or floor, with no external forces on the body (excluding gravity and wind resistance). Runners must modify the stance phase (when contacting the ground) to change speeds. A force plate measures running forces according to Newton's third law of motion (for every action there is an equal and opposite reaction): foot force produces a downward, backward force vector; the ground produces an upward, forward force. The force plate measures this ground reaction force (GRF). Faster running requires shorter stance time plus higher peak forces. Force = impulse / impact time; impulse is relatively constant. Bent knees extend impact time, reducing joint forces and injuries.

## Biomechanics Concepts and Principles

The concept of **force-motion** states that when we produce or change movement, unbalanced forces act upon our bodies or objects we manipulate. **Force-time** states that substantial changes in motion are produced over time, not immediately. **Inertia** defines the property all objects have of resisting changes in states of motion. **Range of motion** is the overall extent of motion a person uses in a movement, described through angular or linear movement of the body parts. **Balance** is an individual's capacity for controlling his or her body position in relation to a base of support. The **coordination continuum** means the goal or purpose of a movement determines the most effective timing of segmental movements or muscle actions. For example, people extend their hips, knees, and ankles concurrently to lift a heavy object but use more sequential movements in the kinematic chain, from legs to trunk to arms, in overarm throwing. **Segmental interaction** means that forces operating in a system of rigid, lined bodies are transferable through joints and links. **Optimal projection** means there is a best range of angles of projection for given goals or purposes in most human throwing and propelling of projectiles.

## Learning Objectives of Biomechanical Principles

When PE teachers instruct students how to apply **biomechanical principles**, students learn to produce and control force in ways that make their movements safer and more effective. For example, on the topic of effects upon objects, PE teachers can instruct students in applying the **concept of force** relative to how

- 102 -

objects move in space. Learning objectives could include calculating and showing how the movements of projectiles are affected by the application of force; explaining and demonstrating how absorbing force increases their control over objects in sports activities, like collecting a soccer ball, bunting a softball, or catching a football; and explaining and demonstrating how efficient movement reduces the likelihood of injuries during various sports activities. For example, in soccer, kicking the ball using the instep rather than the toes can prevent injuries. On the topic of balance, PE teachers can instruct students in analyzing the concept of balance during complex movement patterns. As an example, a general learning objective could be for students to explore how their center of gravity affects their balance and performance during various movement activities.

## Locomotor Skills

Among motor skills, one major category is **locomotor skills**. Locomotor skills are movements wherein we use our legs and feet to move our bodies from one location to another. The basic locomotor skills children develop, in the approximate order they usually learn them, are: walking; running; hopping; jumping; skipping; galloping; sliding, i.e., galloping sideways; and leaping. Most normally developing children typically learn to walk around the age of 1 year. They usually have learned to run, hop, and jump by the age of 2 years. They begin to learn how to gallop, skip, slide, and leap around the age of 3 years. Young children will need to be provided with plenty of opportunities for practicing, though most of them find practicing fun during early childhood. They also will need their parents to provide them with some instruction to acquire the basic locomotor skills, which they do not necessarily just learn on their own.

## Basic Locomotor Skills

Here are some tips for parents to help their young children master the basic **locomotor skills**. **Walking**: Tell children to walk with straight, smooth steps and swing their arms in opposition to their feet. Have them practice different walks, e.g., on tiptoe, low with bent knees, fast and slow, robotic and liquid, etc. **Galloping**: Tell children to use one foot as "leader" and the other as "follower," alternating sides. **Jumping**: Have children keep their feet together, pushing and landing with both feet. Have them try jumping rope; see how high they can jump, how many times in a row, and how quietly they can land. **Hopping**: Have children see how quickly and slowly they can hop, and whether either side is harder. **Side-sliding**: Tell children to spread their arms, lead with one foot, and rise in the middle. **Leaping**: Have children lead with one foot and leap over an object, landing with the other foot. **Skipping**: Tell children to march, raising one knee high and hopping on the other foot—step/hop, step/hop, alternating sides.

## Fundamental Elementary Motor Skills

Some **fundamental motor skills** critical to learn in **elementary school** include running, jumping vertically, leaping, dodging, kicking, overhand throwing, catching, ball bouncing, punting, forehand striking, and two-handed side-arm striking. Some examples of the overhand throw as applied in advanced form in specific sports include baseball and softball pitching, tennis and badminton serving, throwing a javelin, volleyball passing, and basketball shoulder passes. Some examples of the two-handed side-arm strike as applied in advanced sports-specific forms include swinging a golf club, hockey stick, or baseball bat; forehand drives in tennis, badminton, disc golf, squash, or table tennis (ping pong); and cut shots in volleyball, golf, or pool. Running, vertical jumping, kicking, and catching should be introduced in kindergarten. Running, vertical jumping, and catching should be mastered in 2nd grade, kicking in 3rd grade. Overhand throwing, ball bouncing, leaping, and dodging should be introduced in 1st grade. Ball bouncing, leaping, and dodging should be mastered in 3rd grade, overhand throwing in 4th grade. Punting, forehand striking, and two-handed side-arm striking should be introduced in 2nd grade. Punting should be mastered in 4th grade, forehand and two-hand side-arm strikes in 5th.

## Non-Locomotor Skills

Whereas locomotor skills involve moving from one location to another using the legs and feet, **non-locomotor skills** are motor skills that do not involve moving among locations. Non-locomotor skills involve little or no shifting of the base of support, and do not cause changes in position. Lifting a weight and squeezing a ball are examples of non-locomotor skills. Some other common movements that involve non-locomotor skills are balancing, swaying, turning, twisting, and swinging. **Bending** is movement around a joint between two body parts. **Dodging** is sharply avoiding a person or object, e.g., by leaning away or ducking. **Stretching** is extending or hyperextending the joints to straighten or lengthen the body parts. **Twisting** rotates the body or body parts around an axis having a stationary base. **Turning** is moving the body through space in a circle, releasing the base of support. **Swinging** involves circular or pendular movements below an axis of the body or body parts. **Swaying** is like swinging, but above an axis. **Pushing** is applying force against a person or object to move one's body away or move the person or object away. **Pulling** is exerting force to move people or objects closer to one's body.

### Non-Locomotor Skills Grades 1, 2, and 3

In **grade 1**, teachers introduce non-locomotor skills like bending, twisting, curling, and swaying involving a broad range of joints by discussing weight transfer, arm-leg opposition, and other mechanics involved. Teachers have students imitate elephants swaying and trees swaying in wind. Teachers assign small groups to develop warm-up routines using these skills, identify joints used, and name each movement. In **grade 2**, teachers introduce and demonstrate the motions, pair students to perform warm-up and cool-down activities requiring two people using these movements, and have students identify joints and major muscle groups involved and identify exercises targeting each joint in a warm-up routine. In **grade 3**, teachers introduce and demonstrate the skills, work on building student comprehension of principles of improving flexibility, discuss which joints can move, and list exercises targeting each joint in a fitness routine. Teachers design a fitness routine for students to improve range of motion in specified joints, connecting the different movements; and pair students to perform these and improvise exercise that equally stretch opposing muscles in specified joints. Teachers have individual students create and lead warm-up and fitness routines in class.

### Non-Locomotor Skills Grades 4,5, and 6

In **grade 4**, teachers review non-locomotor skills and discuss their importance in physical activities, including bending in tucked, pike, squat, forward, and backward positions; stretching before physical activity, including identifying muscle groups to stretch in warm-up and cool-down; static balancing, with 1-part to 4-part bases and in gymnastic routines; and dynamic balancing, including turning in dance and games and flopping from sitting, kneeling, and standing positions. Teachers guide paired students in mat exercises, have them create routines targeting multiple muscle groups, and have all students perform these. In **grade 5**, teachers review; have students develop skills further through individual and group activities; perform bends, stretches, and rolls on mats; and create warm-up and cool-down routines, and lead the class in performing these. Teachers invite a physical therapist or other professional to discuss stretching and injuries caused by improper stretching. In **grade 6**, teachers review; have students explore non-locomotor movements on mats, pointing out specific movements discovered; assign pairs or small groups to create warm-up routines, recording and displaying activities and muscle groups included on posters; assign homework of short reports with diagrams explaining the relationship of stretching and injury prevention; and emphasize more independent student movement development.

**Manipulative Or Object Control Skills**

**Manipulative or object control skills** are the category of motor skills that involve using objects. They include both fine motor skills, as in buttoning buttons, zipping zippers, fastening and unfastening clasps, twist ties, etc.; using crayons, pencils, pens, and other writing, drawing, and painting implements; using spoons, forks, and other eating utensils; and gross motor skills, as in swinging a baseball bat, a tennis racket, a jai alai cesta, a jump rope, a golf club, a bow and arrow, etc. The actions included in manipulative skills include pushing, pulling, lifting, swinging, striking, throwing, catching, kicking, rolling a ball, volleying, bouncing, and dribbling. A consideration to keep in mind when young children are first learning manipulative skills is not to expect them to be perfectly accurate, for example hitting a target, throwing directly to another player in a game, or catching a ball thrown to them. Children must first master the throwing, catching, hitting, kicking, or other action before they can develop accuracy as well. It can help to have children practice the movements and techniques with imaginary objects to begin, and then progress to real objects.

**Manipulative Movement Activities 5 years**

Teachers can put hoops on the ground or hang them from doorframes or trees with rope for young children to practice throwing things through them. Parents can develop **throwing skills** at home by having children throw rolled socks into laundry hampers or baskets. When they succeed, have them take one step further back for the next throw. Teachers and parents can use pillows or cushions to set up courses (with or without children's participation), placing empty boxes, wastebaskets, buckets, etc. as "golf holes." Have children take turns throwing beanbags into the holes. Children can crumple paper into "snowballs"; adults tape these up and give baskets of them to two groups of children. Mark a line between groups with rope, tape, or chalk. On a signal, children throw "snowballs" over the line for 30 seconds, see who has the fewest snowballs left, switch teams, and repeat. Have children clean up by throwing snowballs into baskets. Adults can cut centers out of empty plastic food tubs to make rings, and have children try to toss rings over plastic bottles. Have children try to toss coins onto paper or plastic plates on the floor or ground. Let children throw a ball trying to knock a stuffed animal off a stool.

**Manipulative Movement Activities 5-12 years**

Older children can practice throwing for **accuracy** or **distance**. Here are some activities to practice throwing for distance.

- **Force Back:** Students face one another in pairs, throwing a ball toward the other as far as they can. The thrower's partner catches or retrieves the ball, throwing it back from where it landed.
- **Three Court Ball:** Assign students to two equally-numbered teams. Each team has one-third of a court and a tennis ball. Students try to throw the ball into the middle third of the court and have it bounce over the other team's goal line.
- **Scatterball**: Use a baseball diamond or any field with several bases arranged in a diamond, circle, square, or other enclosed shape. Divide students into two teams: throwers and fielders. Throwers take turns, one at a time, throwing balls as far away as they can. Then each thrower runs around bases until told to stop. The fielders catch or retrieve the balls thrown and collect them in a basket, bucket, or other receptacle. Switch teams and repeat. The team scoring the most runs wins. Students can also practice catching by throwing and bouncing balls or beanbags in pairs, groups, and teams.

## Playing Baseball, Basketball, and Football

**Baseball** requires locomotor skills for players to run to the bases after a hit, and to run to catch fly balls. It requires non-locomotor skills as players twist their bodies to field the ball, catch the ball, and when batting; lean backward or forward to field balls, lean or bend down to catch low or rolling ground balls; reach out to tag runners out before they reach a base; and go through the movement sequence of pitching that involves leaning back, twisting, raising one leg, etc. Catchers also move their bodies while squatting to catch pitches without changing their base of support. Baseball additionally involves manipulative skills for pitching, catching, fielding, and batting. **Basketball** involves the locomotor skills of running and jumping; the non-locomotor skills of leaning, stretching, and bending; and the manipulative skills of dribbling, passing, catching, and throwing the ball. **Football** involves the locomotor skills of running, and sometimes jumping over other players; non-locomotor skills of bending in the huddle and twisting when dodging tackles; and manipulative skills of holding, passing (throwing), intercepting, and receiving (catching) the ball.

## Playing Tennis, Volleyball, and Golf

**Tennis** involves the locomotor skills of running, walking, and jumping over the net at the end of a match. It uses the non-locomotor skills of bending to pick up a ball, stretching and twisting to prepare for a serve; and stretching, bending, leaning, and twisting and reaching to return the ball in a volley. It uses manipulative skills for swinging the racket to hit the ball when serving and returning. **Volleyball** uses the locomotor skills of walking to take and rotate positions, and running to reach the ball; the non-locomotor skills of stretching, reaching, twisting, and bending to reach the ball in high and low positions; and the manipulative skills of serving the ball using the fist, spiking the ball from above with the palms of the hands, and hitting the ball from below with the fists. **Golf** uses the locomotor skill of walking; the non-locomotor skills of twisting and turning to swing, and bending to retrieve the ball from the cup, green, trap, etc.; and the manipulative skills of swinging the club to hit the ball, retrieving the ball by hand, and writing down scores.

## Locomotor, Non-Locomotor, and Manipulative Skills K-6

**Fourth-graders** should run and change direction dribbling a basketball or kicking a soccer ball. **Fifth-graders** should integrate skills by changing speeds and directions to evade defenders while dribbling a basketball, running with a football, or kicking a soccer ball; or consistently and strategically moving to open spaces to receive passes in small-sided games. **Sixth-graders** should run and leap over consecutive cones or other obstacles without stopping. **Kindergarteners** should be able to volley beach balls or balloons to themselves five successive times and hit balls or balloons up 9-12 inches continuously with different body parts. **First-graders** should be able to vary their striking force and volley 6-10 times upward, alternating left and right palms. **Second-graders** should be able to volley with partners using both hands, and volley underhand while walking forward c. 20 feet. **Third-graders** should make and catch forearm passes to themselves, and volley to partners using overhead passes. **Fourth-graders** should serve underhand or overhand with correct form, and consistently volley using forearm passes to themselves. **Fifth-graders** should serve underhand, overhand, pass overhead, and forearm pass; show correct overhead volleying form against a wall; and consistently serve volleyballs over nets 6 feet high or walls from 15 feet away. **Sixth-graders** should return volleyballs with forearm passes at least 6 feet high.

## Softball vs. Baseball

A variation of baseball, **softball** uses a smaller infield and a larger ball. Two main rule differences from baseball are that, in softball, pitching must be underhand; and regulation softball games have seven innings rather than nine as baseball does. Softballs are 11-12 inches in circumference, which is 3 inches bigger than baseballs. Infields have bases 60 feet apart, not 90 feet apart as they are in baseball. Two types of softball are slow-pitch and fast-pitch. **Slow-pitch**, the kind most often played, has 10 players per team. Slow-pitch softball sometimes uses a ball larger than the usual 12 inches. Slow-pitch softball requires the pitcher to throw the ball in an arcing path. It also does not allow bunting the ball or stealing bases as baseball does. **Fast-pitch** softball has nine players per team, the same as baseball. As its name indicates, it requires faster pitching than slow-pitch softball. Fast-pitch softball also permits bunting and stealing as baseball does. In both slow-pitch and fast-pitch softball, an underhand pitch is required. Pitching distances required are from 46 or 43 feet for men, 39 feet for women, and 35 feet for girls. This contrasts with baseball's 60.5 foot pitching distance.

## Rules and Practices of Soccer

**Soccer** fields are rectangular, with a goal at each end. Soccer teams have 11 players, who score by kicking the ball into the opposing team's goal. Some competition rules stipulate a minimum number of players per team, commonly seven. Only goalkeepers are allowed to touch the ball with their arms and/or hands while it is in play, and only in their penalty areas in front of the goals. Goal posts are 8 yards apart. Outfielders are allowed to contact the ball with their heads and/or torsos in addition to their feet. Whichever team scores more goals by the end of the soccer game is the winner. For tied scores, a draw is declared; there is a penalty shootout; or extra time is designated, depending on the format of the competition. Soccer has 17 official game laws. Soccer balls are 27-28 inches around, weigh 14-16 ounces, and are inflated to pressures of 8.5-15.6 pounds per square inch (at sea level). Adult pitching distances are 110-120 yards long and 70-80 yards wide internationally, 100-130 yards long and 45-90 yards wide non-internationally. Soccer/association football's highest governing body is **FIFA** (Fédération Internationale de Football Association), which organizes the World Cup every four years.

## Characteristics of Tennis

**Tennis** is played with rackets strung with cord hitting a small, felt-covered, hollow rubber ball over/around a net in the center of the court to the opponent's side. Courts are clay, grass, asphalt, concrete, or acrylic, and sometimes carpeted indoors. Nets are 3 feet high in the center, and 3 feet 6 inches high at the posts. The object is preventing opponents from returning the ball within bounds. Returning the ball within bounds earns a point. Tennis is played by opposing single players or doubles (teams of two). One player, behind the baseline between sideline and center mark, serves the ball. Receiver(s) can be anywhere on their side of the court. Legal services must clear the net without touching and go diagonally into the opposing service box. A "let," a serve hitting the net before landing in the service box, is void and retaken. Serves falling wide or long of the service box or not clearing the net are faults. Touching the baseline or extension of the center mark with one's foot before hitting the ball is a foot fault. Two consecutive service faults (double faults) give receiver(s) the point. Legal returns hit the ball before two bounces. Players and teams cannot hit the ball twice consecutively. During rallies, legal returns can hit the net.

## Track and Field

**Track and field** is a sport that encompasses a number of different competitive athletic activities that involve running, jumping, and throwing skills. Among **running events**, it includes sprinting (short, fast running contests), middle- and long-distance races, hurdling (jumping over barriers while running), and relay races. Included among **jumping events** are the long jump (a horizontal distance jumping contest), high jump (a vertical height jumping contest), triple jump, and pole vault (clearing a high bar by propelling one's body with a pole). **Throwing events** include the shot put (swinging and flinging a small, heavy iron shot for the maximum distance), javelin (throwing a long, spear-like projectile for distance), discus (throwing a flat, disc-shaped projectile for distance), and hammer throw (throwing a hammer-like projectile for distance). Track and field also includes events that **combine** multiple sports into a single contest, such as the heptathlon combining seven events, the decathlon combining ten events, and others. Athletes win running events with the fastest time, and jumping and throwing events with the longest heights or distances. Major track and field competition activities include the International Association of Athletics Federations (IAAF) governing body's World Championship, and the Olympics.

## Volleyball

**Volleyball** teams have six players, scoring points by grounding the ball on the opposing team's court, and extensive rules. Serves are from behind the court's rear boundary line with the hand/arm, over a net. The receiving team must keep the ball airborne within their court and return it to the serving team's court. Players can touch the ball up to three times; one player cannot touch the ball twice consecutively.* Grounding the ball on the opposite court is a "kill," winning the rally for that team, which gets a point and the serve beginning the next rally. A team loses a rally by committing a fault. Faults include: catching and throwing the ball, *double hit, four consecutive ball contacts by one team, making the ball touch the floor outside the opposite court or without clearing the net first, touching the net (a net foul), and crossing the boundary line while serving (a foot fault). Common volleyball techniques include spiking and blocking (both requiring vertical jumping skill), setting, passing, offensive and defensive roles, and specialized player positions.

## Dribbling and Shooting Basketballs

**Kindergarteners** should be able to twirl a hula hoop and roll it on the floor. They should be able to drop a ball and catch it at the peak of its bounce. They should be able to dribble a ball continuously with their dominant hand. **First-graders** should be able to juggle two scarves, pass beanbags hand to hand between their legs in a figure 8, and dribble a ball with their dominant hand while moving. **Second-graders** should be able to dribble a ball around stationary objects, and dribble a ball with both left and right hands while standing in place without losing control. **Third-graders** should be able to circle a hula hoop around the waist without using the hands; juggle three scarves or plastic bags in a cascading pattern; and dribble a basketball in a figure-8 pathway, alternating dribbling hands, to the opposite sides of cones set 10 inches apart.

## Dribbling and Shooting, Throwing, Catching, and Rolling Skills

For dribbling and shooting, **4th-graders** should be able to demonstrate a bank shot with a basketball, and dribble the ball around obstacles with good ball control while changing directions at a jogging speed. **Fifth-graders** should be able to juggle small objects like beanbags, tennis balls, etc. in a cascade pattern; dribble a basketball with good control while changing speeds and directions around defensive opposing players who must walk and not use their hands; and demonstrate a basketball layup using the opposing foot on takeoff while moving continuously throughout. **Sixth-graders** should be able to shoot a basketball from anywhere on the court behind the second hash mark*, demonstrating good form. *PE teachers may want to vary the distance they use to assess this skill. **Sixth-graders** should also be able to demonstrate good skills for handling basketballs. For throwing and catching, **kindergarteners** should throw and catch beanbags to themselves and catch teacher-thrown (7-9 inches) foam balls from 5 feet. **First-graders** should roll a tennis ball and scoop up a slowly rolled tennis ball in their hands; throw small, soft balls with hand-foot opposition; and consistently catch big (4-9 inches) balls self-tossed above the head.

## Throwing, Catching, and Rolling Skills

**Second-graders** should catch small, soft tennis/yarn balls at peak, self-tossed above the head; throw balls 7 inches and larger against walls from roughly 8 feet away and catch them before they bounce; and underhand-toss small balls with correct form and accuracy to targets or partners from 15 feet. **Third-**

**graders** should demonstrate correct form in a two-handed overhead/soccer throw, pass balls to slowly-moving partners using chest and bounce passes, catch balls while slowly traveling, and overhand-throw small balls using correct form to partners and targets from at least 20 feet. **Fourth-graders** should throw and catch footballs, Frisbees, and other sport-specific balls or objects with correct form; consistently scoop up rolled balls with hands using mature form (knuckles on ground, pinkies together), moving laterally to get ahead of the ball; and play "keep-away" and other small-sided, low-level throwing-catching games. **Fifth-graders** should throw and catch footballs, basketballs, and other sport-specific balls within skill combinations, e.g., catching, dribbling, and passing to moving teammates; and throw lead passes including chest bounce, overhand, and underhand to moving teammates with mature form and accuracy. **Sixth-graders** should accurately throw and catch footballs, basketballs, and other sport balls to and from partners in dynamic situations with mature form, and advance balls down playing areas passing back and forth in small-sided games.

## Striking With Implements

- **Kindergarteners**: Balance beanbags or objects on rackets and paddles while walking; hit balls off batting tees using implements.
- **First-graders**: Strike beach balls or balloons forward using short implements while walking 20 feet without letting them hit the floor; strike four times without their hitting the floor using short, light implements (e.g., lollipops).
- **Second-graders**: Bounce, then strike balls at walls or targets; strike beach balls or balloons with imple-ments over low nets to partners without their touching the ground or floor; consistently strike balls upward with only one bounce.
- **Third-graders**: Successfully hit balls or objects from close-proximity "soft tosses"; bounce and strike small foam tennis balls with soft, controlled forehand across the gym or into large areas; use long-handled implements to strike objects on the floor or ground to targets.
- **Fourth-graders**: Successfully hit self-tossed objects with one bounce; volley or rally objects using implements over nets and low barriers; receive teacher hockey passes and shoot to targets from about 10 feet.
- **Fifth-graders**: Successfully strike underhand teacher-pitched (3-5 inches) whiffle or foam balls; repeatedly hit balls forehand or backhand against walls at close range; bounce and hit small foam balls with soft, controlled backhand into large areas; dribble and shoot at goals with continuous action using long-handled implements.
- **Sixth-graders**: Successfully strike underhand-teacher-pitched softballs; serve balls without bouncing consistently at target areas; and give-and-go using long-handled implements.

## Manipulative Skills Involving Kicking

- **Kindergarteners**: Dribble a soccer ball slowly with both feet while walking; approach stationary balls and kick with high follow-through without stopping; kick stationary balls with any foot part with high leg backswing and follow-through.
- **First-graders**: Dribble medium/large balls with either foot, walking/jogging; kicking balls with solid contact, high follow-through; approaching stationary balls, kick without stopping with high follow-through.
- **Second-graders**: Dribble balls using both feet, jogging; trap balls when stopping; show correct form kicking balls using insteps; kick slowly-rolled balls to kickers with solid contact and high follow-through.
- **Third-graders**: Dribble soccer balls using feet insides/outsides, running at varying speeds; pass balls to partners or targets using inside-foot kicks somewhat accurately and consistently; punt balls, with or without a bounce, using correct form, 15 feet or more most times.

- **Fourth-graders**: Dribble around stationary opponents or objects without object contact or ball loss; trap teammate-rolled balls; dribble and instep-kick moving balls at large goals.
- **Fifth-graders**: Dribble around lightly resistant, moving opponents; punt soccer balls and/or footballs 30 feet or more with two- or three-step approaches; make lead passes while dribbling with inside-foot kicks to moving teammates.
- **Sixth-graders**: Change speeds and directions to evade opponents while dribbling soccer balls; trap balls from different speeds and heights; show competency with soccer dribbling and inside-foot passes in "keep-away" games.

## Recreational Activities

For people to engage in recreational activities, they must have **free time** when they are not occupied with working, activities of daily living, sleeping, or social obligations. Historically, people had less leisure time than they do today: they needed more time to survive physically and economically. With industrialization, higher standards of living, longer life expectancies, and more commercially offered recreational activities, people now have more **leisure time** available. Although some perspectives see leisure as spare time, others see it as an essential part of civilization and personal development because it enables people to reflect on the realities and values they overlook during daily life activities. Leisure is viewed as both a reward in and of itself and a reward for work, or even the purpose of work. Today, leisure has come to be seen as reflecting a nation's character and values: the United Nations Universal Declaration of Human Rights considers leisure a human right. Recreational activities are pursued for purposes of pleasure, healthy lifestyles, social interaction, competition, physical and mental rehabilitation, and other therapeutic and preventive medical purposes.

## PE Competencies Grades 1-2

- **Body awareness**: demonstrate body movements (flexion, extension, rotation) and shapes. Walk, run, skip, and slide. Stop at boundaries with control. Quickly, safely change direction without falling. Throw underhand, roll, and dribble a ball. Identify walking, running, galloping, skipping, hopping, jumping, leaping, and sliding.
- **Space concepts**: Demonstrate directions, pathways, levels, and ranges during activities; perform locomotor skills while changing these; apply them in simple activities or games (moving to dodge tagging, etc.).
- **Movement quality**: Understand and apply energy and force, time, flow, balance concepts to psychomotor skills, e.g., starting and stopping without falling; bending knees to lower center of gravity; showing understanding of hard and soft, tense and relaxed force variations; controlling personal force, e.g., in tagging, striking; demonstrating fast and slow movement; moving to simple beats and rhythms; following simple, teacher-led rhythmic movements; combining jumping and turning, bouncing and catching; showing smooth transitions between dance or rhythmic movements.
- **Health-related fitness elements**: Begin identifying physiological exercise effects like faster breathing and heart rate; define the four health-related fitness components in their own words. Additional competencies include movement-related problem-solving skills, awareness of personal responsibility for individual wellness, self-confidence and success, safe behavior for self and others, and appropriate social interactions.

## PE Competencies Grades 3-6

- **Grades 3-4**: Describe movements identifying body parts and actions. Identify basic muscle groups and movements. Show awareness of body part relationships (opposition, unison, sequence). Demonstrate leaping, alternating leading foot. Apply space concepts in movements with others. Balance on various equipment with control. Show an understanding of static and dynamic balance. Show comprehension of how bodies create and absorb force. Choose forces appropriate to tasks. Control personal and manipulative force, like dribbling while walking and running. Demonstrate slow, medium, and fast movement. Move with tempo changes. Incorporate various equipment into rhythmic patterns and movements. Combine up to three movements with or without equipment, e.g., jump-roping routines. Demonstrate smooth transitions among sequential motor skills, like running to jumping. Solve movement challenges combining concepts of force, time, and balance, e.g., gymnastics routines. Define, apply, and assess the four health-related fitness components.
- **Grades 5-6**: Identify specific muscle groups and movements. Combine body movements and shapes. Identify major skills in beginning gymnastics, dance, and sports. Recognize similar skills in different activities. Perform movement sequences. Adjust force for tasks projecting objects, using various equipment. Adjust body movements for speed changes. Combine movement concepts and motor skills in series.

## PE Competencies Grades 7-8

Give partners and groups constructive feedback; solve more complex problems with larger groups in simple movement challenges. Describe body movements using more advanced terminology. Show an understanding of body part relationships in performing more complex skills. Identify major skills involved in more complex gymnastics, dance, sports, and/or related activities. Recognize similarities in the use of space in tactics, dance, gymnastics and other advanced activities. Perform more complex movement sequences like low/high ropes exercises. Keep time to music while performing steps and patterns in a variety of dance styles. Adjust movements with partners or groups to a beat. Combine speed, force, directions, levels, and pathways in a dance routine, a sport tactic like dribbling against a defender, or other complex series of movement concepts and motor skills. Demonstrate mature form in various basic skills; adjust skills to more complex situations, e.g., throwing and hitting to different locations. Assess personal performance on Fitnessgram or other nationally accepted instrument. Monitor heart and respiratory rate, perceived exertion, recovery rate during and following activity. Understand basic FITT principles. Play by rules, show appropriate sports conduct, officiate small-group games, appropriately assume leader-follower roles, cooperate with others, show appreciation for appropriate feedback, interact with others from diverse backgrounds.

## PE Competencies Grades 9-12

Recognize personal strengths and weaknesses and develop strategies accordingly. Give partners and groups critical, specific feedback to improve skills and efficiency. Describe body movements using advanced terminology. Identify similar skills in different activities, like volleyball spikes and tennis/badminton smashes. Apply space concepts applicably in varied activities, e.g., dance or gymnastic floor routines and set plays and other tactics in sports games. Recognize similar uses of space among different advanced activities. Apply balance skills in various activities like yoga, skiing, Tae Bo, and volleyball. Demonstrate competency choosing and performing skills in several new activities, e.g., territorial team sports, wall and net sports, target sports, run-scoring games, rhythmic activities, and outdoor adventure or recreation activities. Choose, perform, and apply knowledge and skills proficiently in two different kinds of sports or physical activities. Regularly participate in physical activities to attain and maintain personal activity goals. Assess, refine, maintain comprehensive personal fitness plans based

- 111 -

on nationally accepted assessment. Adjust activities according to knowledge of physiological effects. Analyze characteristics of sports and activities. Persevere to achieve higher performance levels. Anticipate and correct potentially dangerous outcomes (spotting, refereeing, and belaying). Evaluate competition by quality, not results. Show self-discipline and self-direction. Respect feedback and revise actions. Develop leading and following skills. Include diverse others. Help others.

## Participating in Sports with Disabilities

Depending whether an individual has acquired a **disability** later in life or has had it from birth, some individuals will not have had experiences with sports early in life. This presents one **obstacle** to sports participation later and throughout life. Another common problem for people with disabilities is people in their communities, schools, and organizations lacking awareness and understanding of how to include persons having disabilities in sports events they organize and manage. Limited community resources, programs, and opportunities to acquire training, participate, and compete affect people with disabilities. This limitation sometimes results from the aforementioned lack of awareness and understanding about inclusion methods; and sometimes also exists despite community awareness, understanding, and desire, e.g., when funding and support are still missing. Lack of accessible gyms, buildings, and other facilities is another barrier. Dearth of accessible transportation interferes with attending sports events to participate. Social and psychological barriers include parent, teacher, coach, and even disabled people's attitudes and beliefs toward disability and sports participation. Inadequate access to information and resources is another obstacle.

## Current Opportunities for Those with Disabilities

Associations and organizations in the world devoted to accommodating **athletes with disabilities** have grown markedly from the 1970s until now. Many of these are international groups. People with disabilities in some nations also have more opportunities now than in the past for participation in PE in schools, community associations, clubs, and casual recreational activities. In the arena of competitive sports, opportunities include disability-specific and sport-specific world championships; the Parapan American Games and other regional tournaments featuring multiple sports; certain Olympics Games events designated for athletes with disabilities; similar such events in the Commonwealth Games; and additionally, some athletes with disabilities compete against non-disabled athletes in some mainstream competitions. Internationally, 18 or more games now exist for athletes with disabilities. Among the three biggest international competitions, the Special Olympics offer year-round opportunities for training and competition to people with intellectual disabilities at every level; the Paralympic Games include intellectual disabilities, cerebral palsy, spinal cord injuries, amputations, visual impairments, and other disabilities; and the Deaflympics offer competitions for deaf and hard-of-hearing athletes.

## Sports for People with Disabilities

Research evidence in recent decades shows that quality of life and functional abilities are improved for people with **disabilities** by participating in **sports and other physical activity**. Studies have found that physical well-being and health are enhanced across disability groups by participation in physical activity and sports. General affect, as well as physical fitness, are seen to improve through sports and physical activity in psychiatric patients diagnosed with anxiety and depressive disorders. Research studies have also established correlations between physical and sports activity and increased self-esteem, social awareness, and self-confidence in people with disabilities, which can contribute to their empowerment. Also in recent decades, a major focus has developed on including and integrating people with disabilities into mainstream sports. This has resulted in many new opportunities for them to compete or participate. Disability sports participation also contributes on a global scale to national identity and nation-building. After natural and man-made disasters, sports participation helps to rehabilitate people with disabilities.

- 112 -

## Physical Benefits of Recreational Activities

Participating in **recreation** can enhance an individual's **physical health and wellness**. This is especially true of participating in **outdoor recreational activities**. According to the findings of research studies, people who are often active in recreation offered at state parks are found to make fewer visits to the doctor, to have lower body mass indexes (BMIs, i.e., the ratio of their weight to their height), and lower systolic (the top or first number) blood pressure than people who are not active in such recreational parks activities. Moreover, a State Parks report from California (2005) has shown that recreational activities outdoors constitute some of the best opportunities for people to increase the amounts of exercise that they get. In addition, another research study (2001) has found that the amounts of physical activity in which people participate in their communities are directly influenced by how many recreational facilities are available in their area.

## Effects of Recreational Activity

The relationship between **physical and mental health** is reciprocal: Not only does physical wellness promote better mental health, but mental wellness also can have an impact on physical well-being. When people participate in physical, recreational, and leisure activities, it gives them a sense of control over how they spend their time. This is important to busy people who often feel overwhelmed by all of the obligations they must meet. It also offers relief from those required duties in the form of having fun instead of only doing things they have to do. Leisure activities give people opportunities to achieve balance in their lives. Recreational activities help individuals manage stress more effectively, and they decrease symptoms of depression. Parents benefit their children by participating in leisure activities as they model healthy ways of managing emotions and addressing stress for them. One State Parks report (California, 2005) found that simply remembering a past outdoor recreation can elevate one's mood.

## Leisure Recreation

Research studies investigating the effects of **leisure recreation** have found that quality of life is improved by finding balance in life, and one important way people can find such balance is by allocating some of their time for leisure and recreation. In addition, physical recreation is especially related to enhancing **self-esteem**. People who participate regularly in recreational activities are more likely to report greater satisfaction with their lives. Greater life satisfaction is implicated significantly in better mental health. Better mental health is in turn associated with better physical health. As overwhelming evidence of this, in a 2000 study by the American Recreation Coalition, 90 percent of respondents who regularly engaged in recreational activities reported satisfaction with their physical fitness and health. A sharp contrast was the 60 percent of respondents not regularly engaging in recreational activities, who reported dissatisfaction with their fitness and health. Such benefits make recreational therapy (RT) important in rehabilitation programs. The American Therapeutic Recreation Association highlights RT benefits to recovering addicts, psychiatric patients, seniors, and children including better body function, improved cognitive function, stress management, and accelerated healing from medical conditions.

## Rhythmic Movement

The **elements of rhythm** include beat, duration, tempo, accent, meter, phrase, rhythms, and polyrhythms. **Beat** is the underlying pulse that can be heard and counted in music, percussion, and rhythmic movements like tapping toes, clapping hands, snapping fingers, dribbling basketballs, etc. **Duration** is the length or span of time covered by a beat. **Tempo** is the speed or pace at which music and rhythmic movement proceeds, from slow to fast and everything in between. **Accent** is additional emphasis on one or more beats. **Meter** is the rhythmic organization/time signature of music. For example, the 4/4 time signature means there are four beats to each measure and the quarter note gets one count. The 6/8 time

- 113 -

signature means there are six beats to each measure and the eighth note gets one count. Just as a phrase in language is a combination of words, a **musical phrase** is a combination of beats, which can be longer than a single measure. **Rhythms** are combinations of beats, which may be equal in duration/interval ("1, 2, 3, 4") or uneven, mixing fast and slow beats and/or different durations. **Polyrhythms** are multiple rhythms played simultaneously in layers.

## Rhythmic Movement Activity

"Brain Dance" (A.G. Gilbert, 2006), done to music from *Christy Lane's Authentic African and Caribbean Rhythms* (2000) is a warm-up activity for completing the eight motor patterns on the beat in sequence.

- **Breath**: Move arms up and down, coordinating with inhaling and exhaling.
- **Tactile**: To "wake up proprioceptors," i.e., raise awareness and sensation of location in space and body movement, brush, squeeze, tap, and slap body areas and muscles.
- **Core-distal**: Bring all body parts close to center, and then extend outward.
- **Head-tail**: Bring head and tailbone closer front and back; flex, extend, and laterally flex the spine, e.g., rounding, arching, and side-to-side "snake" movements.
- **Upper-lower halves**: Move only the upper body and arms bilaterally first, then move only the lower body and legs bilaterally.
- **Body-side** (left/right halves): Move the left arm and leg together, then move the right arm and leg together.
- **Cross-lateral** (diagonal body division): Make movements in opposition, e.g., lifting the left knee, touching it with the right hand and vice versa, crossing the midline.
- **Vestibular** (inner ear): Disrupt and restore balance by moving off-balance and then stopping, using movements like rocking, spinning, etc.

## Teaching Rhythm

The "hip-hop" activity (Cardinal, 2013) gives students practice in **changing duration** among regular time, half-time, and double-time, plus emphasis on **beat and phrasing**. Recommended musical selections are Pachelbel's *Canon in D* and Jay Sean's *Do You Remember.* Teachers lead students in tapping two fingers together to music, lightly so as not to influence classmates or overwhelm the music, first in half-time, then regular time, and then double-time. Students then repeat each step individually for practice. Then they repeat tapping while marching in place (non-locomotor), then while walking (locomotor) with full motion through each beat's duration—first at half-time; then when the teacher says "Hip," speeding up to regular time; when the teacher cues "Hop," slowing down to half-time; when the teacher says "Hip-hip," speeding up two levels to double-time; and when the teacher says "Hop-hop," slowing down two levels to half-time. Each is performed for two 8-counts, rotating from half-time to regular time to double-time, back to half-time, etc., including full range of arm movements. Tapping-and-walking combinations begin with just walking half-time, then walking regular time while tapping half-time, then walking double-time while tapping regular time, then walking half-time while tapping double-time, etc.

## Accent and Phrasing

An activity (Cardinal, 2013) that emphasizes **accent and phrasing** involves bouncing pinky balls on different beats within a measure or phrase, first while standing (non-locomotor and manipulative) and then while walking (locomotor, non-locomotor, and manipulative). Teachers instruct students to stand and bounce balls on the "1" of each 4-count phrase, then on the "2," then on the "3," then on the "4," practicing repeatedly before changing beats. After enough practice, teachers have students do this while walking. They can then give them different combinations of bouncing with walking, such as step, bounce, step, bounce; bounce, step, bounce, step; step, step, bounce; bounce, bounce, step; etc. Teachers can give students music with a 4/4 time signature and then change to 3/4 (waltz) time music, 2/4 time, etc. The most challenging transition is from the "4" to the "1" count without stopping while walking through space. Recommended music includes: *Beer Barrel/Pennsylvania Polka* from *Christy Lane's Let's Do Ballroom* for 2/4 time; *Edelweiss* from the same source for 3/4 time; *Mad World* by Tears for Fears or the cover by Michael Andrews & Gary Jules for slower 4/4 time; and *Viva la Vida* by Coldplay or *I Gotta Feeling* by The Black Eyed Peas for faster 4/4 time.

## Creative Movement and Dance

According to the National Association for the Education of Young Children (NAEYC – Dow, 2010), within the art form of creative movement, the words "**dance**" and "**movement**" are interchangeable. The human body is this art form's medium. The basic elements of dance/creative movement are:

- the body, its parts and range of motion;
- space;
- time; and
- energy.

Teachers can vary these elements when teaching children, e.g., by assigning variations in body part movements like marching while touching knees; clapping; holding arms up high, with one knee straight and one bent, on tiptoes; lying on the back with legs/feet in the air; etc. They can assign spatial variations, e.g., marching high, low, backward, turning, or in a square; temporal variations, e.g., marching in slow motion or as fast as possible, for a designated number of steps and then freezing; etc. Energy variations include marching as if stomping through mud, as if stuck in quicksand, as if barefoot on hot blacktop, without making any sound, etc.

## Various Forms of Dance

**Ballet** is the foundation for all other Western dance forms, so students taught ballet will be well equipped to learn other forms. The development of core strength, which is essential; the five foot positions; and many steps, turns, and jumps from ballet are shared by jazz, modern/contemporary, tap, and ballroom dance. Some additional techniques not taught in classical ballet include: pelvic rotations and ribcage isolations in **jazz dance**; torso contractions and extensions in **modern/contemporary dance**; loosening the ankles in **tap**, as well as "spanking" and other tap-specific foot movements; specific frames, holds, and other postures in the **Viennese Waltz** and quickstep in **ballroom dance**; specific turns, steps, and other movements in the cha-cha, samba, rhumba, pasodoble, and other **Latin ballroom dances**; and general techniques in ballroom dance bearing weight and leading more on the heels than the toes, and movement down, into the floor instead of up, away from it as in ballet.

## Injury Prevention in Dance Education

Thorough warm-ups and cool-downs are critical. **Warm-ups** must have cardiovascular elements increasing body temperature, heart and breathing rates, blood circulation to muscles, muscle tone, joint flexibility, reaction speed, mental alertness, and motivation to move; and move major muscle groups and angular, gliding, and rotational joints, including internal and external hip rotations. **Cool-downs** lower body temperature, slow breathing and mind, deeply stretch muscles, reward the body for its exertions, and should be followed by recovery periods. Thorough warm-ups and stretching can prevent delayed-onset muscle soreness, cramps, sprains, and tendonitis. Avoiding muscle fatigue prevents inflammation and cramping. Hydration and keeping dietary electrolytes balanced also prevents cramps. Dance spaces should have clean and sprung wood floors, high ceilings, no obstacles, good lighting and ventilation, access to water, separate male/female changing rooms, and wheelchair and telephone access. If only concrete flooring is available, high-impact jumping and running must be avoided to prevent stress fractures. Teacher first aid training and kits are necessary. Student footwear must be appropriate to floor surfaces (slippery, dirty, etc.). Teaching and learning correct body alignment also prevents (or at least limits) injuries and promotes proper dance technique, more effective mechanical functioning, and more energy-efficient movement. Pilates, Feldenkrais, ideokinesis, and yoga improve alignment.

## Types of Music in Dance

Classical ballet commonly employs **classical music**. Many classical compositions were written expressly for the purpose of accompanying ballets. For example, Tchaikovsky was well-known for composing ballet music, including *The Nutcracker, Swan Lake, Romeo and Juliet,* and *The Sleeping Beauty.* Modern classical composer Igor Stravinsky collaborated with choreographer Michel Fokine for Sergei Diaghilev's Ballets Russes production of *The Firebird* (1910). Cincinnati Ballet choreographer Adam Hougland created an opera ballet to Mozart's masterpiece *Requiem Mass in D Minor.* In ballroom dance, the Viennese waltz was/is traditionally performed to **waltzes** by classical Viennese composers like Johann Strauss; however, today's creative choreographers also use diverse contemporary music in 3/4 time, e.g., on TV's *Dancing with the Stars.* Latin ballroom dances traditionally used music specifically for each dance, e.g., rhumba, samba, cha-cha, pasodoble, tango, etc., but *DWTS* also uses other music with appropriate tempi and rhythms. Jazz and tap dances have often been choreographed to/for Broadway show tunes, but can use any compatible music. Contemporary dance choreography frequently interprets song lyrics or expresses **lyrical or evocative music**. **Hip-hop music** most often accompanies hip-hop dance.

## Apparatuses Used in Gymnastics

**Low parallel bars** are 7 feet long, 15 inches high, and 18 inches wide for practicing hand balances. **Standard parallel bars** are adjustable hand rails, made of fine-grained wood, on uprights connected by oval-shaped pressed steel rails. **Rails** go under upright and are completely secured inside the base. **Bars** adjust from 3 feet and 9 inches to 5 feet and 3 inches high and from 15 to 18 inches wide. **Mats** are thick pads covered with canvas or other material, filled with 2 inches of kapok/felt, made in various lengths, widths, and grades, to protect gymnasts when landing or falling. A **side horse** is a cylindrical body with an approximately 14-inch diameter, covered in leather/other material, mounted on steel legs/base, with two pommels, i.e., handles, on top near the middle. Horse height is adjustable from 36 to 57 inches. A **spring board** is an inclined board about 6 feet by 22 inches, over a fulcrum about half its length. It is lightweight, usually made of ash, shod with rubber, and with its upper end carpeted in cork. It is used to spring off from for tumbling, horse and buck vaulting, and to parallel bars.

## Types of Gymnastics

**Olympic gymnastics** are better learned outside school hours. **Educational gymnastics** have different, non-competitive purposes: to teach children to increase their skills for controlling and maneuvering their bodies effectively against gravity's force, on the floor and on apparatus, through learning experiences. It integrates movement concepts, e.g., body and space awareness, force and effort, movement qualities and relationships. It also integrates with skill themes, e.g., balancing, transferring weight, traveling, jumping, and landing. Children must experience these in isolation and/or in dance or game contexts before experiencing them incorporated into gymnastics. Under **traveling**, some introductory themes include travelling independently and safely, to/from and on/off apparatus, changing direction/level, on feet/hands, together/apart, and in shapes. Under **weight-bearing**, included are getting on/off apart, weight on hands, balancing on different surfaces and body parts, balancing and rolling, landing and rolling, changing feet relationships with weight on hands, and while balancing. In **weight transfer**, included are log/side rolling, forward rolls, jumping and landing, and back safety rolls. Under

**relationship**, included are individual sequences; partner sequences together, apart, or side-by-side; and symmetrical and asymmetrical movements.

## Basic Tumbling Terminology

**Tumbling** is a series of acrobatic, controlled large-muscle movements including flips, springs, rolls, falls, dives, twists, etc. **Tumbling stunts** can be on the mat, deck, or ground; semi-aerial, i.e., from the feet to the hands to the feet; or aerial, i.e., from the feet through the air to the feet going forward, backward, or sideways. **Mat stunts** include chest rolls, from a hand balance onto the chest; dives—from a running start, leaping into the air, ending on the chest, back arched, rolling downward; rockers on the stomach, back arched; forward/backward rolls, and sideward shoulder rolls. **Semi-aerial stunts** include front/back walkovers; barrel rolls; cartwheels; cradle rocks to back and shoulders; egg rolls/fish flops, backward to short head balance to shoulders forward, rolling down to chest, stomach, to standing; round offs, changing forward to backward momentum via inward half-turning; front, back, leaping, or one-arm handsprings; headsprings; and shoulder/neck springs. **Aerial stunts** include brandy/Baroni, a handless roundoff; somersault/side somersault/front flip with half-twist/back somersault; spotter, landing on the takeoff spot; cutaway, landing behind it; gainer—backward somersault landing ahead of the takeoff spot; layout; tuck; whipback; bounders; alternates; and Rudolph (brandy with full twist). There are others for doubles and triples.

## Intermediate Movement Themes 4-7

Here are some **intermediate themes** for grades 4-7 educational gymnastics lessons. For **traveling**: moving into and out of balance, and jumping with turns. For **weight bearing**: balancing while curling, stretching, twisting, or otherwise changing body shapes; partner balances; counter-tension (away); platform balance; and counter-balance (together). For body shape: the body shape in flight. For **relationship**: partner matching and copying, small group sequences, and using the partner as an obstacle to move over and/or through. For **traveling into and out of balance**, there are five steps in a learning experience.

- Run and jump onto a vaulting surface.
- Run, placing hands on the apparatus, and land on the same spot.
- Repeat (2), but add a roll upon landing. Practice roll progressions for the backward safety roll.
- Change the relationship of the feet while performing various vaults into the air; move into a balance.
- Hold the balance; then move into another balance.

Refinements for these steps are:

- Move into a balance.
- Take off with feet, and raise the hips as high as possible.
- Use a curved surface area; tuck tightly.
- Spread, cross, or bend the knees.
- Make the sequence parts flow.

## Cooperative Games

In **cooperative games and activities**, students must work together to discover solutions to different challenges presented by the activities. Examples include activities to develop communication skills, teamwork skills, and problem-solving skills. One cooperative PE game activity for developing communication and teamwork skills is "Caterpillar Riot": Teams of 5 or 6 students stand in line, each

- 117 -

wearing a hoop; hoops should touch. Each team is a "caterpillar." The goal is to collect as many objects from the floor as possible by moving the caterpillar forward. To advance, the rear player in each line steps into the hoop of the player ahead, picks up his or her empty hoop, and passes it to the front of the line. The front player puts the hoop down, stepping into it. Each player moves forward into the next hoop. Only the front player may pick up objects; other players must carry objects collected. When all objects are collected, the game ends. Builds include a preparatory race, advancing caterpillars without collecting objects; playing the full version; adding a time limit to the full version; and playing blindfolded.

## Toxic Waste

To play "**Toxic Waste**": The equipment used includes ringette rings, foam balls, jump ropes, cones, and optional blindfolds. Teams of four students each have one foam ball sitting on top of a ringette ring with four jump ropes tied to it. The goal is for students to move the "toxic waste" foam ball from one end of the gym to the other without touching the ringette ring's ball, so students must utilize the ropes. If the ball falls, whichever team dropped it must return to the starting line and start over. After students play the original game, the teacher can add a build wherein one student on each team is blindfolded. After each round, the teacher blindfolds one more player, continuing until all players are blindfolded. One safety rule is that blindfolded students must walk, not run. After playing, the teacher can initiate student discussion by asking them questions such as, "To succeed in moving the toxic waste to the other side, how did you have to coordinate your movements as a team?" "What were the communication challenges in the game?" "How was your communication affected by having one or more players on your team blindfolded?"

## Astronaut

One game PE teachers can have a whole class of children play is **Astronaut**, which involves running and dodging movement patterns and skills. It develops endurance, locomotor skills, non-locomotor skills, and group cooperation. The only equipment is one balloon per child. Teaching tips: The game is best played in a large, grassy area. Include short rest periods for young children, who tire quickly. Do not let children keep balloons afterward. To play, select four children as astronauts. The rest are Martians. Each astronaut has an air supply, i.e., an inflated balloon. On the teacher's signal, the Martians chase the astronauts, trying to destroy their air supplies by popping the balloons. Once all four balloons are popped, start over with four different astronauts. Repeat until all children have been astronauts. One variation is to add flags: once a Martian pulls an astronaut's flag, s/he must surrender the balloon to that Martian.

## Four-Corner Cage Ball

**Four-Corner Cage Ball** involves kicking and crab-walking movements, and develops striking skills, arm and shoulder strength, and teamwork skills. Equipment is four cones and one cage ball. Divide the class into four teams, each forming one side of a square marked by cones. Number off each team; children must remember their numbers. Place a cage ball in the middle of the square. Call a number. All children with that number crab-walk to the cage ball; their goal is to kick the ball over the heads of another team. Other players, also crab-walking, can only block the ball using their feet. Any team having the ball kicked over their heads gets a point. Start again, calling new numbers. The object is NOT getting points. Teaching tips: With this competitive game, children may become excited, forget the rules, and block the ball with their hands. Teams can be given points for doing this if not for safety. For safety, no hard shoes or boots are allowed, and children should remove glasses. If outdoors on grass, carefully check first for debris. If running out of time without everybody getting a turn, extend boundaries as needed; call two or three numbers at once.

## Outdoor Adventure Activities

Some exciting, fascinating, rewarding **outdoor adventure activities** include mountain-climbing; rafting; canoeing; kayaking; whitewater paddleboarding; sailing; driving powerboats; slacklining; rope-climbing; exploring mines; exploring caves; walking long-distance footpaths; backpacking; hiking; running; jungle treks; expeditions through primary rainforests; nature hikes and walks; exploring wild areas in four-wheel drive vehicles; and orienteering, which involves navigating a wilderness environment with a compass and a map, while also racing against others to reach a destination first. Some outdoor adventure enthusiasts pursue these interests close to home, which is most convenient and affordable, while others travel to other countries and exotic locations. Some altruistically-minded adventurers combine adventure expeditions to other lands with **team community service projects** when they arrive. Others find adventure experiences inspire photography, drawing, painting, writing music, writing literature, other artistic pursuits, or scientific/practical inventions. People unfamiliar with and interested in adventure can learn from experienced, credentialed instructors in the outdoor industry—as adventure school faculty or independent freelancers—many with websites advertising their services. In addition to teaching techniques and safety practices, instructors also mentor, motivate, and encourage learners; build their confidence and self-esteem; and foster their skills for teamwork, decision-making, and problem-solving.

## Behavioral and Administrative Outdoor Adventures

Some of the courses offered in the area of **outdoor adventure** include leadership, group dynamics, risk management, conflict management, expedition planning, execution, and evaluation. Classes are offered in specific activities, e.g., backpacking techniques for beginners; slacklining techniques, including choosing the correct trees and avoiding damage to the trees used; learning to set up a line; and learning to stand and balance on a line before learning to walk on it. Multi-pitch climbing techniques include anchoring skills with gear anchors and multidirectional anchors, anchor builds, rappelling techniques, belaying directly off of anchors from above, belay station rope management, belay transfers, efficiently changing leaders, self-rescue techniques, and other hands-on learning. Some outdoor adventure schools and instructors use sports like paddleboarding in whitewater rapids while standing up as facilitation techniques for therapeutic recreation. They advocate these activities for being experienced in natural environments, including elements of perceived or actual danger, and providing challenges to participants. Beginning courses in kayaking techniques teach the basic strokes, e.g., the forward stroke, forward sweep stroke, and low brace stroke, starting in calm lakes. Once learners can paddle in straight lines, they can learn how to turn using the paddle as a rudder and use steering strokes.

## Primary Safety Equipment

**Football players** need heavy shoulder, chest, and elbow pads to protect them from body contact injuries. Helmets are imperative to prevent head and brain injuries from collisions and blows. Recently the NFL began requiring players to wear knee and shin guards; PE teachers should have students follow this practice. **Baseball** does not require body contact through hitting or tackling like football. However, because it involves swinging hard bats and hitting and throwing balls which become projectiles, baseball players must wear helmets to protect against head injury. When traumatic brain injuries do not occur, getting "beaned" by a baseball is still extremely painful—even when wearing a helmet, let alone to an unprotected head. Being accidentally hit by a baseball bat can also seriously injure a student. **Hockey players** use angled wooden sticks, which can cause injuries. Ice hockey uses a small, dense, hard rubber puck, which can be very injurious if striking a player. Helmets, neck guards, shoulder and chest pads, elbow and forearm pads, and shin guards are included in hockey, plus heel guards on skates in ice hockey. Mouth guards are recommended in football and hockey to protect players from lost and broken teeth.

# Risk Management and Safety

The *Outward Bound Wilderness First-Aid Book* (Isaac, 1998) is a manual of standard operating practices for **risk management and safety** in outdoor adventure recreation and education programs. Other outdoor education organizations offer similar books. Additional good resources include government education departments and recreation agencies, which have published outdoor activity risk management guidelines in many countries. Research studies published by various organizations provide data and narratives regarding risk management and incidents. For example, *Adventure Program Risk Management Report, Volume I* (1995) was issued by the Association for Experiential Education. The American Camping Association (ACA) and other outdoor associations have published guidelines, articles, and manuals describing risk management in rope challenge courses and many other specific adventure activities. Adventure Incorporated and others offer risk management specialists as consultants. The National Outdoor Leadership School organizes an annual Wilderness Risk Manager's Conference in America. Every developed nation offers outdoor and adventure risk management and first aid training courses, listed at www.outdoored.com. Professional Outdoor Education listservs also extensively discuss safety and risk management practices.

# Benefits of Dance Activities

**Dancing** increases aerobic fitness, cardiopulmonary and cardiovascular fitness, endurance, muscular strength, muscular endurance, muscle tone, and motor fitness. It strengthens the bones through bearing weight and decreases risk of osteoporosis. It aids in managing a healthy weight. Dancing improves a person's flexibility, agility, and coordination. It enhances spatial awareness, balance, and sense of direction. People who learn to dance enjoy greater physical self-confidence, overall self-confidence, and self-esteem. Dancing improves mental functioning. It promotes better well-being, in general and psychologically. Because of the social interactions inherent in learning to dance, and dancing in classes, groups, and with partners, dance also improves social skills. Serious dancers become very physically fit; even those more casually involved in dance will get more physical activity, improving their health and well-being. Dance can be pursued competitively or socially. Inclement weather does not interfere with dance as it does with outdoor sports. Today there are many places to take dance classes or lessons, including dance studios, dance schools, fitness clubs, colleges and universities, university extensions, dance halls, community recreation centers, etc.

# Learning Tumbling and Gymnastics

Learning **tumbling and gymnastics** skills and routines contributes significantly to children's development in many domains—not only in sport-specific skills, but additionally in academic performance and personality, psychological, and social development. Students meeting challenges in gymnastics, e.g., learning skills for performing on balance beams and parallel bars, gain self-confidence in their own abilities, which extends to school subjects and other life areas. Younger children think concretely, not abstractly; their lives are more physical than mental. The superior body movement and coordination they develop through tumbling and gymnastics give them much of their self-confidence. Children lacking natural talent to be "star" athletes in other sports benefit from success in tumbling and gymnastics as teachers can control the challenges and progress they experience. Students learn to overcome fears and to perform in front of others. The training required in gymnastics builds determination and a hard work ethic; its controlled environment and rules teach discipline. Physical strength and flexibility from gymnastics benefit student athletes playing football, basketball, baseball, and other sports. Athletes typically need more flexibility—which also prevents many injuries. Listening, following directions, taking turns, politeness, and respecting others are social skills learned in gymnastics.

## Outdoor Adventure and Education

**Outdoor learning in nature** affords background benefits of increasing physical, mental, and spiritual health; personal and social communication skills; sensory, aesthetic, and spiritual awareness; sensitivity to one's own well-being; and the ability to exercise personal control. Outdoor learning in the natural environment can also have planned benefits when providers or educators determine or negotiate these. For example, through structured, well-planned, hands-on learning experiences, teachers and providers help students to develop their own self-esteem, take personal responsibility, cooperate with others, and respect others' needs. They help them develop better appreciation of the world and its peoples, which allows them to expand their personal horizons. They teach them to understand why people must establish and maintain sustainable relationships with the environment. They improve students' practical teamwork and problem-solving skills. And they foster knowledgeable, positive student responses regarding personal well-being and health. Outdoor learning allows bonus benefits as well through incidental learning and greater than expected value, which highly supportive learning atmospheres enable. Wider benefits include greater sustainability and other benefits for families, schools, sponsors, society, and future generations, who are all stakeholders in outdoor learning success.

## Modified Movement and Dance Activities

According to experts (cf. Dow, 2013), all children can participate in most **movement activities** when they are modified. Each child can approach movement according to his or her individual abilities, experiences, and imagination. For instance, if a teacher gives children a greeting activity involving their waving various body parts, they can instruct children with physical disabilities to move their fingers, toes, eyelids, or tongues. When leading children in a jumping activity, if the class includes children in wheelchairs, teachers can instruct them to move their heads, shoulders, arms, and/or fingers instead of their legs. If the teacher is instructing children to form the shapes of alphabet letters with their bodies, s/he can guide children with physical disabilities to use their fingers or arms rather than their entire bodies. Children who are unable to do this can point to or hold up a picture or large shape of each letter to participate actively. Children of all/most ability levels can participate in dance stories by exploring and elaborating on characters and events in stories, poems, books, or songs through creative movement, including facial expressions.

## Modifying Educational Gymnastics

Some gymnastics educators state that **inclusion** is not difficult because coaching practices should not really change: in providing opportunities according to individual student needs, **program competencies and strategies** can be preserved while maintaining awareness of **disabilities**. Educators have effected cultural changes by informing coaches at national championships that inclusion tools, tips, and other resources would become available. They find it necessary to raise awareness of and communicate social messages about inclusion before teaching technical elements of coaching students with disabilities. They advocate developing disability action plans. Some agencies and organizations offer funding to support such plans' strategies. Following awareness and education, educators identify the next step as requiring teacher or coach accreditation processes to incorporate mandatory training in inclusion management. They point out that high-performance coaches do this routinely when they assign unevenly-numbered teams and small-sided games and focus on developing specific tactics, techniques, and skills. An inclusive approach, they say, involves the same practices, but simply done for different purposes. Some experts use the **TREE** acronym and principle for modifying and challenging sports players according to individual ability: Teaching style, Rules and regulations, Equipment, and Environment.

## Modifying Curriculum and Instruction

To provide inclusive PE environments, **modifications** are needed to make learning environments safe and meaningful for every student, enable all students' successfully learning appropriate PE skills, and eliminate mismatches between lesson content and student skill levels. To be appropriate, modifications must not make settings or activities unsafe for non-disabled students; not ruin activities or games by precluding fun; not overburden regular PE teachers; and enable safe, meaningful, and successful disabled student participation. **Curriculum modifications** include:

- multilevel selections of different learning objectives in the same domain
- objectives from different domains overlapping in the same activity
- different alternative activities.

Part (1) includes modifying tasks and equipment, e.g., for limited strength, speed, endurance, balance, or coordination; extending skill stations, e.g., holding basketball on lap tray, dropping ball to floor, slapping ball three consecutive times, dribbling while stationary or walking, or dribbling while jogging and or guarded; modifying instruction, e.g., in class format, teaching style, cues and signals, instruction and participation duration, setting, distracters, motivation level, direct instruction, movement exploration, and strategies intervention model. Part (2) includes cooperative learning; class-wide peer tutoring; teaching locomotor skills plus walking, dribbling, and 3-point shooting in a basketball game. Part (3) includes pull-out activities; concurrent multiple activities; and pocket-reference IEP objectives and RPE modifications, arrangements, and activities.

## Adventure PE Adaptations

Experts identify the building-blocks of **adventure PE programs** as the core values of adventure education, which include: emphasizing non-competitive activities; participants' sense of accomplishment from successfully completing a specifically designed activity sequence; trust and cooperation fostered among co-participants; the communication participants exchange to attain their goals; the ability to implement activities at individual participant levels; the combination of enhancing strength, coordination, flexibility, and endurance while having fun; and the fact that activities require participants to cooperate with nature, promoting better appreciation and respect for the natural environment. **Adaptations** include allowing longer times to complete tasks, slowing activity paces, demonstrating activities visually and verbally, employing peer partner assistance, simplifying steps, modifying body positions, removing obstacles and distractions, increasing participation time by using stations, providing ramps, shortening course or activity distance, and using signing gestures along with verbal instructions. Special and regular education teachers must collaborate creatively to assess needs and find appropriate curriculum adaptations that both enable individual success and attain the school's/organization's and individual student's learning goals.

# Physical Fitness in Everyday Life

## Behavioral Development 5-6

Students in **grades 5-6** should show **self-confidence** by identifying PE activities that are personally challenging to them, identifying the skills they need to develop and/or refine personally to succeed, and choosing and practicing specific skills they need to improve. They should demonstrate **safety** for themselves and others and apply the appropriate etiquette in specific sports and activities, e.g., taking turns; avoiding personal fouls, like body contact in basketball; avoiding excessive force to the point of injury in football tackling and blocking; helping up fallen opponents; not teasing teammates or classmates for being out of condition; not celebrating opponent mistakes; not arguing with every call made by referees, umpires, or teachers; not insulting others; not denying fouls; avoiding inappropriate language; and shaking hands after contests. They should follow and help establish rules and procedures, show responsibility for their own actions and the capacity for receiving and providing honest feedback, show willingness to engage with others of different socioeconomic levels, contribute to positive group dynamics, and show cooperation by encouraging and supporting classmates and teammates with different skill levels and abilities.

## Behavioral Development 7-8

**Grade 7-8 students** should demonstrate personal responsibility for their **individual wellness** by acquiring and identifying knowledge about the connections among exercise, nutrition, and fitness, and apply this knowledge in selecting activities for improving and maintaining their fitness goals. They should participate in lifelong and leisure sport or dance activities in and out of school to show they recognize the importance of physical activity to personal wellness. They should further their individual self-confidence and success through identifying how personal performance is affected by attitude, energy, and effort; set personal goals for attaining higher performance levels in challenging and new activities; and show positive attitudes about developing personal skills. They should show positive and supportive behavior to demonstrate safety for self and others. Appropriate social interactions demonstrating responsibility include: playing by the rules and not taking advantage of classmates or teammates; practicing proper sports conduct, e.g., accepting teacher, coach, and referee decisions without argument; and officiating in small-group games. Additional appropriate social behaviors and interactions include: showing appreciation for applicable feedback, being willing to work with others from diverse backgrounds, being able to adopt leader and follower roles as indicated, and cooperating with others within task activity structures.

## Behavioral and Social Development 9-12

**High school students** should show recognition of personal responsibility for individual wellness by demonstrating they understand how personal traits, styles, preferences, and performance change throughout life, and applying this understanding to continually evolving fitness plans. They should also further their achievement and maintenance of personal fitness goals through regular participation in suitable physical activities. To further their self-confidence and individual success, they should be able to analyze the characteristics of the physical and sports activities they personally find challenging, rewarding, and enjoyable, e.g., they are high-risk, competitive, individual, group, socially interactive, aesthetically satisfying, etc. They should also challenge themselves in developing higher or new skill levels, and demonstrate perseverance in pursuing higher performance. By participating in related activities like spotting, refereeing, and belaying, they should demonstrate their ability to anticipate and correct consequences from physical activities that are potentially dangerous. **Appropriate social interactions** include: showing responsibility through sportsmanlike conduct; preventing dangerous

- 123 -

outcomes; using quality of play, not results, to evaluate competition; displaying self-discipline and self-direction; revising their actions to show respect for feedback; exhibiting strategies to include diverse others in physical activities; recognizing and developing their leading and following abilities in group activities; and showing cooperation by helping others participate.

## Leadership and Teamwork

When students must play a game or sport as team members rather than individuals, a **team captain** is often designated. This student must take responsibility for things like choosing team members; planning and organizing plays; developing tactics; providing motivation to team members; encouraging team solidarity; and getting team members to cooperate, collaborate, and function as a unit rather than a collection of individuals. Learning to perform these duties successfully will develop student leadership skills. **Teamwork** is also essential in sports. Purposes and benefits of team sports include winning contests, attaining shared goals, preparing for jobs and wider society, learning to build confidence and manage emotions, learning about oneself and others, and surviving and flourishing in large classes and schools. The power of numbers enables teams to accomplish things individuals cannot. When team members conflict with and/or work against one another, a team thus divided will more likely lose. Supporting each other and working together enables a team to win. Team members must accept their team roles, the team itself, its ground rules, and the individuality of their teammates.

## Fair Play

In virtually all sports, **fair play** is a universal standard. Thus, when students learn sports in PE classes and activities, they are held to the same standards that adult athletes are to behave fairly by following the established rules of the game; not cheating by breaking or circumventing those rules; and treating their peers fairly by not taking advantage of their weaknesses, unfairly exploiting their strengths, or making fun of their shortcomings or difficulties. Sports have structures and rules to promote fairness. Playing sports can help young students learn to be fairer in their behavior, for example, by not choosing team members preferentially out of friendship or enmity; not rejecting students because they have disabilities or are shorter, slower, weaker, or have less experience; and not excluding students from diverse cultural, ethnic, or socioeconomic backgrounds. When students play team sports or games in PE, they must develop and refine skills for cooperating with others. When they respect and listen to others, help others participate, and work jointly as a team, they develop cooperative skills that will enhance their social interactions outside of PE activities in their schools, families, communities, current and/or future jobs, and everyday lives.

## Good Sportsmanship

When students learn to play individual and team competitive sports, the meaning of **competition** is better construed as striving for excellence than exhibiting adversarial hostility. While individualistic American culture places great emphasis on competition in contrast to collectivist cultures' emphasis on cooperation, American sports also emphasize **good sportsmanship** and **fair play**. In this spirit, students should view other teams and individual competitors as worthy opponents rather than enemies, and the object of play as a challenge to exceed opponents' strategies and performance rather than a mission to destroy them or pound them into the ground. Good sportsmanship includes being a good winner by respecting opponents' efforts and acknowledging the competition they offer, and being a good loser by giving winners the credit they deserve for superior strategy and performance. Consideration promotes mutual respect and enabling healthy competition rather than antisocial or destructive behavior. Another element of sportsmanlike conduct is helping others, e.g., helping up an opposing player that has been knocked down. Supporting teammates teaches students to be supportive in friendships and workplace, family, and intimate relationships.

## Student Respect for Peers

PE experts assert the importance of teaching not only information, skills, and strategies, but equally teaching **effective skills and objectives**. Without these, they say students, despite having the knowledge and skills, may not want to participate in PE activities. Values, attitudes, feelings, and interpersonal behaviors affect student motivation. Hence, the National Association for Sport and Physical Education's (NASPE) National PE Standards include "responsible personal and social behavior that respects self and others in physical activity settings" (2004). As role models, PE teachers should never show favoritism among students or marginalize students with lesser motor skills. They should also not limit the health benefits of PE activities for students with either lower or higher skills, but provide challenges to all levels. When designing PE activities and curriculum, teachers should deliberately include ways to teach respect for self and others, cooperation, teamwork, skills, and techniques. As examples, students can practice teamwork along with meeting individual and group goals during modified game play; students can learn to value safety for themselves and classmates while learning or practicing educational gymnastics skills and routines.

## Peer Acceptance

Children and teenagers judge their own competence in large part through **social comparison** to their peers and **evaluations** from those peers. Moreover, students' beliefs of self-worth, approaches to motivation, participatory behaviors, and emotional experiences are all influenced by their peers. One type of relationship that researchers have investigated relative to student behavioral and psychosocial results in sports and physical activities is **peer acceptance**. This represents the extent to which members of a peer group like or embrace an individual, varying from rejection to popularity. Research has consistently revealed strong relationships between students' degrees of perceived physical competence and their degrees of peer acceptance. For instance, teens and children find competence in sports an important factor in peer group popularity and status. Investigators have found that students who are perceived as physically skilled by both themselves and their teachers were also rated as liked by their peers by both themselves and their teachers.

## Practicing Inclusion of Peers

A common requirement in many PE standards is for students, particularly at the high school level, to demonstrate positive social interactions by including **diverse types of students** with them in their PE activities. Student diversity includes **disability**. Students with disabilities, especially physical disabilities, have historically been excluded from many PE activities because they could not participate in typical ways. However, modern federal laws mandate including students with disabilities in all aspects of education. One way students can include disabled peers is for PE teachers to instruct them to be peer facilitators, enabling them both to assist and participate. For example, non-disabled students can use hand-over-hand assistance to enable students with upper-body or limb disabilities to hit balls with bats and racquets; hit balloons with noodles; throw Frisbees at bowling pins; hit balls off tees at bowling pins; hit hockey pucks with hockey sticks; drive wheelchairs while dribbling balls with hockey sticks attached to the chairs; or catch whiffle balls, sponge balls, or beanbags in boxes. There are also many modified games wherein non-disabled students and those in wheelchairs or lacking upper-body control can participate together, and activities that include students with intellectual disabilities.

## Understanding and Appreciation of Diversity

Experienced PE teachers have observed that students and teachers alike often suffer from **unrealistically stereotypical views** of diverse students. This is detrimental even when the stereotype appears positive. For example, many Americans view Asian-Americans as the "model minority" for being intelligent, academically successful, quiet, well-behaved, and hardworking. However, not every Asian-American is intellectually gifted, an excellent student, a model of good behavior, or even an English speaker. Making stereotyped assumptions can hurt such students by depriving them of needed behavioral and academic support. When teachers ask students the first thing they think of when they name Asian-Americans, students say "smart"; when they name African-Americans, students say "good athletes." Yet not every African-American person is athletic. Even in their own culture, some African-American students excelling academically may be stereotyped as "acting white." Educators call for the necessity for teachers to examine and challenge their own stereotypical beliefs, and understand their own diversity, in order to teach students to do the same.

## Diverse Cultural Implications

PE teachers need to realize some **cultural differences** they will encounter when teaching diverse students. For example, Hispanic students tend to learn kinesthetically. While this is a natural fit with PE activities, some Anglo-American teachers who introduce new activities using verbal information may need to adjust instruction to begin with movements, which Latino students need to engage in learning. Hispanic and Asian students not raised in America are likely to avoid eye contact with teachers, and teachers should not demand it. Latino students may not be expressing agreement when they nod; their silence may not indicate understanding or agreement, but confusion or embarrassment. For all **English language learners (ELLs)**, teachers should include visual aids in demonstrations and employ peer facilitators to bridge language barriers. American teachers accustomed to encouraging competition must realize Latin, Asian, Native American, and other collectivist cultures frown on competing and value cooperating, and should accordingly deemphasize aggressive competition. Knowing what teachers expect of them makes Asian students more comfortable, as do cooperative learning environments; positive reinforcement benefits them. Culturally, they communicate nonverbally, e.g., leaning forward or backward; they rely on this more when they are ELLs.

## Benefits Diverse Students Contribute

PE classes and teams incorporating students from **heterogeneous sources** benefit from a wider variety of contributions than those with narrowly homogeneous origins. For example, although American teachers and students might view the non-competitive cultural values of the collectivist traditions in which Hispanic, Native American, and Asian students have been raised as detrimental to winning in competitive team sports, this is not the only way to view them. Because they value cooperation for the good of the group, subsuming individual identity in favor of group identification, and helping others to promote collective harmony, students from these cultures can actually make better team players than some highly individualistic American students who behave more like high-profile athletes than they do like equal team members. Students from collectivist cultures are also more likely to engage in respectful sportsmanship than compete in overly aggressive ways. Deferring individual accomplishments and attention for being important parts of a group make them valuable contributors to team solidarity and success.

## Diverse Cultures and Physical Activity

**Asian cultures** often have a **holistic** view of physical activity and sports. They value the connection between mind and body, and practice various sports and disciplines to develop spiritual awareness as well as physical skills. Yoga, tai chi, and the many martial arts are examples of Asian traditions combining physical and spiritual discipline this way. PE teachers should realize that Asian students previously accustomed to these traditions may view playing sports or games in PE for fun as irrelevant and spiritually unsatisfying, view playing them for aggressive competition as against their values of cooperation and group harmony, and view competing in sports for individual attention and fame as

- 126 -

inappropriate. American cultural groups also view physical activity and fitness differently. For example, research finds that, compared to white girls, **African-American girls** are less physically active; tolerate, accept, prefer, and are more satisfied with larger body sizes or weights; and do not view celebrities as physical role models. The time and expense of hair and nail maintenance, lack of urban neighborhood safety, and school and extracurricular time constraints also limit their participation in structured physical activities.

## Personal Challenges and Satisfaction

Although mainstream American culture emphasizes competition in sports, students need not always compete to excel in PE activities. The concept of a **"personal best"** can be even more consistent with individual excellence, as it does not depend on comparisons or differences with other students and teams. Also, social psychologists studying achievement motivation have found students with a higher **internal locus of control**—i.e., they attribute their successes and failures to their own internal factors, not external influences—are more likely to maintain motivation to achieve more constantly across time, settings, and situations than those with a more external locus of control—i.e., they attribute their successes or failures to the help or interference of people, things, and events outside themselves. Students who strive to run faster than their last or current time, farther than their last or current distance; lift more weight or complete more repetitions; jump higher; and even in team sports, score more points than before, etc., compete with themselves, not others. Thus changes or differences in opponents will not affect their motivation or efforts. Also, in contrast with being on a losing team, students who achieve their own personal physical activity goals experience satisfaction regardless of what others do.

## Competition and Achievement

When children are young and in earlier motor development stages, they may learn, practice, and enjoy running, jumping, hopping, skipping, balancing, etc., individually or in groups, but not **competitively**. As they grow, though, they will be exposed both in and out of school to running races to see who finishes first, experiencing their first taste of competition. Soon they will learn to play games and sports in PE classes. Individual activities include comparisons like who can hang from a high bar the longest, jump the highest and farthest, or make the most baskets, as well as run the fastest. While competitive themes pervade both individual and team activities, when students begin learning team sports, the inherent object is for one team to win by scoring more points, gaining more yards, making more runs or goals, etc. While some students may already have met "personal best" goals, if they find all their peers exceed them in certain activities, competition can motivate them to increase their **standards and efforts** accordingly. Because American education also compares academic achievement against national averages, PE competition and achievement can inform and transfer to other school subjects.

## Positive Social Interactions

When younger children are first taught to play **organized games** with peers, they must learn to follow rules; take turns; share; cooperate with others; and refrain from hitting, kicking, biting, punching, and other antisocial behaviors. These are novel experiences to many youngsters. The structure and rules of organized games are ideal contexts to teach them to control aggressive behaviors; and to reinforce the pro-social, unselfish, helpful, and cooperative behaviors young children also naturally display at times. By participating in games, sports, dance, etc., older students learn not to reject, ignore, insult, tease, taunt, assault, or take advantage of peers; to offer helping hands when they need them; include peers with different backgrounds and abilities in physical activities; detect when and how to assume leader or follower roles; and include, invite, and help other students participate. When students improve their physical fitness, they gain self-esteem and physical well-being that often discourages incompatible habits like overeating, smoking, drinking, and taking drugs. Spending time being physically active leaves less unoccupied time for dangerous pursuits. Students interact socially through sharing sports, games, and dance instead of substance abuse or other risky behaviors.

## Major Human Body Systems

The **skeletal system** provides the body's structural framework of bones to support it, protects the soft vital organs from harm, collaborates with muscles to produce body movement, stores calcium in the bones, and produces red blood cells in the bone marrow. The **integumentary system** includes the hair, nails, and especially skin, which is the body's largest sensory organ. It provides tactile sensation, including pain, heat, cold, pressure, and pleasure; regulates loss of blood and other fluids; synthesizes vitamin D; and protects deeper tissues. The **muscular system** maintains body posture, creates body movements with the support of the bones, generates heat, and consumes energy. The **immune system** is composed of parts of many other systems, including parts of the lymphatic system, the cardiovascular system, the respiratory system, the gastrointestinal system, etc. It works to protect and defend the body against disease organisms and other foreign elements.

## Major Human Body Systems Functions

The **lymphatic system** retrieves fluids that leak from the capillaries (small blood vessels) and contains the white blood cells, hence supporting parts of the immune system. The **cardiovascular system** transports nutrients containing oxygen and other necessities throughout the bloodstream, transports gaseous wastes for elimination, and supports immune functions. The **urinary system** regulates balances of fluids, electrolytes, and pH; and removes nitrogenous wastes from the blood. The **digestive system** breaks foods down into proteins, sugars, amino acids, and other building blocks for the body's metabolic processes, growth, replenishment, and repair. The **respiratory system** performs gas exchanges by taking in, warming, and moistening environmental air, delivering oxygen, and expelling carbon dioxide. The **nervous system** provides sensory input, interprets the sensory information, evokes and signals responses, and coordinates muscle functions. The **endocrine system** secretes hormones that regulate the body's growth, metabolism, and general functionality. The **reproductive system** produces hormones enabling reproduction and creates, nurtures, and delivers offspring.

## Muscular System

Among cardiac, smooth, and skeletal muscles, **skeletal muscles** are used in voluntary body movement. They are wrapped in several layers of connective tissue, which join to form tendons attaching to bones. **Tendons** extend connective tissue around muscles, giving individual muscle fibers support and stability. **Ligaments** connect bones at joints, and exercise is thought to strengthen ligaments. Tendons and ligaments, combined with muscle and skin elasticity and joint structure, determine flexibility, which can be enhanced through stretching exercises. **Type I/red/slow-twitch muscle fibers** are needed for endurance activities like long-distance running and cycling, and need more aerobic energy. **Type II/white/fast-twitch muscle fibers** need less oxygen and are used in short-term, maximum-force exertion like sprinting, jumping, and weight-lifting. Both types are activated in activities needing maximal force production. Lesser force requirements activate slow-twitch fibers first, then fast-twitch if needed. Muscle fibers are always activated in groups called motor units, which include motor neurons. Dumbbell curls use more motor units than picking up a pencil, for example. Resistance and weight training increases muscle fiber size, and strengthens and thickens connective tissues, resulting in larger muscles and greater muscular strength and endurance.

## The Cardiopulmonary System in Exercise

The heart's right side receives blood from the veins. When the heart muscle contracts, it pumps blood from its **right ventricle**, through the **pulmonary arteries**, to the **lungs**. This blood acquires fresh oxygen in the lungs from atmospheric air the individual has inhaled, and releases carbon dioxide into **pulmonary capillaries**. Exhaling expels this $CO_2$. The freshly oxygenated blood travels through the pulmonary veins, to the heart's left atrium, to the left ventricle. When the left ventricle contracts, it pumps blood through the **aorta**, the largest artery, to the entire body. The left and right ventricles contract simultaneously, so the cardiopulmonary system functions in a perpetual cycle. Oxygen consumption directly affects cardiorespiratory fitness: heart and lung function determine oxygen transportation to body tissues. The volume of air inhaled and exhaled each minute is pulmonary ventilation, which typically increases when exercising. The differential between oxygen inhaled and exhaled is the measure of oxygen consumption. Its maximum, **$VO_2$max**, equals maximal aerobic capacity, frequently regarded as indicating cardiorespiratory fitness. It defines the cardiovascular system's greatest ability to deliver oxygenated blood to working muscles, and how quickly the body can produce adenosine triphosphate (ATP) to supply energy to muscles.

## Hierarchy of Neural Systems

Many areas of the brain, including parts involving motivation, emotions, and memory, are included in the **highest level** of the **motor control hierarchy**. In this level, command neurons formulate the intention to move the body and its parts. This message is sent to the hierarchy's **middle level** in the cerebral cortex's sensorimotor cortex, subcortical nuclei's basal ganglia, cerebellum, and brainstem. The highly interconnected structures in this level determine postures and movements needed to perform an action. Midlevel neurons additionally receive input from receptors in the eyes, vestibular system, skin, joints, and muscles regarding current surroundings and body posture. The middle level uses this complex of data to produce a motor program, which defines the information necessary for performing the activity. It sends this program information along descending pathways, originating in the sensorimotor cortex and brainstem, to the **lowest hierarchy level**, the motor neurons and interneurons. These determine joint angles and degrees of muscle tension. Continuous monitoring and updating of movements allow for unexpected events. Initial motor programs generate rapid, crude execution of movements. Repeating a movement allows the middle level to supply more accurate information, requiring fewer corrections and enabling learning.

## Fundamental Processes of Life

- **Organization**: Labor is divided at every level of life, each part cooperatively performing its function. Loss of organization, i.e., integrity, causes death, even to a single cell.
- **Metabolism**: All the chemical reactions in the body, e.g., breaking substances down to simpler components and releasing energy.
- **Responsiveness**: Also known as irritability, detecting changes in external and internal environments and reacting to them—sensing and responding to stimuli.
- **Movement**: At the cellular level, molecules move among locations. Blood moves among body parts in the circulatory system. As we breathe, our diaphragms move. Our muscles produce movement through contractility, i.e., ability to shorten.
- **Reproduction**: Specifically, transmitting life across generations by creating new organisms. Generally, cellular reproduction means new cell formation to repair or replace old cells and affect growth.
- **Differentiation**: How unspecialized cells developmentally become specialized, with distinct structures and functions, e.g., into tissues and organs.
- **Respiration**: How oxygen and carbon dioxide are exchanged between cells and the environment, including ventilation, diffusion, and transportation in blood.
- **Digestion**: Breaking down foods into simple molecules for absorption and use.
- **Excretion**: Removal from the body of digestive and metabolic waste products.

## Major Body Systems

The **nervous system** includes the brain, nerves, and spinal cord. It interprets sensory input, enables thought and emotion, and sends messages to the rest of the body. The **circulatory system** includes the heart and blood vessels. It delivers blood to and from the lungs and the rest of the body to supply oxygen and remove carbon dioxide. The **respiratory system** includes the lungs, bronchi, diaphragm, trachea, larynx, and pharynx. It enables us to breathe. The **skeletal system** includes the bones, cartilage, tendons, and ligaments. It protects the organs, structurally supports the body, and collaborates with the muscles in body movement. The **digestive system** includes the salivary glands, esophagus, stomach, intestines, liver, gall bladder, pancreas, rectum, and anus. It breaks down and processes food we eat; extracts nutrients to build tissues and supply energy; stores fats, amino acids, etc. for future use; and eliminates waste products. The **lymphatic system** includes the lymph nodes and vessels. It produces white blood cells for the immune system and transports lymph between the tissues and the bloodstream.

## Major Body Systems Identification

The **immune system** includes the white blood cells (leukocytes), tonsils, adenoids, thymus, and spleen. It protects the body against organisms and other agents that cause diseases and infections. The **muscular system** includes all of the many muscles in the body. It enables the body to move with support and cooperation from the skeletal system (bones). In addition to the head, neck, chest, back, arm, hand, leg, and foot muscles, the heart is also a muscle, which pumps blood to and from the lungs and the rest of the body to supply oxygen and remove carbon dioxide. The **integumentary system** includes the skin, nails, and hair. The skin protects the tissues from injury and fluid loss, provides sensation, and synthesizes vitamin D. The nails protect the fingertips and toes. The hair protects the skin, particularly on the scalp. The **reproductive system** includes the ovaries, fallopian tubes, uterus, vagina, and mammary glands in females; and testes, vas deferens, seminal vesicles, prostate, and penis in males. It enables reproduction via the conception, gestation, and delivery of babies. The **endocrine system** includes the hypothalamus; pituitary, pineal, thyroid, parathyroid, and adrenal glands; and pancreas. It secretes hormones regulating various body functions.

## Food Calorie

A **food calorie**, also called a dietary calorie, nutritional calorie, kilogram calorie, or large calorie, equals the approximate amount of energy required to increase the temperature of one kilogram of water by one degree Celsius. (Another calorie term, the gram calorie or small calorie, refers to the approximate amount of energy required to increase the temperature of one gram of water by one degree Celsius. The food calorie/large calorie/kilogram calorie equals 1,000 small calories, or one kilocalorie [Kcal].) Because energy produces heat, we describe "burning" calories. Foods have calories, i.e., potential energy. When we digest food, build and repair body cells, engage in physical activity, and use our brains, we expend energy, or "burn" calories. When people or animals ingest more calories than they expend, surplus calories not used get stored as **body fat**. Hence overeating results in extra fatty tissue and weight gain. When one expends more calories than one eats, initially the body burns fat for fuel, resulting in **weight loss**. When no extra fat exists, the body metabolizes muscle for protein and energy, causing muscle wasting. Additional energy expense without sufficient food causes weight loss, emaciation, and ultimately starvation.

## Movement During Physical Activity

The **skeletal system** gives our bodies their structural framework. The bones interact with the muscles to allow our body parts to move when the muscles contract. The skull is a bone that protects the brain, which regulates all body functions including movement. The vertebrae protect the spinal cord in general, including during movement. The joints where bones meet contain sensory receptors that send information about the body's position to the brain. The brain controls the contractions of the muscles to regulate the positions of the bones. The brain interacts with the cardiovascular system to regulate the heart rate and blood pressure, increasing these during physical activity. Baroreceptors in the cardiovascular system send the brain blood pressure information. Receptors in the muscles send the brain body position and movement information. The brain interacts with the **respiratory system**, controlling breathing rates and monitoring respiratory volume and blood gas levels. The respiratory system provides oxygen to and removes carbon dioxide from blood during breathing, whose rate increases during exercise. The integumentary system's skin receptors send temperature and other sensation information to the brain. The **autonomic nervous system** controls sweat gland secretions and peripheral blood flow during exercise.

## Energy for Muscular Contraction

**Adenosine triphosphate (ATP)** is a molecule with an adenosine nucleotide attached to three phosphate groups, providing energy for muscular contractions, converted via cellular respiration from food energy. Its energy store is released for muscles to access when the bond is broken between its second and third phosphate groups. When this bond is broken, the third phosphate group is released by itself, reducing the ATP molecule to **adenosine diphosphate (ADP)** with two phosphate groups. Replacing the third phosphate group, i.e., rephosphorylization, restores ADP into ATP again. The process of cellular respiration that converts food energy to ATP depends largely upon how much oxygen is available. Exercise intensity and duration affect the amounts of oxygen the muscle cells demand and the oxygen supply available to them. Depending on the amount of oxygen available, any one of three exercise energy systems can be accessed selectively: the alactic anaerobic energy system, the lactic anaerobic energy system, or the aerobic energy system.

## Energy to Muscles: When and How

Short-term (10 seconds or less), high-intensity, explosive exercise recruits the **alactic (not producing lactic acid) anaerobic (not using oxygen) energy system**, e.g., a 100-meter sprint or one weightlifting set. Also called the **ATP-PCr (adenosine triphosphate-phosphocreatine) or phosphagen energy system**, this is the first accessed for exercise. It uses ATP stored in muscles and then rephosphorylizes the resulting ADP via phosphocreatine. It stops supplying energy when PCr is depleted until muscles have rested and regenerated PCr. High-intensity exercise for up to 90 seconds, e.g., one ice hockey shift or an 800 meter sprint, uses the lactic anaerobic energy system. It functions when the alactic anaerobic system is depleted and the aerobic system cannot handle the exercise intensity's demands. It produces lactic acid as a byproduct in the muscles but does not use oxygen. It directly accesses cellular respiration to convert food energy to supply ATP. Continuous/long-term (beyond 2-5 minutes), lower-intensity aerobic exercise, e.g., running marathons, accesses the aerobic energy system, which depends upon how efficiently oxygen can be sent to and processed by the muscles. It also recruits cellular respiration to get ATP from food energy; however, oxygen is available to the muscles, so no lactic acid is produced.

## Principle of Specificity

The **principle of specificity** in exercise science means one must exercise the specific body part, muscle(s), or sport movements and techniques that one wants to improve. To strengthen the upper body, one must do exercises targeting the upper body, and the same for the lower body; one will not help the other. Someone who wants to play football must practice the skills specific to this sport; general body conditioning, while it might be a prerequisite, will not improve specific football skills. While core and cardio workouts are necessary to conditioning for improving overall endurance and strength, and the principle of specificity dictates that attaining one's specific goals requires tailoring one's exercise

- 131 -

regimen, neither one of these cancels out the other. The principle of adaptation means the body adapts to exercise, so that with regular practice, certain activities become easier. To continue improving, one must vary one's workouts with different training and/or routines. The body adjusts to demands made of it. **Adaptation** also means the body adapts to the processes of executing specific tasks.

### Principles of Overload and Individual Differences

The **principle of overload** means the body only responds beyond its normal level if new stimuli or additional pressures are introduced. Stopping within comfort zones maintains current skill levels, but brings no improvement. This is true for gaining strength, improving athletic ability, or losing weight. To increase what muscles can do, we must require them to function in unaccustomed ways. This is one reason exercise science professionals are helpful: they can push and motivate clients to work past their comfort zones. The principle of individual differences means not everybody will attain the same results from the same training programs and levels. Every individual has different body chemistry: some must work harder than others for the same results. Another aspect of this principle is that some people are more predisposed to succeed in certain sports or workouts than others, who in turn are more predisposed to other activities. The **principle of individual differences** indicates the importance of personal training: individuals must tailor their exercise programs for meeting goals at their own paces. Even individuals with stronger talents or skills in a certain activity or sport need to practice it to enable their bodies to adapt.

### Principles of Progression and Exercise Science

The **progression principle** means, one must progress at a certain, individual rate to get results. While people must push past their comfort zones to improve, pressing oneself overly hard negates natural progression and can cause injury. An appropriate exercise routine is a science. While there is no "one-size-fits-all" formula, there is a formula determining how one should push oneself. The principles of progression and **overload** balance delicately: progression indicates specific times of being unready for overload, or benefiting from it. The **principle of use/disuse** means one must use muscles to sustain muscular strength—the proverbial "use it or lose it." When we do not practice a sport we want to improve in or use muscles we want to develop, we lose our skills and strength. Anytime we stop exercising or exercise less and notice we are no longer seeing results, this is evidence of the use/disuse principle. With disuse, muscles lose definition; the body compensates for the lack of practice. This is also called the **reversibility principle**. At times disuse can be valuable: muscle overuse requires healing. Otherwise, moderately high year-round fitness levels are better than seasonal detraining or retraining.

### Physical Training and Health

**Motivation** to follow and continue physical fitness routines can be supported by both the **short-term** and **long-term effects of exercise** on the body, including the brain. For example, training energetically accesses the body's glycogen stores to supply energy. Glycogen depletion then triggers the release of endorphins, hormones that bring feelings of well-being and euphoria (the word endorphin comes from Greek root words meaning "morphine within") in the short term. Additionally, in the long term, exercising regularly can both prevent and relieve depression. Some research studies comparing exercise to antidepressant medications have found exercise equally effective. In addition to the brain, exercise improves cardiovascular health. Physical activity requires the heart rate to increase to deliver oxygenated blood to the muscles. People new to exercising may initially feel dizzy and winded. However, in the short term, exercise increases blood circulation. In the longer term, exercising for a few months can lower one's blood pressure and pulse. Exercising regularly significantly predicts heart health. People who perform cardiovascular (aerobic) exercise consistently lower their long-term risks of heart attacks, strokes, and other cardiovascular disorders.

## Individual Differences on Learning

Research has shown that **situational interest** can help motivate students to become engaged in the process of learning. Studies find that teachers can change and arrange task presentation, the structuring of learning experiences, and instructional strategies to enhance student situational interest. Although most research into motivation in physical education is related to theories of achievement goals, these reportedly are not very predictive of motivation or performance. However, researchers find **student interest** to have greater influence on student learning behavior, as well as on student intentions for future participation. Despite educator recognition of the importance of interest to learning, researchers find teachers still lack clarity in understanding the roles they can play in helping to stimulate and develop students' interest. When individuals interact with the environment, two kinds of interest emerge: situational and individual. Both kinds have two phases. Situational interest has a phase when interest is **activated**, and an ensuing phase when interest is **sustained**. Individual interest has a phase when interest emerges, and an ensuing phase when interest is defined.

## Performance in Physical Education Activities

One element of individual differences is **age**. Some activities are not appropriate for students who have not attained physical maturity. Students also need to understand what their bodies can and cannot do as they pass through different developmental stages and periods. Students of very different ages should not be expected to compete against one another. Age affects strength, aerobic capacity, reaction time, flexibility, and experience. Humans do not attain full strength until about age 20. Humans are most flexible in their teens. Experience, which increases with age, is a crucial element in sports. Another individual difference is **somatotype**, i.e., body shape. This informs appropriate sport choices. There are three basic somatotypes.

- **Ectomorph**: a long, narrow, thin shape with minimal muscle or fat. Good sports for ectomorphs include long-distance running and the high jump.
- **Endomorph**: fat, and often pear-shaped, with narrow shoulders and wide hips, with small ankles and wrists but more fat on the torso, arms, and legs. Good sports for endomorphs include shot-putting and wrestling.
- **Mesomorph**: muscular, often wedge-shaped, with wide shoulders and narrow hips, strong limbs, and little body fat. Good sports for mesomorphs include gymnastics and swimming.

## Physical Education Performance

**Individual differences** include biological, physiological, and environmental factors affecting performance. For example, muscular tissue composition will influence individual strength, flexibility, and endurance. Individual deficits in rod and cone development in the eyes would inhibit perceptual-motor ability, which could alter reaction times. Children participating more in formal schooling will develop their verbal and reasoning skills further, while children participating more in physical education and/or sports will develop their motor skills further. Development rates across and within individuals vary by maturation and growth differences. **Perceptual-motor abilities** affecting individual skill performance include: control precision, e.g., hockey-puck handling; rate control, like racecar driving; aiming, e.g., texting; response orientation and choice reaction time, e.g., football quarterbacking; reaction time, e.g., sprinting; manual dexterity, e.g., basketball-dribbling; finger dexterity, e.g., typing; arm-hand steadiness, e.g., performing surgery; and wrist and finger speed, e.g., speed-stacking. Physical proficiencies affecting performance include: explosive strength, e.g., standing long jumps; static strength, e.g., weight-lifting;

trunk strength, e.g., pole-vaulting; extent flexibility, e.g., yoga; dynamic flexibility, e.g., squat-thrusts; limb movement speed, e.g., javelin-throwing; static balance; dynamic balance, e.g., gymnastics; object-balancing; multi-limb coordination, e.g., stick-shift driving; gross body coordination, e.g., hurdling; stamina, e.g., marathons; and dynamic strength, e.g.

## Positive Effective Physical Education

In the **psychomotor domain**, effective PE enhances student movement skills for participating in sports and other physical activities, and for being a spectator as well. It affords skills for applying cultural and intellectual pursuits to use leisure time, and skills for preserving the natural environment. In the **cognitive domain**, effective PE supports higher-order thinking processes through motor activity, enhances academic performance, provides understanding of the human body and knowledge of health and illness and of exercise, enhances understanding of the roles of sports and physical activity in American culture, and supports knowledgeable consumerism with goods and services. In the **affective domain**, effective PE supports a healthy response to physical activity. It adds to student aesthetic appreciation of beauty. It contributes to student self-esteem and facilitates self-actualization. It helps students direct their lives for setting worthwhile goals. PE reinforces humanistic values. It enables students to use the medium of play for enjoying rich social experiences. PE also informs cooperative play and social interactions. It teaches students fair play, good sportsmanship, and courtesy. Moreover, it supports humanitarian ideals and behaviors.

## Risks Associated with Physical Inactivity

According to Johns Hopkins medical experts, research has definitively proven that a **lack of physical activity** is a risk factor for cardiovascular disease and other health conditions. People who are less physically fit and less physically active are at higher risk of developing hypertension (high blood pressure). Research shows that even after eliminating the factors of smoking tobacco, drinking alcohol, and eating an unhealthy diet, people who are physically active are still less likely to develop coronary heart disease than people who are physically inactive. Moreover, depression and anxiety can be caused or exacerbated by lack of physical activity. Additionally, scientists think physical inactivity may raise risks for certain cancers. Studies have found obese or overweight people decreased their risks of disease significantly through physical activity. Scientists say lack of physical activity causes many thousands of deaths annually. People tend to become less active as they age. Women are more likely to live sedentary lifestyles than men. White, non-Hispanic adults are more likely to be physically active than Hispanic and black, non-Hispanic adults.

## Health Benefits and Disease

**Obesity** and **type 2 diabetes** are two common results of physical inactivity. While obesity contributes greatly to type 2 diabetes, there are also individuals who are not even overweight, but due to their being physically sedentary, combined with poor nutritional habits and other behaviors like smoking tobacco and drinking alcohol, and interacting with genetic predispositions—some of which are much more prevalent within certain racial/ethnic populations—have developed type 2 diabetes as well. Current research studies that find sitting for most of one's waking hours is as harmful to health as habits like smoking. Even when exercising an hour each day, sitting for the rest of the day still has significant negative health impacts. People who drink, smoke, never exercise, spend most of their time sitting, and experience high levels of emotional and/or psychological stress are at much higher risks for hypertension, heart attacks, strokes, type 2 diabetes, some cancers, mental and emotional disorders, poorer quality of life, and earlier mortality. Physical activity can aid weight control, lower risks for heart disease and some cancers, strengthen the muscles and bones, and enhance mental health. While physically active people are not immune to disease, they lower their risks for many illnesses.

## Injury Prevention and Cause

Research studies show that up to one half of all hip fractures could be prevented by engaging regularly in enough **moderate physical activity**. Physical activity that bears weight strengthens the bones and prevents them from becoming porous, brittle, and more prone to breaking. Another consideration is that regular physical activity improves coordination, balance, and flexibility. Better coordination, balance, and flexibility can lower a person's likelihood of falling during everyday life activities as well as during sports and recreational physical activities. Stronger bones can prevent fractures in the event of a fall, while improved coordination, balance, and flexibility can avert many falls in the first place. Studies have also proven that people who are physically inactive in general sustain more accidents and injuries than people who are physically active. Children who are physically inactive risk higher stress, anxiety, and lower self-esteem and are likelier to smoke and take drugs. Sedentary workers are absent from work more than active ones.

## Healthy Lifestyle

Because most American students today do not receive PE at the frequencies or durations recommended for optimal health, they must engage in **physical activity** outside of PE classes and outside of school. To constitute physical activity, brisk walking or other pursuits must use energy by moving the body at a level of intensity sufficient to raise one's body temperature to feel warmer, and to cause one to breathe somewhat deeper than normally. Some students who live close enough can walk to and from school daily. They can play intramural and outdoor sports at school. Outside school, they can vacuum the house, wash the car, cut the grass, do gardening, clean up their rooms, and help their parents with other housework. These combine the benefits of contributing to smooth household and family functions with being more physically active for better health. Students can ride bicycles, go swimming, dance, and take weekend nature walks as more physically active forms of recreation than playing video games or watching TV. Experts recommend that children and teens build up to at least an hour of moderate physical activity most days of the week, while adults should aim for at least a half-hour most days.

## Health-Related Physical Fitness

There are five major **components of physical fitness** that are directly related to health:

- **Cardiorespiratory endurance**. This is the ability of the circulatory system, i.e., the heart and blood vessels; and the respiratory system, i.e., the lungs, trachea, bronchi, pharynx, larynx, and diaphragm, to supply the muscles and the rest of the body with oxygen during continuing physical activity over time.
- **Muscular strength**. This is the greatest amount of force that any given muscle can generate during a single attempt.
- **Muscular endurance**. This is how long a given muscle is able to continue to perform an exercise or activity without becoming fatigued, i.e., becoming unable to perform the movement anymore.
- **Flexibility**. This is the ability to move the joints of the body through the full range of motion, e.g., when bending, turning, twisting, stretching, reaching, contracting, extending, etc.
- **Healthy body composition**. This refers to the ratio of lean muscle tissue to fatty tissue in the body. The amount of muscle should be greater in proportion to the amount of fat, though there should be at least enough fat to enable normal body functions.

## Kinds of Physical Fitness Training

**Weight training**, aka strength/resistance training, can use measured weights; exercise bands, exercise balls or other resistance gear; or one's own body weight. By exercising the musculoskeletal system,

- 135 -

resistance training improves neurological control of muscle functions and enlarges muscle fibers. This promotes both muscular strength and muscular endurance—strength by increasing the maximum force a muscle contraction can produce, and endurance by increasing the maximum amount of weight one can lift repeatedly and/or the maximum number of repetitions one can lift the same weight. **Cardiorespiratory endurance** is not simply aerobic training, as it requires overload, accessing both aerobic and anaerobic energy systems through circuit/interval/other training. **Stage training**, e.g., a three-stage model, involves:

- Developing baseline aerobic fitness at 65-75 percent of maximum heart rate, gradually increasing intensity and duration up to 30 minutes two or three times a week.
- Raising intensity to 65-85 percent of maximum heart rate/14-16 RPE or, in other words, raising the level of intensity from "challenging" to "difficult." Work-to-rest ratios progress from 1:3 to 1:2, then 1:1, gradually increasing interval durations.
- Short, high-intensity exercises (like sprinting) alternating with active recovery (like jogging), at 65-95 percent of maximum heart rate/17-19 RPE, or boosting the intensity from "difficult" to "impossible." Transitioning from stage (2) to (3) can take 2-3 months or more.

### Developing Flexibility

**Flexibility** not only improves muscular and aerobic training and sports performance and prevents athletic injuries, but also facilitates everyday life activities and prevents age-related mobility loss. **Flexibility training** releases muscle tension that builds up during workouts and reduces stress in working muscles; balances joint tension, improving posture; and makes muscles more pliable, decreasing injury risk. **Stretching exercises** should follow each workout, four to seven days weekly. Intensity should create slight muscular tension without causing pain. Instructors should remind learners to continue their breathing patterns throughout stretches. Duration varies according to individual motivation and needs, but generally should be at least 5 to 10 minutes per session. Instructors should design organized workouts to include stretching, as learners most frequently cut this short when pressed for time. **Static stretching**, done seated, is easy, safe, and (once learned) doable virtually anywhere without equipment or assistance; but limited in efficacy for competitive athletes or increasing flexibility in multiple ranges of motion (ROMs). **Dynamic stretching**, done standing, uses reciprocal inhibition of opposing muscles to develop active ROM, gradually increasing in intensity and speed. Best for athletes and as warm-ups for movement-based sports and activities, it should be taught and learned gradually with appropriate movements to prevent trauma from excessive ROM or speed.

### National PE and Sports Organization's Definitions.

The National Association for Sport and Physical Education (NASPE)'s Council on Physical Education for Children (COPEC) identifies **quality PE** as both developmentally and instructionally appropriate for the actual children involved. This council defines developmentally appropriate PE practices as acknowledging the changing abilities of children for moving, and as promoting those changes. **Developmentally appropriate PE programs** are defined as addressing developmental status, body size, age, fitness levels, previous experiences with movement, and other various individual student characteristics. NASPE's COPEC defines **instructionally appropriate education** as including both research-based and experience-based best known practices in programs that give all children maximal opportunities to learn and succeed. The council identifies the result of a PE program that is both developmentally and instructionally appropriate as a "physically educated" individual. NASPE (1990) defined a physically educated individual as someone who has learned the necessary skills for performing varied physical activities, participates regularly in physical activity, is physically fit, knows the benefits and implications of engaging in physical activities, and values physical activity and what it contributes to healthy lifestyles. NASPE deems appropriate PE programs significant first steps in becoming physically educated.

## Appropriate Vs. Inappropriate Practices

**Appropriate PE curriculum** enhances all students' physical, motor, cognitive, and affective fitness by balancing concepts, skills, games, educational gymnastics, and rhythm and dance experiences with an observable sequence and scope determined by goals and objectives appropriate for all students. **Inappropriate curriculum** is based on teacher backgrounds, preferences, and interests, e.g., mainly playing large-group or whole-class games without developed learning goals and objectives. Practices inappropriate for developing motor skills and movement concepts limit the number of activities, games, and opportunities for developing basic motor skills and concepts. Appropriate practices frequently offer students meaningful, age-appropriate opportunities to practice locomotor, non-locomotor, and manipulative motor skills, developing confidence in their ability to perform these. Students also develop functional comprehension of body awareness, spatial awareness, effort, relationships, and other movement concepts. Practices inappropriate for promoting cognitive development through PE do not give students opportunities to integrate PE with classroom, art, music, and other school experiences; and do not enable students' learning to move while moving to learn. Appropriate practices design PE activities considering both physical and cognitive development by enabling students to analyze, communicate, question, integrate, apply concepts, and attain multicultural worldviews, thereby integrating PE into the whole educational experience.

## Inappropriate Vs. Appropriate Practices

PE practices **inappropriate for promoting affective development** include teacher exclusion of activities that help students develop social skills, and overlooking opportunities to help children understand emotions they experience from PE participation. **Appropriate practices fostering affective development** include purposely designing and implementing activities through the school year, enabling students to collaborate, cooperate, and develop emerging social skills and positive self-concepts; and helping every student feel and appreciate joy and satisfaction from participating regularly in physical activity. Inappropriate approaches to fitness concepts include requiring participation in fitness activities without helping students understand why. Appropriate approaches include designing activities that aid students in understanding and valuing significant physical fitness concepts and how these contribute to healthy lifestyles. Inappropriate uses of physical fitness tests include testing twice yearly, only as required by states/districts, or to qualify students for awards; requiring testing without students understanding why or what their results imply; and/or requiring testing without sufficient conditioning or preparation. Appropriate practices include conducting ongoing fitness assessment to help students understand, maintain (or improve), and enjoy physical well-being; sharing results privately with students and parents to develop knowledge, competence, and understanding; and preparing students for tests as part of ongoing PE programs.

## Principles of Cardiorespiratory Endurance

PE teachers should explain to students that **cardiorespiratory fitness** is considered the most important component of physical fitness because it indicates effective functioning of their hearts, lungs, and blood vessels. They can tell them the heart is a pump with two sides: the right side supplies blood to the lungs, the left sends blood to different body systems. The vascular system provides body tissues with blood, which carries oxygen and carbon dioxide through the bloodstream. Cardiorespiratory fitness lowers risk of cardiovascular disease—America's foremost cause of death. It also reduces body fat and raises energy. PE teachers should encourage students to do all they can to avoid dying from **cardiovascular disease**, particularly if their families have histories of heart disease and/or diabetes. Cardiovascular disease screening measures total cholesterol, LDL, HDL, and triglycerides, which directly affect heart disease risk. Teachers should have students exercise aerobically, continuously using large muscles, to improve cardiorespiratory fitness, three to five days per week, at 60-85 percent of maximum heart rate, for 20-60

- 137 -

minutes continuously. Good exercises include walking, jogging, cycling, swimming, rowing, in-line skating, spinning, step aerobics, and dancing aerobically to music sustained at the necessary intensity.

## Fitness Testing and Cardiorespiratory Endurance

According to the National Association for Sport and Physical Education (NASPE, 2010) position statement, PE programs not only develop student physical skills and cognitive understanding about physical activity to inform physically active, healthy lifestyles, they also teach students the significance of **health-related fitness**. NASPE states that, for students to achieve these goals, they must acquire knowledge about health-related fitness components, and a required part of that learning process is the assessment of those components. A philosophy of fitness testing includes that **purposeful measurement** is a necessary part of quality PE, and fitness education is a component of the PE curriculum conforming to exercise physiology standards. Additionally, **assessment** and **measurement** should be integrated with instruction. Moreover, educators should develop plans for applying individual student fitness data to inform their instruction. **Cardiorespiratory endurance** can be tested in elementary schools using a mile or half-mile run, e.g., the PACER (Progressive Aerobic Cardiovascular Endurance Run) Test. Measurements are number of PACER laps run, and time in minutes taken to complete a mile. Some schools require assessment twice yearly (beginning and end), but require instruction and practice throughout the school year. Baseline and subsequent data enable monitoring student progress.

## Cardiorespiratory Endurance Safety

When exercising to develop greater **cardiorespiratory endurance**, students need not engage in strenuous activity. Teachers should start them slowly doing activities they enjoy, and supervise them in gradually increasing the intensity of their pace. Activities to improve cardiorespiratory endurance should elevate the heart rate for an extended duration of time, but at a safe level. These include activities like walking, bicycling, or swimming. PE experts say it is impossible to overemphasize the importance of drinking water before, during, and after exercising. Sweating during exercise depletes the body of fluid and electrolytes, which can disrupt heart rhythms, so hydration and rehydration are paramount. It is also important to pay attention to the heat index—i.e., the effect that higher humidity has of raising the actual temperature to a functionally higher heat—when exercising outdoors, and modify workouts accordingly. Not only does humidity make temperatures effectively higher, it also prevents perspiration from evaporating, which keeps bodies from cooling off efficiently and can result in overheating, heat exhaustion, and heat prostration. Clothing unsuited to the weather can also cause serious health problems.

## Benefits of Flexibility Training

**Flexibility** is the ability to move the body freely. It encompasses two parts: **range of motion (ROM)**, which is the extent of direction and distance that one's joints are able to move; and **mobility**, which is the ability of the muscles to move with restrictions around the joints. By pursuing flexibility training, one realizes benefits including increasing one's range of motion; decreasing one's risks for becoming injured during physical activities by making muscles more pliable, less stiff, and less prone to pulls, tears, ruptures, sprains, etc.; decreasing the soreness of muscles following exercise by keeping muscles more relaxed and looser; and enhancing overall athletic performance by using less energy for body movement through having more flexible muscles and joints. Flexibility not only improves sport performance, it also facilitates activities of daily living like lifting objects or children, squatting down, reaching high shelves, getting out of bed, and turning fully to see behind oneself when backing up or parking a car.

## Stretching Exercises

**Stretching** is an equally important part of fitness as strength and aerobic capacity, although some people often overlook it in training programs. Stretching before and after performing other conditioning exercises promotes flexibility and prevents stiffness, soreness, and even injuries. Before stretching, one should always warm-up. Injuries are more likely from stretching cold muscles. One should stretch the whole body, not just selected parts. Each stretch should be held for 15 to 30 seconds or more, but should *not* include bouncing, which can cause injuries. One should stretch until one feels some mild tension in the muscle or the joint, but not actual pain. Pain is a signal to stop whatever one is doing. When resuming, do not stretch as far, as hard, or as quickly; or stretch in a different manner or direction. While stretching, one should never hold one's breath, but should always continue to breathe normally.

## Different Basic Full-Body Stretches

Arms above head, palms up, stretch arms upward: stretches forearms, front upper arms, chest, and upper side muscles. Arms behind back, hands turned inward, stretch arms backward: stretches chest, shoulder, upper arms. Raise arm, bend elbow, place hand on the back. With other arm, grasp opposing elbow, pull upward toward opposite side: stretches outer upper arm, side, and back on raised-arm side. Arms outspread at sides below shoulders, move arms inward, stretching chest, shoulder, front and back arms. Sit with one leg straight, one knee bent upward, lower leg across straightened leg, foot on floor. Turn upper body away from crossed leg, placing hands on floor to side: stretches ribcage, leg, and outer hip. Sit with knees bent outward, as low to floor as possible, feet together, clasping feet with hands: stretches hips, inner thighs. Sit, legs together straight in front, feet flexed. Lean forward, stretching hamstrings. Stand, one hand touching surface; bend opposite knee behind; pull ankle up with same-side hand, stretching quadriceps. Bend from hips/waist; touch toes, stretching backs of legs, lower back. Hands on wall, one foot back, step forward with opposite foot: stretches back lower leg. Perform all one-sided stretches on each side.

## Muscular Strength and Endurance

**Muscular strength** equals how much force one can produce within one effort. **Muscular endurance** equals how many times one can repeat a movement before muscles become too fatigued to work. As examples, the amount of weight an individual can bench-press signifies that person's muscular strength; the number of times that individual can bench-press that weight repeatedly before fatiguing indicates that person's muscular endurance. The two are not necessarily equal in the same person. Some people can lift enormous amounts of weight, but only a few times, showing high muscular strength but low muscular endurance. Some people can lift a lesser amount of weight, but can repeat it many times, meaning lower muscular strength and higher muscular endurance. Others are high or low in both muscular strength and endurance. People can develop both muscular strength and muscular endurance through strength training, e.g., lifting weights or using resistance, by both executing many repetitions of the same action, gradually increasing the number of repetitions; and also gradually increasing the amount of weight or resistance used. One may build muscular strength and endurance in all muscle groups of the body, or concentrate on specific muscles or muscle groups.

## Upper-Body Muscular Strength and Endurance

In lifting weights, one can work each arm **individually** using dumbbells, or both arms **together** using barbells. One thing to remember is that training each arm individually can result in slightly different levels of muscular strength and endurance in each arm. To begin workouts for the arms, use a general strength-training routine. Starting with weights of 20 pounds or lower, lift them 12 times; 12 repetitions (reps) equal one set. Do two or three sets of 12 repetitions each. As this becomes easier, start to lift heavier weights in small increments. Also gradually increase the number of sets performed. Increasing the weight builds muscular strength. Increasing the sets builds muscular endurance. One excellent exercise to increase upper-body muscular strength and endurance is doing push-ups. These build the pectoral muscles in the chest, the triceps muscles at the backs of the upper arms, and the deltoid muscles at the fronts of the shoulders. Even a few push-ups can be difficult for people lacking upper-body strength. Perform 10 repetitions, beginning with only one or two sets. Increase by two repetitions per week. Building upper-body strength enables more forceful arm extensions for bench-pressing, swimming, throwing, and more push-ups.

## Lower-Body Muscular Strength and Endurance

Among the best **lower-body and leg exercises** are squats and lunges. These increase strength and endurance in the gluteus maximus, gluteus medius, gluteus minimus, and tensor fasciae latae muscles of the buttocks; the hamstrings along the backs of the legs; the quadriceps at the fronts of the thighs; and the gastrocnemius and soleus muscles in the calves. Strengthening these muscles improves running speed, power, distance, and stamina. A variation of squatting and lunging is to perform these holding dumbbells in both hands to increase weight resistance. To build muscular strength and endurance in the buttocks and legs, do three to five sets of 10 squats and/or lunges per set every other day. Some trainers recommend engaging in boxing and martial arts as sports that require high intensity and increase muscular strength and endurance. Striking opponents or punching bags with force requires muscular strength; going through 12 rounds in a boxing match requires endurance. While martial arts can involve the hands, arms, legs, and weapons, these sports also require strength and endurance to win. Learning both boxing and martial arts involves combinations of various cardiovascular, strength-training, and mental conditioning activities.

## Body Composition

**Body composition** is basically the ratio of fatty tissue to non-fatty tissue, especially lean muscle tissue, in the body. For people who are overweight, improving their body composition entails both decreasing their total proportion of **body fat** and increasing their total proportion of **lean muscle tissue**. For people who are underweight, it can include both gaining some body fat and also more muscle tissue. For people with normal weights and without excess fatty tissue but lacking muscular development, it involves increasing the proportion of lean muscular tissue in the body. While isolation exercises work only one joint at a time, **compound exercises** use movements that require articulations of multiple joints at a time. Compound exercises are best for improving body composition. Compound pushing exercises improve upper-body composition through resistance movements of the arms and shoulders. Those using horizontally loaded resistance include push-ups and weighted flat, incline and decline bench-presses, which work the pectorals, triceps, serratus, and lateral deltoid muscles. Exercises using vertically loaded resistance include the shoulder press and military press, which work the anterior deltoid, upper pectoral, and trapezius muscles.

## Aerobic Exercise

While strength training increases muscle and decreases fat, **aerobic training** is also effective for decreasing body fat. **Visceral fat**, surrounding the vital organs and concentrated in the abdomen, is more of a threat to health than subcutaneous fat, found elsewhere just below the skin. Recent research finds that high-intensity exercise reduces more visceral fat than moderate-intensity exercise. The "HIIT" method stands for "high-intensity interval training." **High-intensity interval training** involves exercising at high intensity and also to develop endurance. It can include running, sprinting, climbing stairs, running up and down stadium steps, or any other aerobic exercise performed at intensity levels of seven out of 10 or above. An example of high-intensity interval training would be running on a track, road, path, or treadmill at 70-95 percent of maximum capacity for 30 seconds to 5 minutes; resting for a duration equal to or greater than the exercise duration; and repeating the interval, for a total of approximately 22 minutes, at least three days of the week.

## Safety Practices to Observe

Before beginning any kind of exercise program, one should discuss it with a doctor or **healthcare provider(s)** to ensure types and amounts of exercise are safe for one's individual health, and learn whether s/he advises avoiding any particular activities because of specific health conditions (e.g., heart conditions) and/or previous injuries (e.g., not using arm poles while walking on a treadmill following a recent shoulder or upper-back injury). Then one should also have a consultation with a **personal trainer** who can assess body composition and develop an individualized training program targeting types of conditioning most needed and body parts needing contouring and what kinds, e.g., building muscle, increasing definition, reducing fat, changing shape, etc. Everybody should always warm-up for at least 10-15 minutes first. After warming up properly, they should then perform stretches with all muscle groups and joints to increase flexibility and lower risks for injuries. People should not eat large meals immediately before exercising, but they should eat a small meal 2-3 hours before, or a snack 30-60 minutes before. Drinking water before, during, and after working out is imperative.

## Muscular Endurance

- The **continuous tension** form of muscular endurance makes demands on the muscles to be under continuing tension for extended durations of time. Some continuous tension activities appropriate for middle school students include tug-of-war, isometric muscle contractions, extremely slow muscle contractions, isolation exercises, compound exercises without lockouts, beginning weight training, and supervised mountain climbing or wall climbing.
- The **repetitive dynamic contraction** form of muscular endurance requires repeated muscle contractions over time periods. Some middle-school activities include running, bicycling, swimming, rowing, skating, and weight training involving many repetitions and/or supersets using the same muscle.
- The **prolonged, intense contractions with short rest periods** form of muscular endurance involves contractions for longer durations with brief recovery periods between bouts. Some activities include playing football; handball; ice hockey; and weight training that involves circuit training (going from one exercise or machine to another in a circuit), performing multiple sets of repetitions, and/or performing multiple different exercises to work the same muscle.

## 4-9 Gymnasium or Outdoor Activities

**Body core strength** provides a foundation for all sports and physical activities. Here are some gym/outdoor activities with core-strengthening exercises for grades 4-6 and 7-9. Equipment includes one basketball, volleyball, soccer ball, or medicine ball per student; jump ropes; folding mats; ribbon sticks, scarves, pom-poms; exercise bands; and masking tape. Have students warm-up first and then choose partners and balls. Teachers review exercises for core strength and stability. Considering any student physical limitations or injuries, teachers offer variations and/or have students suggest variations. Exercises include abdominal crunches with feet on floor, feet raised 90 degrees, and elbow-to-opposite-knee; V-sits (legs and torso form a V); twisting V-sits; same-sided hand-to-heel touch sit-ups; bicycles; hip raises; dolphin kicks; side planks; alternating leg-lowering from 90 degrees; and "superhumans" lying prone, raising opposite arm and leg alternately. Partners alternate: one performs, one gives feedback. Students may roll dice to decide repetition numbers, or repeat to muscle fatigue. Individual students record activities and repetitions they completed. Use these for future reference to monitor progress. Ribbon sticks, scarves, pom-poms and exercise bands can help some students extend their movements.

Teachers encourage students to practice their favorite activities every 15 minutes for 30 seconds while watching TV, doing homework, or using computers.

## K-6 Gymnasium Activity

This **creative dance activity** for grades K-3 and 4-6 builds endurance and develops spatial awareness and concepts. Equipment needed includes audio player, recorded music, and pathway signs. Teachers review space concepts of direction and pathways, e.g., combining locomotor movements with directions. Teachers call out forward, backward, and sideways directions for students to take while moving around the gym; then combine a locomotor pattern and direction, e.g., walking backward, skipping sideways, galloping forward, etc. Teachers draw these patterns on pathway signs and post on the walls. Teachers point at pathway pictures and have students move using these, first using two body parts and then three, for example, straight, zigzag, small curves, larger curves; small spirals, larger spirals. Teachers lead students around the gym in a large spiral pathway. Have students move in pairs to pathways they choose; have some pairs demonstrate. Have students combine three or more pathways and directions to create "movement stories." Remind them to notice others' movements, shoulder-check while moving backward, and avoid collisions. Have some students demonstrate stories and others identify directions and pathways included. Use music with strong beats during story creation and presentation. For more complexity, have students add shapes (square, rectangular, circular, triangular, figure-eight, or favorite letter, for instance) into stories.

## Improving Overall Physical Fitness

When students who have been inactive want to lose weight and/or become more physically fit, their initial enthusiasm assures their motivation to pursue these goals; however, they must be counseled to **moderate** their eagerness to obtain results quickly or they will strain their muscles or overwork their entire bodies. Particularly when they are not already conditioned, they must be warned not to begin at high intensity or repeat initial workouts obsessively. These practices cause injuries, derailing fitness efforts early. Students should be taught to begin **slowly**, paying attention to their bodies' feedback; when they feel ready, they can increase their intensities, speeds, repetitions, and durations gradually, a little at a time. **Incorrect form** is also a hazard for inexperienced exercisers. They should begin working out in front of mirrors to observe and modify their body positions as needed. Teachers and trainers can help correct form. Students should determine they are using proper form before increasing the speed of their repetitions. Another consideration is **not focusing overly on body parts**. Students may think exercises to tone and build specific muscles will give them their desired appearance; however, regular exercise combined with healthy nutrition more effectively shape bodies overall.

## Safety and Efficacy for Strength Training

- Never hold your breath, which can cause lightheadedness, dizziness, and fainting.
- Never lock elbows, knees, or other joints; this produces tremendous stress and can cause injuries.
- When lifting barbells, always use bar collars.
- Concentrate on lifting and lowering weights slowly with control to maximize effectiveness and prevent injury.
- When using free weights, always have a spotter to help prevent injuries and with using correct form.
- When using free weights, always keep both hands at equal distances from the middle of the bar. Unequal distances can stress and injure one side of the body.
- Never overly bend or twist the spine; this can cause lower back problems and injuries.
- While using weights standing up, always keep the knees slightly bent to prevent undue stress on the lower back.

- When doing leg exercises with weights or resistance, always keep the knees in alignment with the toes to avoid leg injuries.
- Always replace weights so others will not trip over them. Always place weights on the correct racks so others do not mistakenly pick up the wrong weights.

## Biomechanical Principles

Using **biomechanics** correctly ensures safety. For example, lunges with knee aligned over ankle are safe; lunges extending the knee past the ankle are mechanically incorrect and unsafe. Consider individual differences, e.g., a healthy 18-year-old female can safely do a squat-jump, but a 66-year-old female with osteoporosis cannot. **Biomechanical changes** informing ineffective, inefficient, or unsafe movements include: movement pattern changes, indicating fatigue and compensation with other body parts; body weight shifts, indicating fatigue or excessive difficulty; forward body flexion, indicating fatigue preventing muscles from overcoming gravitational pull; and flexed or bent joints, shortening muscles to be ineffective and inefficient, also indicating fatigued working muscles. According to the force-length curve, muscles generate their greatest force when slightly stretched or just past resting length. To choose safe, effective, and efficient exercises, incorporate walking, cycling, and other natural movement patterns. Repeat the same movements during and between lessons. Design lessons and programs in logical sequences or increments. Minimize degrees of freedom, i.e., number of joints involved. Minimize intersegmental coordination, i.e., different simultaneous arm and leg movements, such as an overhead press plus a squat. Select bilateral exercises for equal, opposite workloads. Distribute forces evenly across the body to minimize impact point. Apply forces horizontally or parallel, not vertically or downward to the body.

## Physical Fitness and Activity

A definition of **physical fitness** that applies to most people rather than only to professional athletes is being able to actively complete all of one's daily living tasks without becoming overly tired and still having enough energy to pursue leisure activities for enjoyment. **Physical activity** should include both planned, structured activities, and movement that is integrated into daily life as an essential part of it. Regularly engaging in physical activity and exercise are not only required for being athletic, but for basic well-being and health. To be effective and safe, any comprehensive physical fitness program should incorporate the three major components of

- **aerobic exercise**, to promote cardiovascular health, endurance, and to manage weight;
- **resistance training**, which decreases risks for lower-back injuries and pain, improves posture, builds strength and muscular endurance, and also manages weight; and
- **flexibility** to stretch the muscles and move the joints, which prevents sore muscles, decreases the chances of injury, and maintains and/or improves the range of motion of the joints and the mobility of the muscles.

## Aerobic Activity Levels

In fitness plans for most individuals, **aerobic activity** at a **moderate level** is recommended to add up to 150 minutes, or 2.5 hours per week. Aerobic activity at a **vigorous level** is recommended for half that duration, i.e., 75 minutes per week. Individuals may also choose to combine or alternate moderate and vigorous aerobic activities for equivalent durations. During activities at moderate intensities, people are able to speak but unable to sing. During activities at vigorous intensities, people can only utter a few words before needing to pause for breath. Examples of moderate-intensity activities include walking briskly, 3 mph or faster; bicycling at less than 10 mph; playing doubles tennis; doing water aerobics; ballroom dancing, and dancing in general. Examples of vigorous-intensity activities include running, jogging, race-walking; bicycling at more than 10 mph; playing singles tennis; swimming laps; aerobic dancing; doing heavy, continuous gardening that raises the heart rate; hiking with a heavy backpack or uphill; and jumping rope.

## Personal Fitness Plan

To **assess** individual current status, define fitness goals, and identify what one is able or willing to do to achieve them, identify the following: current age; indicators of the current body fat, e.g., a "six-pack," a small belly, or a large belly; and an index of current strength, e.g., one can do a few push-ups and pull-ups, at least 10 good push-ups and five good pull-ups, or at least 20 good push-ups and 10 good pull-ups. Define a **fitness goal**, e.g., wanting people to perceive you (a) are trim and healthy, (b) must work out, or (c) must compete athletically. Define how soon you want or need to accomplish this goal, e.g., in a few months to a year, 1-2 years, or 3-6 years. To define what you are able or willing to do, identify whether you have about 2-4 hours, 5-10 hours, or 11-21 hours weekly to devote to fitness. Nutritionally, are you willing to substitute a few healthy for unhealthy foods, or consistently avoid junk food and eat produce, whole grains, and lean protein? Or eat six small meals daily and follow a strict dietary plan? Individuals should also identify their available exercise equipment and partners.

## Health-Related Fitness

PE programs and teachers instruct students not only in sport skills, but also in the significance of **health-related fitness**. PE teachers need to help students develop both comprehension cognitively and competence physically to engage in regular physical activity to enable them to follow physically active, healthful lifestyles. To do so, students need to learn about health-related fitness needs, principles, and goals. One required component of this learning process is the assessment of fitness through **testing**. Some examples of fitness tests often used to assess elementary school student fitness include measuring the number of push-ups, curl-ups, and chin-ups they can do, and how well they can repeat these to a beat, to assess muscular strength and endurance. To assess flexibility, PE teachers may measure how far in inches a student can reach while sitting and how far s/he can stretch. To assess cardiorespiratory endurance and aerobic capacity, a common measure is how many laps a student can run, and the time in minutes it takes a student to run a mile or a half-mile.

## Fitness Assessment Data

**Fitness assessment data** furnishes students, teachers, parents, and other stakeholders with student fitness feedback. Comparing baseline to subsequent data enables PE teachers to **monitor student progress**. PE teachers can also use fitness testing data to inform their curriculum development decisions about which program content will best address students' strengths and needs. Students can make use of their own fitness testing data to inform measurable goals they set for personal fitness plans. PE teachers can use fitness testing results to individualize and differentiate their instruction for each student to help them achieve their goals. Fitness assessment data can also be used **motivationally**: identifying skill improvements and attaining goals give students incentive to live active, healthy lives. When PE teachers conduct authentic fitness assessments, the results inform the context for the curricula and activities they plan. This helps students comprehend the reasons for PE activities, rather than assuming PE is simply playing games. Student motivation for physical activity; understanding of how to evaluate and improve personal fitness levels; self-assessment, data analysis, and development of personal fitness goals and plans are also enabled by using fitness data.

## Conducting Fitness Assessment

According to the National Association for Sport and Physical Education (NASPE), **fitness assessment** is one of the components of the continual process of enabling students to comprehend, maintain, improve, and enjoy physical fitness that PE teachers should use. PE teachers should physically prepare students in each fitness component and testing protocol of the assessment instruments used to ensure safe participation. Teachers should do everything needed to establish non-threatening, private, encouraging, and educational testing circumstances. For example, they should explain to students what each test is designed to evaluate. They should encourage students to use test results as springboards for personal progress, not to compare themselves with others. Teachers should ensure the privacy of students and parents when sharing test results and not post these publicly to compare. They should use these results as tools to help students and parents develop individual goals and strategies to sustain and improve fitness measures. Teachers should also report student progress regularly to students and parents. Students should be informed immediately after testing of their scores, and use these during instruction throughout the school year. Parents should receive student fitness reports following completed assessments.

## Personal Fitness Programs

Statistics show that half of all people who embark upon exercise programs **abandon** them within only six months of beginning. Therefore, personal trainers recommend assorted techniques to adopt that will increase the likelihood of sticking with an exercise program long enough to make it a **permanent lifestyle change** and reap its benefits to health and well-being. One technique is to identify the best **location** for exercising. Students who do not get enough exercise through school PE classes need to choose places best suited for them. Some will find working out at a gym offers fewer distractions and better facilities, equipment, and trainers; others will find exercising at home more convenient. Distantly located gyms decrease the likelihood of attendance. Students should also identify the **time(s)** with the most convenience and fewest distractions for exercising; and the activities they enjoy most because the more convenient and fun a program is, the more likely they are to continue it. Starting exercise at overly high **intensities** and/or durations predicts dropout. Those who work out with more experienced partners may also overdo it.

## Establishing and Monitoring Fitness Goals

Adults and students alike should set **fitness goals** that lead to long-term changes in lifestyle and are realistic. Goals should include both **results** and **behaviors**. For example, jumping 1 inch higher by the next sport season and losing 12 pounds within three months reflect outcome goals. Exercising every weekday at 7:30 p.m. for 20 minutes is a behavioral goal. To set suitable behavioral goals, students should understand the underlying objectives. Students can have far more control over accomplishing behavioral goals than outcome goals, so they should focus on attaining those target behaviors. If they do not meet short-term outcomes by their original goal deadlines, they should not let this discourage them. When they do accomplish outcome-related goals, students should change their behavioral goals accordingly. If they are not sure they can meet behavior goals consistently, or if they find more effective ways of meeting their objectives, students should re-evaluate their fitness plans.

## Motivation and Commitment to Fitness

Planning specific workout times and establishing a **routine** helps physical activity become a habit. Students can enter these in their smartphone or tablet calendars like appointments; set alarms to remind them when to exercise; and pack workout bags or lay out exercise clothes and gear in advance. If they sometimes don't feel like exercising, they can agree with themselves to do just a short, light workout. Once prepared and warmed up, they will often become motivated for a full session. They should not give up hope if they miss a session, but reevaluate their fitness behavior plans, adjust strategies to prevent future omissions, recommit, analyze past barriers and identify new strategies to surmount them, and make backup plans for unexpected events or situations. Doing a variety of activities and exercises maintains interest. This includes fun activities like playing sports, kayaking; practical ones like walking dogs, yard work, walking to the store; and trying out new activities. Planning activities for the week or month helps. So does changing workouts according to changing interests and moods. Music, TV, and/or reading while walking, jogging, or cycling prevent boredom. Partners provide social support. Pedometers, stop watches, heart monitors, etc., and logging activity in writing or on digital devices help monitor progress.

## Diet, Physical Activity, and Health

**Regular physical activity** aids in weight control; strengthens the heart, blood vessels, lungs, muscles, bones, and joints; and lowers risks for heart disease, stroke, diabetes, and various cancers. However, physical activity must be combined with good **nutrition** to be most effective. In fact, improper nutrition can even undermine any benefits of physical activity. For one thing, the body requires fuel to be physically active. People who eat too little and/or eat food that is not nutritious will not have enough energy to exercise. For another, foods high in refined sugars and flours and saturated fats will actually cause fatigue, depriving a person of energy and motivation to be active. In addition, people who want to build muscle cannot do so through strength training alone; they must eat lean proteins to supply the amino acids that are the building blocks of muscle. Foods high in refined sugars and flours and saturated fats are also very high in calories. Exercising, even vigorously for hours, is usually insufficient to burn as many calories as one can easily consume from the junk foods, fast foods, and restaurant foods so prevalent in modern society. Improper nutrition can derail the health benefits of physical activity.

## Physical Activity, Weight, and General Health

To lose weight, you must expend more calories than you consume. In other words, weight loss requires a **calorie deficit**. Although most people lose weight by reducing the calories they eat, research evidence also finds regularly engaging in **physical activity** necessary for maintaining that weight loss. This explains why so many people who do not engage in enough regular physical activity regain weight after losing it. Even when people have lost weight, if they are physically active on a regular basis they lower their risk of diabetes and cardiovascular disease beyond the risk reduction afforded by weight loss alone. To put the relationship between diet, exercise, and weight into perspective, consider that a Big Mac from McDonald's has about 550 calories. A person who weighs about 150 pounds would have to run at a speed of 5 mph for an hour to burn that many calories. Few if any people who just ate a Big Mac will want or be able to run that fast for that long. Moreover, its high saturated fat content, refined white flour, etc. all contribute to cardiovascular disease, diabetes, and cancers.

## Deficiencies in Nutrition and Physical Activity

According to the Centers for Disease Control and Prevention (CDC), **physical inactivity** and **poor diet** are major causes of chronic non-communicable diseases, from which hundreds of thousands of people die every year. In addition to deaths, disabilities caused by strokes, obesity, diabetes, and osteoporosis are the results of improper nutrition and sedentary lifestyles. The Healthy People initiatives have found that almost two-thirds of Americans eat too much saturated fat, three-quarters do not eat enough fruit, and more than half do not eat enough vegetables. People who are inactive physically have nearly twice the probability of developing heart disease as people who are active regularly. This makes physical inactivity approach high blood pressure, high cholesterol, or smoking cigarettes as a risk factor for heart disease. However, physical inactivity is a more prevalent risk factor than any of those others. Sedentary people who are also obese and have high blood pressure, and hence have multiple risk factors, can especially benefit from becoming physically active.

## Diet for Healthy Weight

According to the US Centers for Disease Control and Prevention (CDC) and the federal Dietary Guidelines, a **healthy diet** should place the most emphasis on fruits and vegetables, whole grains, and fat-free or low-fat dairy products. It should also include lean protein sources like beans, fish, eggs, nuts, poultry, and lean meats. It should eliminate or limit trans fats, saturated fats, salt, added sugars, and cholesterol. In addition, a balanced diet should not contain many more or fewer calories than an individual needs every day to function optimally. Eating fresh produce in season, especially produce grown locally, is best. When favorite fruits are out of season or unaffordable, they are available frozen, canned, or dried. One caveat is to avoid canned fruits with heavy, sugar-laden syrups and find those canned in their own juices. If fresh vegetables are unavailable, many are flash-frozen at their peak nutritional value without added sodium or fatty sauces. For canned vegetables, avoid those with added sodium. Some ways to enjoy vegetables more include steaming them; adding different herbs, which provide flavor without salt or fat; sautéing in non-stick pans with a little cooking spray; and trying a new or unfamiliar vegetable every week.

## Weight Management Strategies

The healthiest diets involve **balance** rather than completely eliminating foods we enjoy. Many people's favorite "comfort foods" happen to have high caloric, sugar, and/or fat content. To lose weight and/or maintain weight loss, it is not necessary to give up these foods entirely, though. One strategy is to indulge in fattening foods, but less often. For example, instead of every day, eat them once a week, or even once a month. Not eating high-calorie foods as frequently reduces overall calories. Another strategy is enjoying fattening foods in smaller portions. For example, if a favorite comfort food is a candy bar, only eat half of it or buy it in a smaller size. Manufacturers offer many miniature, "snack size," or "fun size" candy bars. Sometimes taste and texture provide enough enjoyment rather than amount. Another strategy is comfort food "makeovers." For example, macaroni and cheese can be remade with skim milk instead of whole milk, low-fat cheese, and less butter. Some people incorporate healthier foods to lower calories while adding fiber and nutrients, e.g., cauliflower in macaroni and cheese, puréed spinach or beets in brownies, etc.

## Maintaining Current Weight

Some individuals are not overweight, but will need to plan to avoid gaining weight. Others are overweight, but currently not ready to lose weight. In either case, **weight maintenance** has the benefits of preventing many chronic diseases, as well as minimizing the need for future weight loss. The number of calories needed to maintain weight varies individually. Variables affecting this include height, weight, gender, age, levels of physical activity, and muscle-to-fat ratio. Muscle tissue burns more calories than fatty tissue, even at rest. Thus some people have higher basal metabolisms than others; these people can afford to consume more calories without gaining weight. Some of this body composition is natural, some lifestyle-related. More physically active people burn more calories and can eat more than sedentary people. To maintain current weight, it is useful for people to weigh themselves regularly. It is easier to lose a gain of 2-3 pounds discovered sooner than 10 pounds discovered later. If weight creeps up, it helps to self-examine changes in physical activity and eating. People can keep food diaries, activity logs, and use numerous available digital apps for self-monitoring.

## Participating in Physical Fitness

Experts say that, to be healthy, children and teens need to engage in **moderate physical activity** for around an hour a day, adults around half an hour a day, about five days a week. But most Americans fall far short of these parameters. Increasing the frequency and duration of physical activity improves health even more. People who want to lose weight or maintain their weight loss may need 40-90 minutes of physical activity daily. Modern conveniences plus school and occupational work primarily done seated interfere with physical activity. Lack of financial resources is another obstacle. People living in socioeconomically disadvantaged communities lack not only money, but often also accessible community recreation facilities like safe outdoor parks, indoor recreation centers, facilities, equipment, and clubs or other social groups focusing on physical activities. There are solutions, however. For time, physical activity like walking can be divided into small, 10-minute sessions three times daily. For motivation, family outings, free or low-cost group activities, and walking and exercise partners offer social support.

## Discuss Some Factors That Encourage Physical Activity in Communities and Families

Research finds people are more likely to engage in physical activities for recreation when they are located **near their homes** and are **free or inexpensive**. Even in communities containing beautiful state parks and other natural areas, citizens still prefer recreation that is closest to home and most affordable. People are more likely to exercise regularly when they live within 1 mile of a recreational facility. Another factor affecting physical recreation is safety. People who ride bicycles and walk or jog for recreation often must use public roads and streets, where motor vehicle traffic threatens their safety and discourages their participation. Some communities have obtained funding to create local bike, walking, and/or jogging paths separate and safe from road traffic. Because low-income families are less apt to enjoy access to recreational facilities, experts recommend that establishing free or low-cost facilities in low-income communities would make an appreciable difference in their physical activity levels, improving their health and enjoyment in life.

## Physical Activity Levels Among Diverse Populations

Experts recommend that **local government offices** should work together with members of their **communities** who represent people with disabilities, low incomes, and culturally and ethnically diverse backgrounds. Incorporating the input and insight these community members can contribute, they can **collaborate** to make organized plans; identify, secure, and prepare or renovate suitable sites; construct community recreation facilities; and staff, operate, and manage them. When families have access to recreational facilities that are close to their homes and provide safe environments, appropriate space and equipment, and beneficial social interaction, they are much more likely to engage in physical activity for recreation, benefiting their physical, mental, and social health and well-being. Some neighborhoods have organized local walking groups and activities in ethnically diverse communities. These combine greater physical activity with safety and social interaction. Residents report greater neighborhood pride and ownership and stronger sense of community. Mexican-American citizens have reported in focus groups that they value family-based physical activities. For culturally competent responses, recreation facilities should organize family exercise programs rather than individually targeting women, men, seniors, youth, etc.

## Physical Activity Addresses Stress

One way in which **physical activity combats stress** is by directly reducing it. Moving at moderate intensity long enough to increase the heart rate, breathe more deeply, work the muscles, and break a light sweat releases **endorphins**. These hormones, named from the Greek meaning "the morphine within," produce a naturally occurring "high," or sense of euphoria. Endorphins also alleviate physical and mental pain. People feel physically and mentally relaxed after expending energy; working the heart, lungs, and muscles; and perspiring and releasing toxins. Family and friends often observe someone they know well seems and feels much more "mellow" after exercising. Worries and negative attitudes are frequently dissipated by exercise. Another way physical activity affects stress is by improving the ability to **cope** with it. While some stressors are inherent in life and cannot themselves be eliminated, people's attitudes toward them can change markedly through being physically active. Increased physical strength, stamina,

- 148 -

and flexibility afford greater senses of personal competence and empowerment. Increased blood circulation enables clearer thinking, hence more effective problem-solving. Enhanced physical and mental health synergistically improve capacities for dealing with life's challenges.

## Enjoyment and Challenge

Enjoyment:

- A high school boy never interested in traditional intramural and team sports offered in PE classes sees a brochure on kayaking and decides to enroll in lessons at a local outdoor adventure training company. He finds navigating rapids thrilling and enjoys interacting with nature.
- Some low-income urban kindergarteners have done unstructured running, jumping, etc., and played simple games like Simon Says at home, but never learned any physically active games with rules. Their teacher introduces them to a variety of games wherein they must walk, run, change directions, link arms, jump, tumble, do extensions; throw, bowl, and fetch balls; touch things, etc., following teacher directions and rules. They enjoy these new experiences.

Challenge:

- A middle school girl can only do a few sit-ups. Her PE teacher assigns 30 sit-ups to alternating pairs. While spotting her partner—a pretty, thinner friend she admires, she sees the effort on her face with each sit-up. She is inspired to complete all 30 during her turn. A high school student has run 500-yard dashes, but never a marathon, and doubts her ability. Her PE teacher encourages her. After training regularly for three months, she successfully completes a full 26-mile race.

## Social Interaction and Healthcare Expenses

Social interaction:

- Two high school girls have free periods at the end of the day and don't want to wait for the bus. They decide to walk to one of their homes instead. During the 3-mile trip, they enjoy conversing and interacting in the outdoors more than on a noisy, crowded school bus.
- A boy in elementary school gets good grades but is socially introverted and lacks physical self-confidence. His parents offer to enroll him in Little League baseball. As he learns and succeeds he gains confidence, teammates applaud and encourage him, and he makes new friends.

Healthcare expenses:

- A diabetic child's mother is overprotective about exercise. The school nurse and PE teacher collaborate with her on a plan for regular blood sugar testing during the school day, suitable exercise, and appropriate snacks before and after exercising. As a result, her family doctor reduces the child's insulin dosage.
- A PE teacher, collaborating with a dietitian and school nurse, designs a safe fitness program for an obese high school student. With significant weight loss, his type 2 diabetes symptoms abate. He needs less medication and fewer doctor visits; as a result, his parents' health insurance co-pays decrease.

## Self-Concepts and Self-Esteem

International Council for Sport Science and Physical Education President and professor Margaret Talbot has written that challenging physical activities like sports and dance are powerfully influential for helping **youth** "learn to be themselves." She finds that, when presented appropriately, such activities teach young people to question assumptions they have held that limit them, and to perceive themselves and their potentials anew. In *Run Like a Girl: How Strong Women Make Happy Lives* (2011), Mina Samuels writes that once she discovered running, she not only gained self-confidence, but she found she was stronger than expected. As a result, she perceived herself differently, as someone with greater potential and a bigger future who could take risks and push herself—not just in sports but other life areas—by competing with herself rather than others, and setting and meeting higher expectations and standards for herself. Psychologists find physical self-worth, sense of autonomy and self-efficacy enhanced through developing competence in sport skills. Studies have found elementary, high school, and Latino students benefit with higher **self-esteem** from school sports participation and other physical activity.

## Mental and Emotional Well-Being

Many research studies find improvements in **mood**, with fewer symptoms of **anxiety and depression**, resulting from physical activity. Experiments have compared participants with major depression, giving some psychotropic medication and others an aerobic exercise intervention. The exercisers demonstrated more significant improvements and lower relapse rates than those taking the drugs. Other research has shown that walking programs increase positive mood. Six-month resistance training programs have decreased anger, tension, and confusion while elevating moods in participants. Investigators comparing the effects of yoga, dance, or lecture on participants' psychological well-being found significantly lowered negative affect and stress perception in the groups with the physical activities. Large-scale studies with adolescents find correlations between increased leisure-time physical activity and decreased symptoms of depression. In addition, research with 4th-grade Hispanic children from low-income families has found their self-esteem and cardiovascular fitness increased while their depression decreased when they participated in an aerobic intensity physical activity program.

## Self-Management Skills

**Self-assessment skills** enable: self-evaluating fitness and interpreting results, e.g., choosing and self-administering good fitness assessments; goal-setting and plan-making; and success, new thinking, and learning skills. Self-monitoring skills entail keeping records, enabling viewing one's behavior more objectively and accurately, and gauging progress toward goals. For example, if you cut calories yet aren't losing weight, record-keeping can reveal you are eating more than you thought. Keeping progress records also promotes adhering to fitness plans and programs. These skills supply information and feedback, help change beliefs, aid planning and goal-setting, and raise success probabilities. **Goal-setting skills** are particularly important for beginners at behavior change. They enable establishing achievable, realistic future objectives. For example, success is more likely for someone wanting to reduce fat with a process goal to eat 200 fewer calories and burn 200 more calories daily than an outcome goal to lose 50 pounds. These skills facilitate planning and feedback, build confidence, change attitudes and beliefs, and increase enjoyment and success. **Planning skills** enable independently designing fitness programs, reinforcement, self-confidence, success, and enjoyment. **Performance skills** enhance competence, self-confidence, attitudes, success, and enjoyment. An example is learning stress-management and relaxation skills. Balancing attitudes enhances planning; goal-setting; beliefs; and enjoyment, e.g., emphasizing exercise's positive aspects, not its negative.

# WEST-E Practice Test

1. The National Health Education Standards (NHES) were developed in response to what?
   a. Standards being developed in hospitals
   b. Standards being developed in education
   c. Standards being developed in public health
   d. Standards being developed in private practice

2. Which of the following is MOST accurate regarding the components of a coordinated school health program?
   a. School health education should be comprehensive.
   b. Physical education is separate from such a program.
   c. School health services are only for emergency care.
   d. Community and family are not part of this program.

3. Of the following diseases, which one is NOT caused by the Epstein-Barr virus?
   a. Infectious hepatitis
   b. Burkitt's lymphoma
   c. Infectious mononucleosis
   d. Nasopharyngeal carcinoma

4. According to Piaget's developmental theory, when do children first achieve mental operations?
   a. During the sensorimotor stage
   b. During the preoperational stage
   c. In the concrete operations stage
   d. In the formal operations stage

5. About 80 percent of all deaths from noncommunicable diseases are caused by four types of disease. Which of these four types causes the majority of these deaths?
   a. Diabetic
   b. Cancerous
   c. Respiratory
   d. Cardiovascular

6. Which statement is MOST accurate regarding the nature of decision-making for teenagers?
   a. The decisions teens make are unlikely to affect their long-term futures.
   b. Social contexts change; hence, teens must evaluate and adjust decisions.
   c. Teens generally have enough life experience to make difficult decisions.
   d. Intervention programs to improve decision-making skills are ineffective.

7. What is true about the privacy of records protected under Family Educational Rights and Privacy Act (FERPA)?
   a. Student health but not immunization records are protected by FERPA.
   b. Student health and immunization records are protected under FERPA.
   c. Student health but not public school nurses' records are protected under FERPA.
   d. Student special education records are protected under Individuals with Disabilities Education Act (IDEA), not FERPA.

8. What is a valid claim when comparing Rosenshine and Stevens' model of direct instruction with the Direct Instruction method of Engelmann and colleagues?

    a. Both are teacher directed, but only one is skills oriented.
    b. Both are face-to-face, but only one uses small groups.
    c. Both use task analysis, but only one is sequenced.
    d. Both teach explicitly, but only one is generic.

9. Of the following research methods for gathering health-related data, which one is most applicable to collecting aggregate information on large population groups?

    a. Questionnaires
    b. Observations
    c. Interviews
    d. Surveys

10. Among the life skills of values clarification, decision-making, communication, and coping skills, which of the following responses to stressful life events MOST reflects decision-making skills?

    a. Considering positive aspects of the situation
    b. Evaluating the pros and cons of the situation
    c. Expressing your feelings about the situation Com
    d. Positive behaviors to deal with the situation

11. According to Erikson's theory of psychosocial development, which ability must be achieved during the period of adolescence?

    a. Identity
    b. Intimacy
    c. Industry
    d. Autonomy

12. How is cardiorespiratory endurance best defined?

    a. The ability to perform dynamic exercise using large muscles over long times
    b. The ability to perform dynamic exercises using small muscles for short times
    c. The ability to perform static exercises using all muscles for average durations
    d. The ability to perform any kind of exercising using any muscles for any time

13. What is a common misconception among teenagers that health educators should correct?

    a. That conception cannot occur by body rubbing without vaginal or vulvar sperm contact
    b. That conception will not occur without penetration and ejaculation inside the vagina
    c. That teenage males should put on condoms before sex and wear them continuously
    d. That kissing or oral or anal sex will not cause pregnancy if no sperm touches the vulva or vagina

14. Within personal hygiene, which of these is a fact about oral care?

    a. Gum disease can cause serious disorders of the heart valves.
    b. Unhealthy gums can cause gum infections but not tooth loss.
    c. Brushing one's teeth prevents tooth decay, not gum disease.
    d. Gum disease affects soft tissues rather than the jaw's bones.

15. We get _____ from _____ in our diet and _____ from _____.
    a. Energy, protein; amino acids, carbohydrates
    b. Energy, vitamins; muscle repair, amino acids
    c. Energy, carbohydrates; amino acids, protein
    d. Energy, minerals; tissue repair, saturated fat

16. Which of the following correctly sequences the stages of change in the stages of change model of health behavior?
    a. Precontemplation, contemplation, preparation, action, maintenance
    b. Preparation, precontemplation, contemplation, action, maintenance
    c. Maintenance, preparation, precontemplation, contemplation, action
    d. Preparation, action, maintenance, precontemplation, contemplation

17. Of the four types of diseases—cancers, cardiovascular diseases, diabetes, and respiratory diseases—that cause the majority of deaths from noncommunicable diseases, which risk factors do they all share in common?
    a. Smoking and drinking
    b. Poor diet and inactivity
    c. All of these risk factors
    d. None of these factors

18. Teaching the idea that saturated fat in the diet contributes to heart disease is MOST developmentally appropriate to which stage of Piaget's theory of cognitive development?
    a. Sensorimotor
    b. Preoperational
    c. Formal operations
    d. Concrete operations

19. Which statement is accurate concerning U.S. laws governing immunizations?
    a. Federal laws specify immunizations for children to enter public schools.
    b. Laws regulating child immunizations for public school vary in each state.
    c. Certain states have laws about immunizations for school; others do not.
    d. As laws vary by state, there is no central data repository for these laws.

20. Which of the following major muscles controls the chewing functions of the jaws?
    a. The orbicularis oris muscle
    b. The zygomaticus muscles
    c. The trapezius muscles
    d. The masseter muscles

21. What is correct about the hormones that stimulate male and female organs to produce male and female sex hormones?
    a. Female organs are stimulated by female hormones and male organs by male hormones.
    b. The same hormones that produce male or female sex characteristics stimulate the organs.
    c. The same hormones stimulate both male and female organs to produce sex hormones.
    d. The hypothalamus stimulates the pituitary gland's secretion of male and female hormones.

- 153 -

22. What is true about guidelines for making emergency 911 calls?

    a. Call 911 for uncontrollable bleeding or unconsciousness but not allergic reactions or chest pains.

    b. Situations needing immediate help from police, fire departments, or ambulances merit 911 calls.

    c. Prank calls to 911 are a great nuisance and interfere with actual emergencies but are not illegal.

    d. When a person calls 911 in an emergency, he or she should hang up immediately to free up the lines.

23. What has been found by research into teacher influence on children's peer relationships as a social context factor?

    a. Teachers who believe in and relate positively with attention deficit hyperactivity disorder (ADHD) children can modulate peer dislike of them.

    b. Teachers have difficulty relating to children with ADHD; therefore, they cannot change peers' dislike.

    c. Teachers cannot affect dislike of ADHD children by peers rejecting them despite improved behavior.

    d. Teachers who create classrooms improving peer relationships eliminate all dislike of ADHD children.

24. When comparing the federal Healthy People 2000, 2010, and 2020 initiatives, which applies MOST?

    a. The 2000 initiative aimed to decrease health disparities, 2010 to eliminate them, and 2020 to establish health equity.

    b. The 2000 initiative aimed to eliminate health disparities, 2010 to establish health equity, and 2020 to improve health.

    c. The 2000 initiative aimed to improve American health, 2010 to reduce health disparities, and 2020 to eliminate them.

    d. The 2000, 2010, and 2020 Healthy People initiatives all have aimed to improve health for all Americans.

25. Which of the following is MOST appropriate concerning extracurricular activities for student health needs?

    a. A student should expect to feel overextended when participating in activities.

    b. A student should discontinue an activity if he or she cannot keep up with all things.

    c. A student should join only those activities that he or she already knows how to do.

    d. A student should consider trying new things but not the time that is available.

26. Of the following, which is accurate regarding personal hygiene in adolescence?

    a. The majority of teens experience acne regardless of skin care habits.

    b. Teens should not need to shampoo hair more but do so out of vanity.

    c. The same oral hygiene they used as children should suffice for teens.

    d. Teens who learned good bathing habits as children need not change.

27. Of the following, which is accurate regarding modes of human immunodeficiency virus (HIV) transmission?

    a. HIV cannot be transmitted by oral sex.

    b. HIV cannot be transmitted genetically.

    c. HIV cannot be transmitted via nursing.

    d. HIV cannot be transmitted perinatally.

28. Of the following, which is NOT a sign that an individual may need to get help from a professional for emotional or mental health problems?

    a. Persistent insomnia
    b. Pervasive depression
    c. Difficulty concentrating
    d. Any or all of these are signs

29. Among signs of domestic abuse, physical violence, isolation, and psychological symptoms of being abused, which of the following is more specifically a sign of domestic abuse than of the others?

    a. Constantly reporting one's locations and activities to the partner
    b. Often exhibiting or trying to hide injuries, claiming accidents
    c. Marked changes in a person's personality traits or behaviors
    d. Few or no public outings, no car or money use alone, or no visiting with others

30. Which of the following are used as formative assessments?

    a. Student final class projects
    b. Tests given at the ends of units
    c. Curriculum-based measurement
    d. Standardized state examinations

31. What is a result of regular and substantial alcohol use?

    a. It impairs judgment over the long term but not in the short term.
    b. It distorts the perceptions but not the senses of vision or hearing.
    c. It damages both the cardiovascular and central nervous systems.
    d. It causes liver damage but not impotence or stomach disorders.

32. Which of the following correctly identifies the big five personality traits?

    a. Introversion, detail-orientation, responsibility, psychoticism, and kindness
    b. Extraversion, agreeableness, conscientiousness, neuroticism, and openness
    c. Oral traits, anal traits, phallic tendencies, latency tendencies, and genital traits
    d. Assertiveness, prosocial behaviors, impulse control, moodiness, and imagination

33. Among tactics typically employed by domestic abusers to control their victims, what is destroying the victim's property an example of?

    a. Isolation
    b. Humiliation
    c. Dominance
    d. Intimidation

34. In a coordinated school health program, which of the following is a factor?

    a. Psychological, counseling, and social services are parts of a different program.
    b. This program is for promoting the health of students, not of school personnel.
    c. Healthy physical, emotional, and social school environments support learning.
    d. Coordinated school health programs incorporate physical education but not nutrition services.

35. In professional development (PD) for health educators, which of the following organizations offers a national PD conference for educational support professionals (ESPs)?

    a. Society of Health and Physical Educators (ShapeAmerica)
    b. The Centers for Disease Control and Prevention (CDC)
    c. The American Public Health Association (APHA)
    d. The National Education Association (NEA)

36. When health educators teach their students eight steps for establishing and meeting health goals, which of the last four is MOST related to monitoring progress for accountability?

    a. Asking friends to help or forming a club
    b. Using journals, diaries, charts, or graphs
    c. Healthy self-rewards for meeting goals
    d. Making revisions in plans and time lines

37. Which of the following is accurate regarding the history of U.S. regulations addressing pollution?

    a. The Environmental Protection Agency (EPA) first developed standards, laws, and regulations in the 1980s.
    b. The EPA's focus shifted from the remediation of existing pollution to preventing it during the 2000s.
    c. Congress's policy to prevent and reduce pollution is declared in the Pollution Prevention Act of 1990.
    d. National policy shifted in the 1990s from reducing pollution sources toward treatment and disposal.

38. In which human body system do the white cell blood cells function?

    a. Respiratory
    b. Circulatory
    c. Lymphatic
    d. Endocrine

39. Which statement accurately reflects recommended refusal strategies for children and teens?

    a. Walking away from a pressure situation is avoidant.
    b. Standing up for others being pressured is meddling.
    c. Proposing alternative activities is coping effectively.
    d. To say "no," one often needs to be very aggressive.

40. Of the following, which correctly reflects how teenagers make decisions?

    a. Internal, not external, variables influence teen decisions.
    b. Adolescents usually make decisions in isolated conditions.
    c. Feedback influences the decisions that adolescents make.
    d. External, not internal, variables influence teens' decisions.

41. According to research studies, what is true about the impact of physical activity (PA) on health risks?

    a. Similar amounts of PA lower heart disease, stroke, diabetes, and colon and breast cancer risks.
    b. Enough regular PA reduces risks of heart disease and stroke but not of diabetes or any cancer.
    c. Sufficient, consistent PA reduces risks of all these diseases, but amounts for each vary greatly.
    d. Regular PA in adequate amounts improves overall well-being but does not lower disease risks.

42. According to current research, what is true related to diabetes prevention?

    a. Supplements and foods control blood sugar equally well.
    b. Overall hours of sleep are unrelated to insulin sensitivity.
    c. Research does not connect stress with insulin resistance.
    d. Exercise in cooler temperatures can help glucose control.

43. From birth to three years, children typically grow to reach _____ of their previous height; during puberty, they typically attain around _____ of their growth in height.

    a. 175 percent; 50 percent
    b. 300 percent; 75 percent
    c. 200 percent; 25 percent
    d. 150 percent; 30 percent

44. How many deaths does smoking cigarettes cause annually in America compared to other causes?

    a. More than alcohol and drug use, car accidents, human immunodeficiency virus (HIV), and gunshots together
    b. More than alcohol and drug use combined or more than HIV and gunshots
    c. More than alcohol and drug use and HIV combined, not including gunshots
    d. More than gunshots and HIV combined, but less than alcohol and drug use

45. Which of the following accurately represents findings about how stress interacts with interpersonal communications on health care and other important subjects?

    a. We can control a problem better by limiting discussions of it.
    b. Being able to explain a problem affords more control over it.
    c. Sensitive discussions have outcomes worse than we expect.
    d. Quantity supersedes quality for discussing important issues.

46. Which statement is MOST accurate concerning differences between type 1 and type 2 diabetes?

    a. Type 1 involves children and teens; type 2 involves onset in adulthood.
    b. Type 1 involves more lifestyle factors; type 2 involves genetic elements.
    c. Type 1 involves insulin insufficiency; type 2 involves insulin insensitivity.
    d. Type 1 involves obesity and inactivity; type 2 involves nutrition deficits.

47. Among domains of development throughout life stages, what does Piaget's theory focus MOST on?

    a. Emotional development
    b. Developing relationships
    c. Intellectual development
    d. Developing independence

48. Which of the following is recommended for teachers to deal with an individual student who is always misbehaving in class?

    a. Speaking with the student in private
    b. Disciplining the student during class
    c. Differentiating behavior versus the student
    d. (A) and (C) but not (B) unless necessary

49. Regarding contraception methods, which of the following is correct?

    a. A condom or spermicide is effective enough by itself.
    b. Vasectomy is never reversible; tubal ligation always is.
    c. None of these choices is correct about contraception.
    d. Women insert IUDs, diaphragms, and pills themselves.

50. Which of Howard Gardner's multiple intelligence styles would learn best through group instructional activities?

    a. Interpersonal
    b. Intrapersonal
    c. Visual-spatial
    d. Mathematical

51. What is the School Health Index (SHI)?

    a. A tool that the Centers for Disease Control (CDC) uses to rate school health policies
    b. A tool that the CDC uses for (C) and (D) but not for (A)
    c. A tool to help schools in their health self-assessments
    d. A tool to help schools create health policies and plans

52. Among the following instructional techniques, which is equally amenable to individual or multiple student work and also to student work with or without the teacher's active involvement?

    a. Role-playing
    b. Brainstorming
    c. Guided discovery
    d. Cooperative learning

53. In his developmental theory, what did Erikson identify as the positive outcome of successfully resolving the nuclear conflict of basic trust versus mistrust?

    a. Will
    b. Hope
    c. Purpose
    d. Competence

54. Which of the following foods is classified in two food groups by the U.S. Department of Agriculture (USDA)?

    a. Legumes
    b. Seafood
    c. Cheese
    d. Eggplant

55. In the majority of U.S. states and territories, which of these professions are identified as mandated reporters of child maltreatment?

    a. Probation or parole officers, substance abuse counselors, and film processors
    b. Camps and recreation and youth center employees, directors, and volunteers
    c. School, health care, child care, mental health, and law enforcement employees
    d. Domestic violence workers, humane or animal control officers, and college faculties

56. To write learning objectives in planning health instruction, which of the following verbs represents a measurable student action?

    a. Learn
    b. Explain
    c. Understand
    d. Any of these

57. In the nuclear family emotional system Dr. Murray Bowen describes in his Family Systems Theory, which basic relationship pattern is represented if a parent shows excessive anxiety about a child, and the child responds by regressing to increased dependence and immature demands on the parent?

    a. Dysfunction in one spouse
    b. Impairment of a child(ren)
    c. Emotional distance pattern
    d. The marital conflict pattern

58. In the reflective process of teaching, which tools would MOST help a teacher to self-analyze his or her own body language and movement within the classroom and adjust these to be more effective?

    a. Journals and diaries
    b. Video recordings
    c. Audio recordings
    d. Peer observation

59. What is a definition of body mass index (BMI)?

    a. The ratio of weight to height squared
    b. The ratio of abdominal fat to total fat
    c. The ratio of body fat to muscle cubed
    d. The ratio of total fat to overall weight

60. What have physical education teachers found about using apps like Coach's Eye, iCoachview, and so on with their students?

    a. Student enthusiasm helps them appreciate constructive criticism.
    b. Students typically cannot use apps after only brief demonstration.
    c. Students are uncomfortable seeing their performance postgame.
    d. Students experience delayed feedback when teachers play videos.

61. A part of which body system controls fluid loss, protects deep tissues, and synthesizes vitamin D?

    a. The skeletal system
    b. The muscular system
    c. The lymphatic system
    d. The integumentary system

62. What is true about how teachers can engage community members and groups in physical education (PE) programs?

    a. It would be inappropriate to solicit funds from local health agencies to buy sports equipment.
    b. Local trophy companies are in business to make money and will not donate for school events.
    c. Local governments lack departments that could talk to students about community resources.
    d. When PE teachers plan Olympics-themed events, they may find volunteers from local colleges.

63. The frog kick is used in which swimming stroke(s)?
   a. The breaststroke
   b. The butterfly
   c. The crawl
   d. All these

64. Which of the following describes the most appropriate physical education self-assessment activity for kindergarten through Grade 2 students?
   a. Students write entries in journals describing the fitness activities they are doing.
   b. Students pictorially illustrate their activities in each of several fitness categories.
   c. Students keep notebooks of progress notes and give them to teachers regularly.
   d. Students record their progress on index cards they give to teachers at intervals.

65. Regarding perceptual-motor abilities, which is a performance skill that would be MOST affected by individual differences in control precision?
   a. Playing quarterback in football
   b. Handling a hockey puck
   c. Dribbling a basketball
   d. Driving a race car

66. Compared to naturalistic observations, structured observations are _____ in physical education assessment.
   a. more objective and less subjective
   b. more subjective and less objective
   c. more to see social than motor skills
   d. more realistic regarding behaviors

67. For cooperative learning activities to be more productive than competitive or individual learning activities, one of five necessary elements is positive interdependence among the members of a student group, including student awareness of it. What is accurate about the other four required elements?
   a. The students occasionally engage in productive, face-to-face interactions.
   b. The students are accountable for group goals collectively, not individually.
   c. The students use task-relevant interpersonal and group skills frequently.
   d. The students process group functioning to sustain current effectiveness.

68. A physical education teacher addresses a wide range of skill levels in one class by setting up several learning stations to teach a lesson in throwing. Which station activity represents the highest student skill level?
   a. Throwing lead passes
   b. Throwing at a stationary target
   c. Throwing to teammates while defended
   d. Throwing all these ways equally

69. Regarding communication with athletes, which statement is recommended by experts for coaches to consider?
   a. Coaches must not only get athlete attention but also explain, so athletes understand easily.
   b. Coaches must determine if athletes understood them but not whether they believed them.
   c. Coaches must get athletes to understand and believe, not necessarily accept, what they say.
   d. Coaches must disregard athletes' individual and group nonverbal cues for controlling them.

70. Which of these locomotor activities is most appropriate for children younger than five years old?
- a. Blob tag
- b. Musical hoops
- c. Follow the leader
- d. Any of these equally

71. Relative to spatial awareness, which movement concept involves vertical, horizontal, and circular paths of movement?
- a. Locations and levels
- b. Personal space
- c. Directions
- d. Planes

72. A physical education teacher has included an objective for student heart rates to reach a target range when they play a sport. The teacher discovers the majority of students did not reach that target. Which teacher response to this discovery is the best example of using reflection to inform instruction?
- a. The teacher decides students were not playing hard enough and gives them a pep talk.
- b. The teacher experiments with having the students play the next game at faster speeds.
- c. The teacher changes the rules of the game so all students will participate more actively.
- d. The teacher might do either (B) or (C) or even both of these but is less likely to use (A).

73. Compared to regular baseball, softball has a _____ ball, a _____ infield, _____ innings, and _____ pitch.
- a. smaller; bigger; more; the same
- b. bigger; smaller; fewer; a different
- c. bigger; bigger; fewer; a different
- d. smaller; smaller; more; the same

74. For a student who has joint problems but wants to be physically active, which is the best extracurricular activity?
- a. Skiing
- b. Swimming
- c. Skateboarding
- d. Playing soccer

75. Which statement about physical education (PE) class safety and teacher liability is a valid one?
- a. PE classes can include advanced gymnastics safely by having group spotters.
- b. PE classes as well as extracurricular activities can include trampolines safely.
- c. PE teachers must instruct students in calling for and backing away from fly balls.
- d. PE teachers commonly and safely discipline students with strenuous exercise.

76. Regarding indications that a student should be evaluated to determine eligibility for adapted physical education (APE), which of the following (in addition to referral) correctly states a criterion?
- a. The student performs at his or her ability level in group settings but not on an individual basis.
- b. The student's social behaviors impede his or her or others' learning more than half of class time.
- c. The student has scored below average in at least one part of the state physical fitness test.
- d. The student scored at least one standard deviation low on the norm-referenced test used.

77. One teaching method for managing kindergarten through Grade 12 physical education classes uses three steps to address student noncompliance with class rules. In which of the following sequences should these steps be applied?

    a. An oral warning; a brief time-out; a time-out with written response
    b. A brief time-out; a time-out with written response; an oral warning
    c. A time-out with written response; an oral warning; a brief time-out
    d. A brief time-out; an oral warning; a time-out with written response

78. Of the following, which elementary school activity best integrates physical education skills with English language arts (ELA) skills within the same lesson?

    a. Students perform movements and then look up adverbs and write synonyms and antonyms.
    b. Students look up and write adverbs, synonyms, and antonyms and then perform movements.
    c. Students identify adverbs in teacher-read sentences and describe movements using adverbs.
    d. Students perform movements in ways described by recently learned adverbs on given cards.

79. Within the TARGET model, which physical education teaching strategy is an example of the R in the acronym?

    a. Varying the difficulty levels among several different activities
    b. Giving students some responsibility for the choice of activities
    c. Acknowledging process and improvement rather than product
    d. Avoiding peer comparison through rapid and variable grouping

80. Of the following statements, which is true about aerobics?

    a. Aerobics originally focused on the flexibility of the body.
    b. Aerobics originally focused on the strength of the muscles.
    c. Aerobics originally focused on cardiorespiratory endurance.
    d. Aerobics originally focused on one thing as it still does today.

81. Which of the following is a recommended strategy for physical education teachers to plan effective class behavior management?

    a. Announce at least ten expectations to the students in oral format.
    b. Enforce expectations occasionally for intermittent reinforcement.
    c. Define expectations in terms of what they want students not to do.
    d. Define expectations in terms of what they want the students to do.

82. According to national physical education (PE) standards, to show respect, which of the following should PE teachers do to address a student's behavior problem?

    a. The teacher describes the student's behavior, why it was disruptive, and solutions for the problem.
    b. The teacher has a classmate describe the behavior, why it was disruptive, and solutions for the problem.
    c. The teacher has the student describe the behavior, why it was disruptive, and solutions for the problem.
    d. The teacher avoids discussing it but provides concrete consequences and solutions for the problem.

83. When someone bench presses weights to strengthen the arms and upper body, this is an example of which exercise science principle?
    a. Overload
    b. Specificity
    c. Adaptation
    d. Progression

84. What advantages does Fitbit technology include for physical education teachers and students?
    a. Weight control but not sleep quality
    b. Self-monitoring but not competition
    c. Fashion appeal as well as motivation
    d. Stand-alone fitness progress tracking

85. The respiratory system _____ oxygen and _____ carbon dioxide.
    a. inhales; exhales
    b. delivers; expels
    c. creates; absorbs
    d. exhales; inhales

86. Among the following divisions of biomechanics that involve physics concepts, which one is MOST closely related to Newton's first three laws of motion?
    a. Coplanar vectors
    b. Kinematics
    c. Kinetics
    d. Forces

87. Among the following common areas of negligence in physical education, in addition to first aid emergencies, which one can teachers and coaches MOST mitigate by enlisting the help of students?
    a. Instruction
    b. Supervision
    c. Transportation
    d. Class environments

88. Of the following assessment approaches, which one is traditional rather than alternative?
    a. Students write down their personal fitness plans.
    b. Students perform a series of dance movements.
    c. Students show learning by playing a sports game.
    d. Students label the team's positions on a diagram.

89. Research finds that motor skills training, endurance training, and strength training all share which neuroplasticity effects in common?
    a. New blood vessel formation
    b. Motor map reorganization
    c. Spinal reflex modification
    d. New synapse generation

- 163 -

90. When a physical education teacher gives a defense cue of "Match up" to students during basketball practice, what does this mean?

    a. Students always should pair up with another player on the court for defense.
    b. Students should stay near to offensive players that they defend on the court.
    c. Students should defend players more like them in size than fitness or skill level.
    d. Students should defend players similar to them in size, fitness, and skill level.

91. Concerning the impacts of various resources on student physical education (PE) outcomes, what has research found?

    a. Class size and student–teacher ratio correlate inversely with activity levels, time, safety, and learning.
    b. Students receive a higher quantity and quality of PE from teachers who also teach different subjects.
    c. Student physical activity is the same whether PE curriculum is based on educational standards or not.
    d. PE facilities and equipment are valuable resources but do not change the amount of student activity.

92. Among the most prevalent challenges to kindergarten through Grade 12 physical education, which has recently become even more challenging than the others?

    a. Inadequate resources and parental support
    b. Overly large class sizes and teacher burnout
    c. Violence, student drug abuse, and discipline
    d. Reductions in school curriculum times for physical education

93. Regarding feedback that physical education teachers and coaches give students and athletes, which of the following is an example of prescriptive feedback rather than descriptive feedback?

    a. "You can do this!"
    b. "Follow through!"
    c. "That was great!"
    d. "Way to play ball!"

94. Among fundamental movement skills (FMS), which two are both part of the same main category?

    a. Locomotor and manipulative
    b. Manipulative and rotation
    c. Rotation and balance
    d. Balance and stability

95. Related to summation of forces, which is accurate about how body parts move?

    a. The largest body parts are the slowest and move last.
    b. The smallest body parts are the fastest and move first.
    c. The largest body parts are the slowest and move first.
    d. Regardless of speed, all parts move at the same times.

96. According to experiences reported by physical education teachers, what are some characteristics of technology in applications such as GradeBookPro?

    a. Apps like this enable physical education teachers to use most of their time for teaching.

    b. Apps like this reduce final grade disputes by consolidating student data.

    c. Apps like this can exponentially speed up the task of taking attendance.

    d. Apps like this streamline all these and a great many more teacher tasks.

97. Which of the following is an example of the short-term effects of exercise on health?

    a. Exercising releases endorphins, generating euphoria.

    b. Exercising regularly prevents and relieves depression.

    c. Exercising lowers the risk of heart attacks and strokes.

    d. Exercising can reduce one's blood pressure and pulse.

98. Which non-English language is shared in common by some of the terminology in both ballet and ballroom dancing?

    a. French

    b. Italian

    c. Spanish

    d. Russian

99. Which kinds of physical education activities are both appropriate for boys and girls to participate in together and are less dependent on team assignment by student skill levels?

    a. Activities that involve participant body contact

    b. Activities that require more upper-body strength

    c. Activities that require agility and lower-body strength

    d. Activities of all these types

100. Which of these describes a function of formative assessments?

    a. They enable teachers to show accountability for adequate yearly progress and similar requirements.

    b. They enable teachers to compare student achievement to population averages.

    c. They enable teachers to adjust instruction in progress to address student needs.

    d. They enable teachers to see if they helped students meet curriculum standards.

101. Which development in human manual skills emerges the earliest?

    a. Successfully reaching for objects

    b. Coordinated arm–hand movements

    c. Arm flapping and jerky arm extensions

    d. Changing hand shapes before touching objects

102. Of the following, which is a valid principle of physical education (PE) coaching for teaching movement and sport skills to students?

    a. Asking think-about questions gives an advantage to students.

    b. Reading tasks or steps aloud only will delay the setup of players.

    c. PE teachers should alternate practice plan sequence for variety.

    d. PE teachers should either describe or demonstrate but not both.

103. Compared to the amount of time in moderate to vigorous physical activity (MVPA) the Institute of Medicine recommends for children to spend daily, how much do research studies find they actually spend in school physical education classes?

    a. About one-sixth of what is recommended
    b. About one-third of what is recommended
    c. About one-half of what is recommended
    d. About the same as is recommended

104. What amount of quality physical education time most reflects the National Association for Sport and Physical Education (NASPE) recommendation for elementary school students?

    a. A minimum of 15 minutes per day
    b. A maximum of 30 minutes per day
    c. A minimum of 30 minutes per day
    d. A maximum of 60 minutes a week

105. Regarding appropriate physical education (PE) teaching practices, which statement is MOST valid?

    a. PE teachers must use extrinsic motivations to teach student responsibility for learning.
    b. PE teachers should ignore certain inappropriate student behaviors to extinguish them.
    c. PE teachers do not necessarily need to obtain or renew certification in cardiopulmonary resuscitation (CPR) or automated external defibrillator (AED) use.
    d. PE teachers must regularly and consistently inspect facilities and equipment for safety.

106. Regarding physical education teacher communication with parents, what is MOST effective related to posting and communicating class rules to students at the beginning of the school year?

    a. Giving rules to students, but not parents, so students feel they can trust teachers
    b. Giving copies of rules to students with instructions to take them home to parents
    c. Sending the rules by postal mail with a cover letter asking parents to review them
    d. E-mailing the rules to the parents with a cover letter asking them to review them

107. Which of the following is true about center of gravity (COG)?

    a. COG is in the same location for each human body.
    b. COG varies according to the body parts' positions.
    c. COG varies among bodies but is constant for each.
    d. COG is the same as center of mass or of pressure.

108. The MyFitnessPal, Endomondo, and Fitbit digital fitness apps all share what in common?

    a. Sync
    b. Recipes
    c. Audio feedback
    d. Social networking

109. Of the following, which most accurately represents an aspect of the relationship between nutrition and fitness?

    a. Exercising regularly and energetically enables you to eat anything you want.
    b. Eating a diet rich in calcium prevents bone density loss, but exercise cannot.
    c. Eating right provides energy for exercise, while exercise can control appetite.
    d. Exercising prevents high blood pressure and cholesterol more than diet does.

110. Among examples of how physical education (PE) teachers can collaborate with other educators, which one applies most to taking advantage of administrator support to improve student motivation and learning?

    a. Reading *A River Runs Through It* to study fly-fishing and character development and relationships
    b. Watching *Footloose* to study dance movements and themes of freedom, rebellion, and repression
    c. Designing a joint PE and Family and Consumer Sciences unit that combines nutrition and exercise
    d. Developing a morning walk/run project together with the principal to help students focus better

111. Regarding individual differences that affect physical education activity performance, which of these sports is most appropriate for the ectomorphic somatotype (body type)?

    a. Wrestling
    b. Gymnastics
    c. Shot-putting
    d. High jump

112. When using an assessment instrument meant to measure aerobic endurance, physical education teachers find that maximum student repetitions are limited not by their becoming winded but by specific muscle fatigue. After obtaining the same results over repeated administrations, they conclude that this test measures muscular endurance instead. What have they discovered about this test?

    a. The test is neither a reliable nor valid test.
    b. The test is a valid test, but it is not reliable.
    c. The test is a reliable test, but it is not valid.
    d. The test is valid and reliable, but misused.

113. Among physical proficiencies that affect individual performance, which type of strength is most involved in the activity of kayaking?

    a. Static strength
    b. Trunk strength
    c. Dynamic strength
    d. Explosive strength

114. A physical education teacher designs a student volleyball activity to meet National Association for Sport and Physical Education (NASPE) standards for setting, spiking, forearm passing, defensive strategies, officiating; aerobic capacity; and cooperating and accepting challenges. Which of the following represents the correct sequence of steps in this activity?

    a. Rotational positions; serve; base positions; defend against attack
    b. Base positions; rotational positions; defend against attack; serve
    c. Serve; base positions; defend against attack; rotational positions
    d. Defend against attack; serve; rotational positions; base positions

115. In three stages of motor learning, which of these is characteristic of the associative stage?

    a. Understanding an activity's goal and nature
    b. Making attempts that include major errors
    c. Making fewer and more consistent errors
    d. Effortless automaticity in performance

116. If a student has the condition of atlantoaxial instability, which of the following activities would be safe for a physical education teacher to assign to the student?

a. A log roll would be safest for this student.
b. A forward roll would be better for this student.
c. No kind of roll should be assigned to this student.
d. It is irrelevant because atlantoaxial instability is so rare.

117. According to experts, what is true about the primary functions of nonverbal communication?

a. Nonverbal communication serves a function of performing social rituals.
b. Nonverbal communication shows personalities rather than relationships.
c. Nonverbal communication is used to replace, not help, verbal interaction.
d. Nonverbal communication is not used like words for expressing feelings.

118. A physical education teacher writes an entry task on the board before class. How does this relate to teacher communication toward student understanding and ownership of high expectations for themselves?

a. This is not recommended because the teacher will not be supervising the students for this activity.
b. This supports high classroom expectations because students can begin the activity independently.
c. This supports student independence for activities but not student comprehension of expectations.
d. This is not recommended because the teacher did not structure the learning activity for students.

119. In quality of movement, _____ is bound/interrupted or free/sustained.

a. flow
b. effort
c. speed
d. rhythm

120. Professional development at its best accomplishes which of these?

a. Improves primarily the teacher's own knowledge and skills
b. Improves both a teacher's and his or her colleagues' expertise
c. Improves primarily the expertise of the teacher's colleagues
d. Improves teaching practices primarily at the classroom level

121. Which statement best characterizes the role of posture in theories of motor development?

a. As evidence of growing cerebral control, posture was more important to classical theories.
b. As the biomechanical basis of action, posture is more important to contemporary theories.
c. For different reasons, posture has been equally important to both earlier and later theories.
d. In both classical and contemporary theories, posture is a minor part of motor development.

122. Which of the following biomechanics subjects are based on calculus?

a. Vector composition and resolution
b. Differentiation and integration
c. The parallelogram method
d. None of these topics

123. Which of these is a typical effect of substance abuse on student behavior?

    a. A shy student becomes more sociable.
    b. An outgoing student becomes withdrawn.
    c. An inhibited student becomes more impulsive.
    d. These are all typical effects of substance abuse.

124. Of the following, which accurately reports research findings related to how physical fitness affects academic achievement?

    a. Cardiovascular fitness and body mass index (BMI) correlate positively with test scores in achievement.
    b. More physically fit children react more quickly but not necessarily more accurately.
    c. Children burn more calories during active gaming than teacher-led fitness activities.
    d. Intense exercise is followed by a significant temporary decline in cognitive function.

125. In one instructional method to promote psychomotor learning, a physical education teacher clearly explains learning goals and skills to be learned to the students; demonstrates the skills for the students; and provides the students with practice time, frequently and regularly monitoring their progress during practice. This describes which of the following      methods?

    a. The contingency or contract method
    b. The command or direct method
    c. The task or reciprocal method
    d. None of these methods

126. When is performing the Heimlich maneuver on a student indicated?

    a. The student says he or she is having trouble breathing.
    b. The student is choking and is not able to breathe.
    c. The student has trouble breathing and is coughing.
    d. The Heimlich should not be done until cardiopulmonary resuscitation (CPR) is tried.

127. Which of these is an effective strategy for physical education teachers to enhance students' perceived physical competence?

    a. Specify the number of trials to complete during a certain time period.
    b. Specify the length of time for practicing but not the number of trials.
    c. Specify the technical errors students make in instructional feedback.
    d. Specify a certain activity without varying it to keep students on task.

128. When students learn to fall sideways and land using their hands, which of the following should be the last activity they do in a sequence of increasing difficulty?

    a. Falling sideways from kneeling
    b. Rolling sideways down a wedge
    c. Falling, rolling, and standing up
    d. Running, falling, rolling, and standing

129. When does physical education instruction necessarily require giving feedback to students?

    a. When a skill requires specific correction
    b. When a skill gets environmental feedback
    c. When a student has experience with a skill
    d. When a teacher can comprehensively demonstrate a skill

130. What is MOST accurate about how physical education teachers can use bulletin boards to communicate instructional information to students?

    a. Schools must provide real bulletin boards for physical education teachers to utilize them.
    b. A time-lapse bulletin board accesses student participation and creativity.
    c. A time-lapse bulletin board is a project only the physical education teacher can complete.
    d. Physical education teachers must communicate orally, as students ignore bulletin boards.

# Answers and Explanations

1. B: The original impetus for the National Health Education Standards (NHES) was that health education, physical education, public health, and school health authorities observed standards being developed for other subject-area content in education (B) and decided that the subject area of health education needed similar standards developed. Health educators were not influenced by standards developed in hospitals (A), public health (C) agencies, or private medical practice (D).

2. A: A coordinated school health program includes comprehensive school health education addressing physical, cognitive, affective, and social health domains, differentiated for every developmental and age level to promote health knowledge, skills, and attitudes, decrease health risk behaviors, and enhance student health. Physical education is not separate (B) but is an essential component of a coordinated school health program. So are school health services, which include not only emergency care (C) but also prevention, education, referral, and acute and chronic health condition management. Another essential component of a coordinated school health program is family and community involvement (D).

3. A: Infectious hepatitis is caused by different viruses depending on which type it is: three separate viruses cause hepatitis A, B, and C. Burkett's lymphoma (B), infectious mononucleosis (C), and nasopharyngeal carcinoma (D) all can be caused by the Epstein-Barr virus under different conditions.

4. A: During the latest part of the sensorimotor stage, from around 18 to 24 months of age, Piaget said children develop early representational thought when they begin using symbols to represent other things, like playing make-believe by pretending to be adults or fictional characters and using objects to represent other things or beings, for example, pretending a broom is a horse, a block is a phone, and so on. This is the first instance of mental operations. In the preoperational stage (B), children display more intuitive than logical thinking. Though capable of basic mental operations, they do not perform logical ones. In concrete operations (C), they begin performing logical mental operations but only concerning concrete objects or events. In formal operations (D), they begin performing mental operations that are abstract as well as logical.

5. D: Cardiovascular diseases like strokes and heart attacks were found in 2013 by the World Health Organization (WHO) to cause 17.3 million deaths yearly. Diabetes (A) was found to cause 1.3 million deaths yearly. Cancers (B) were found to cause 7.6 million deaths annually. Respiratory (C) diseases like asthma and chronic obstructive pulmonary diseases (COPD) were found to cause 4.2 million deaths a year. Thus (D), (B), (C), and (A) is the order of most to least causes of mortality, with (D) far exceeding all the others.

6. B: Because the social contexts in which teenagers make decisions are subject frequent change, they must learn to evaluate and adjust those decisions in response to such changes. A challenging paradox for teens is that the decisions they make are frequently critical, with long-term consequences affecting their futures (A); yet they commonly lack enough life experience to inform these decisions (C). Research has found intervention programs to improve teen decision-making skills effective (D) in enhancing positive, responsible, prosocial, constructive and self-sufficient behaviors and decreasing negative, irresponsible, antisocial, destructive and self-destructive behaviors.

7. B: Student health records in educational institutions and agencies receiving federal Department of Education funding are protected under the Family Educational Rights and Privacy Act (FERPA); immunization records are not excluded (A). Neither are records kept by public school nurses (C) on students, whose privacy is also protected under FERPA. Student special education records, including

records of services they receive under the Individuals with Disabilities Education Act (IDEA), also are defined as "education records" by FERPA; hence, their privacy is also protected by FERPA (D).

8. D: The model described and named *direct instruction* (lower-case) by Rosenshine and Stevens in 1986 is a generic instructional model; the Direct Instruction (capitalized) model pioneered in the 1960s by Siegfried Engelmann and his colleagues is a specific instructional model. However, both share in common the characteristics of teacher-directed, skills-oriented (A), face-to-face, small-group (B) instruction that uses task analysis, deliberate sequencing (C), and explicit teaching (D).

9. D: While questionnaires (A) can be sent to large groups of people, they also can be used to collect data on an individual and small group basis equally well or better (i.e., not all recipients return mailed questionnaires, whereas individuals and small groups, when given these directly in clinical, public health, or other settings, are obligated to complete them). Observations (B) are most useful for gathering data about individuals or small groups as they require researchers to watch their actions and interactions directly (overtly or covertly). Interviews (C) typically require one-to-one question-and-answer interactions between researchers and respondents. The survey (D) method enables researchers to collect large-scale data on entire population groups, often through a combination of these other methods, by obtaining the same information from a much greater number of respondents.

10. B: Carefully weighing and evaluating the pros and cons of a stressful life situation facilitates making decisions that aid coping with stress and most reflects the decision-making life skill. Considering the positive aspects of the situation (A) most reflects the life skill of values clarification. Expressing feelings about the situation (C) most reflects the life skill of communication skills. Engaging in positive behaviors that raise self-esteem or develop interests to enable dealing with the situation (D) most reflects the life skill of coping skills.

11. A: Erikson identified a nuclear conflict to be resolved in each stage of psychosocial development. Babies confront basic trust versus mistrust, toddlers autonomy (D) versus shame and self-doubt, preschoolers initiative versus guilt, school-aged children industry (C) versus inferiority, adolescents identity (A) versus role confusion, young adults intimacy (B) versus isolation, middle adults generativity versus stagnation, and older adults integrity versus despair.

12. A: Cardiorespiratory endurance is best defined as the ability to perform dynamic, that is, movement, exercise rather than static (C) or passive exercise using the large, that is, limb and trunk muscles, not small (B) muscles like those in the hands and feet, or both large and small, that is, all muscles (C), or any muscles (D) for extended time periods. Cardiorespiratory means involving the heart and breathing. Endurance requires long, not short (B), average (C), or any (D) durations.

13. B: A common misconception among teenagers is that only vaginal penetration and ejaculation will cause pregnancy. Health educators should inform them that small drops of pre-ejaculate they may not detect can be released before as well as during sex. Pre-ejaculate also contains sperm; males cannot control its release; and vulvar contact alone can cause conception. Thus, there is a smaller but real chance of impregnating a girl without penetrating or ejaculating inside her vagina [a reason to do (C)]. Choices (A), (C), and (D) are all facts, not misconceptions, of which health educators can inform teens.

14. A: Gum disease can develop when oral bacteria build up due to poor oral hygiene and can cause serious heart valve disorders when the bacteria travel from the gums directly to the heart. Unhealthy gums cannot only lead to periodontal (gum) infections; they also can cause loosening and loss of teeth (B). While flossing and gum massage are important for preventing gum disease, brushing the teeth also prevents both tooth decay and gum disease (C). Gum disease not only affects the soft tissues of the gums but also causes irreversible bone loss in the jaw (D).

15. C: Carbohydrates in our diet (e.g., from fruits, vegetables, and grains) are sources whereby our bodies make glucose, which supplies energy. Our bodies get amino acids, which they use to repair cells, muscle and other tissue, and organs by breaking down protein in our diet (e.g., from meats, poultry, seafood, dairy, and beans). Our bodily functions require 20 to 35 percent of our diet from fats but not saturated fat (D). Unsaturated fats are healthier for the heart, blood vessels, body composition, weight, and organs.

16. A: In precontemplation, individuals have no plans to act anytime soon. This can be caused by lack of information, lack of motivation, and resistance. In contemplation, individuals plan to make changes within roughly six months but are not ready to act immediately. They have acquired awareness of both the costs and benefits of change, causing ambivalence that fuels procrastination. In preparation, individuals usually have made some significant action in the last year; plan to act within a month; and have developed some plan of action. In action, people have accomplished obvious lifestyle changes in the last six months, sufficient to reduce disease risk according to professional and scientific criteria, for example, quitting smoking. In maintenance, people devote more effort to preventing relapse than initiating change processes, which they have already largely done. This stage can last six months to five years.

17. C: Smoking tobacco, drinking alcohol (A), poor nutrition, and lack of physical activity (B) are all risk factors shared in common by all four types of illnesses that cause the majority of deaths from noncommunicable diseases. Therefore, (D) is incorrect.

18. C: The idea that saturated fat in the diet contributes to heart disease is an abstract concept. This would be most appropriate to teach to students in Piaget's stage of formal operations (typically preadolescent and adolescent ages), who can understand abstract concepts. Babies in Piaget's sensorimotor (A) stage and toddlers in Piaget's preoperational (B) stage cannot grasp abstract concepts. Preschoolers are best taught using single, simple subjects one at a time and intuitive or animistic ideas. Middle childhood students in Piaget's concrete operations (D) stage can think logically and perform mental operations but only related to concrete objects and events; they still have not developed the facility for comprehending completely abstract ideas that emerge during the formal operations stage. They are best taught using concrete illustrations of food groups, digestion and energy processes, the food chain cycle, weight gain and loss, and so on rather than future nutritional benefits or abstract relationships.

19. B: There are no federal laws in the United States concerning immunizations required for children to enter public schools (A). These laws vary from state to state (B). However, all 50 U.S. states do have such laws (C). Because the laws vary by state, the U.S. Centers for Disease Control and Prevention (CDC) does offer a database of all state immunization laws (D) for schools, hospitals, health care facilities, provider practices, child care providers, long-term care facilities, facilities for the developmentally disabled, and correctional facilities.

20. D: The masseter muscles in the sides of the face connect the jaws and control their chewing functions. The temporalis muscles in the side of the head also are involved in chewing. The orbicularis oris muscle (A) encircles the mouth and is used to make facial expressions, open and close the mouth and pucker the lips to kiss, and blow trumpets and other musical horns, but not to chew. The zygomaticus major and minor muscles (B) are in the cheekbones, running between the cheek below the eye and the corners of the mouth; they control smiling, not chewing. The trapezius muscles (C) are large, triangular muscles extending from the neck, across each shoulder, and down the upper back and thus not in the jaws or face.

21. C: In both females and males, the brain's hypothalamus stimulates the pituitary gland to secrete luteinizing hormone (LH) and follicle-stimulating hormone (FSH). In females, these two hormones stimulate the ovaries to produce estrogen; in males, they stimulate the testes to produce testosterone. Hence, both female and male organs are stimulated by the same hormones, not each by female or male hormones (A). LH and FSH, the hormones that stimulate the male and female sexual organs, are not the

- 173 -

same as estrogen and testosterone, which respectively stimulate the male and female organs to produce these sex hormones (B). The pituitary gland does not secrete these (D); it secretes LH and FSH.

22. B: Emergencies that warrant 911 calls are identified as any situations needing immediate help from the police, a fire department, or an ambulance. People should call 911 not only for uncontrollable bleeding or unconsciousness but also for allergic reactions, which can be fatal; for chest pains (A), which can indicate heart attacks; and if someone is not breathing or having trouble breathing. Prank calls to 911 are not only nuisances and interfere with actual emergencies; they are also illegal (C) in most U.S. states and subject to law enforcement. When a person calls 911 in an emergency, he or she should not hang up until instructed to do so by the call taker, who will first need to get information from or give instructions to the caller.

23. A: Research has found that, although teachers do have difficulty relating to children with attention deficit hyperactivity disorder (ADHD), this does not mean they cannot change peer dislike of these children (B). Peers do tend to continue rejecting ADHD children based on their existing negative reputations, even after those children improve their behavior, but this also does not mean teachers cannot affect this (C). Teachers who create classroom environments that promote better peer relationships do not eliminate all dislike of ADHD children (D), which classmates continue to display; however, they do influence peer interactions to enable more variation and less consistent dislike.

24. A: The federal Healthy People 2000 initiative had as its main goal to decrease health disparities in America. The Healthy People 2010 initiative made its main goal to eliminate those disparities rather than just decrease them. The Healthy People 2020 initiative established goals not only to eliminate health disparities but moreover to establish health equity and improve health for all Americans.

25. B: When students engage in extracurricular activities, if they begin to feel overextended, they should not expect (A) or consider this normal; it is a sign that they should quit at least one activity (B). Students should consider not only the abilities and skills they already have (C) and familiar interests but also trying new things in which they are interested as well as the time they have available (D) before they choose extracurricular activities.

26. A: At least 80 percent of adolescents develop acne. This is not due to inadequate or incorrect facial skin care but to hormonal changes. Health educators should inform teen students how to treat and not treat acne. Hormonal changes in puberty also frequently make teens' hair oilier, so they are likely to need to shampoo it more often (B). Many teenagers have to wear braces, which makes oral hygiene more complicated and challenging; additionally, fresh breath becomes more important to them in adolescence. Therefore, the same oral hygiene they practiced in childhood usually will not suffice (C). Hormonal changes also cause increased perspiration, so adolescents need to bathe more often than in childhood (D).

27. B: It is impossible for parents to pass the human immunodeficiency virus (HIV) genetically to their children as it is not a genetic disease. However, HIV can be transmitted by oral sex (A) as well as genital and anal sex. Infected nursing mothers can transmit HIV to their babies (C) in breast milk. Infected mothers also can transmit HIV perinatally (D) to their unborn children.

28. D: If an individual has insomnia, not just occasionally but persistently (A); feels sad, depressed, discouraged, or hopeless more of the time than not (B); or has enough difficulty concentrating to impede home or work functioning (C), these are signs that the person should probably consult a mental health professional. Uncontrollable fears, negative thinking, or self-destructive thoughts are additional signs. Preoccupation with death and suicidal ideations are also warning signals to seek professional help. Qualified professionals can help when self-help measures cannot.

29. A: Constantly reporting one's locations and activities to the partner is a sign of being domestically abused as well as appearing desperate to please the partner; agreeing with all the partner's words and actions; often receiving harassing partner contacts; and mentioning partner possessiveness, jealousy, or temper. Often exhibiting or trying to hide injuries or excusing them as accidents (B) or clumsiness is a sign of being physically abused. Marked personality and behavioral changes (C) are psychological symptoms of being abused. Making few or no public outings, use of the car or money, or visits with friends and family (D) are signs of being isolated by an abuser.

30. C: Curriculum-based measurement (CBM) is a standardized measure that is used as a formative assessment to evaluate student progress during instruction. Final projects (A), end-of-unit tests (B), and standardized state examinations (D) are used as summative assessments to evaluate student learning after instruction.

31. C: The short-term effects of regular, substantial alcohol use include impaired judgment (A); distortion of perceptions, vision and hearing (B), and emotions; impaired coordination; bad breath; and hangovers. The long-term effects of heavy alcohol use include liver damage, sexual impotence, stomach disorders (D), vitamin deficiencies, skin problems, loss of appetite, loss of memory, damage to the heart and entire cardiovascular system, and damage to the central nervous system (C).

32. B: The big five personality traits are extraversion, agreeableness, conscientiousness, neuroticism, and openness. All people are said to possess some greater or lesser degree of each along a continuum; for example, very introverted (A) people are low in extraversion; very irresponsible people are low in conscientiousness; very emotionally stable individuals are low in neuroticism, and so on. Detail-orientation (A) is a characteristic of conscientiousness. Kindness (A) is a characteristic of agreeableness. Assertiveness (D) is a characteristic of extraversion. Prosocial behaviors (D) are characteristic of agreeableness. Good impulse control (D) is characteristic of conscientiousness. Moodiness (D) is characteristic of neuroticism. Imagination (D) is characteristic of openness. Oral, anal, phallic, latency, and genital traits or tendencies (C) are concepts from Freud's psychosexual theory of personality, not the big five trait theory of personality.

33. D: Destroying the victim's property is an example of domestic abusers' typical tactics of intimidation, which they use to frighten victims into submission by indicating the violent consequences they will suffer if they do not comply with the abuser. Examples of isolation (A) include cutting their victims off from contact with family and friends to make the victims dependent on the abusers. Examples of humiliation (B) include making victims feel worthless, undermining their self-esteem by shaming them both in private and public. Examples of dominance (C) include giving their victims orders, treating them like children, servants, slaves, or even possessions and expecting them to comply unquestioningly.

34. C: Components of a coordinated school health program include psychological, counseling, and social services (A); health promotion for school personnel as well as for students (B); healthy school environments that support learning through physical, emotional, and social safety and health (C); and school nutrition services as well as physical education (D).

35. D: The National Education Association (NEA) offers a national professional development (PD) conference for educational support professionals (ESPs), its Leaders for Tomorrow program, and various other PD trainings. ShapeAmerica (aka American Association of Health, Physical Education, Recreation, and Dance [AAHPERD]) (A) offers a PD webinar series on various topics, a Researcher's Toolkit, a Distinguished Lecture Series, and workshops. The Centers for Disease Control (CDC) (B) has a Division of Scientific Education and Professional Development (DSEPD), its Learning Connection containing thousands of public health learning products and continuing education (CE) courses through CDC TRAIN, online resources, Quick-Learn lessons for mobile devices, and Facebook and Twitter links to public health

topics. The American Public Health Association (APHA) (C) has a Center for PD, Public Health Systems, and Partnerships.

36. B: Students can use journals, diaries, charts, or graphs to keep track of their progress toward their health goals and ensure accountability. Asking friends to help or forming a club (A) is related to developing a support system for meeting health goals. When students give themselves healthy rewards for meeting their goals (C), this is related to positive reinforcement. Revising their action plans or time lines (D) is related to ensuring success in meeting health goals by adjusting the means or time by which they need to achieve them.

37. C: The Environmental Protection Agency (EPA) first developed standards, laws, and regulations to address environmental pollution during the 1970s, not the 1980s (A). Its focus shifted from remediation in the 1970s toward prevention in the 1980s and 1990s, not the 2000s (B). In 1990, Congress's national policy to prevent and reduce pollution was declared in the Pollution Prevention Act (C). This law called for the national policy to shift away from emphasizing treatment and disposal and toward emphasizing source reduction, not vice versa (D).

38. C: White blood cells are known as lymphocytes, a clue to the fact that they function in the lymphatic system to produce antibodies and destroy virally affected or foreign cells. While they are also found within the circulatory (B) system, that is, in the bloodstream, they do not function there but are only in transit from the bone marrow to the lymphatic system. The endocrine (D) system includes the pancreas, male testes, female ovaries and uterus, and all of the body's glands, which secrete hormones regulating bodily function, metabolism, and growth.

39. C: Experts advise children and teens particularly to use refusal strategies when others try to pressure them, including walking away from the situation (A); standing up for others who are being pressured (B); proposing alternatives to whatever unwanted activity others are pressuring them to engage in (C); and not being overly aggressive when saying "no" (D).

40. C: Teenagers' decisions are influenced by both internal variables (A), like self-concept and locus of control, and external variables (D), like their relationships with their parents and friends. They do not make decisions in isolated conditions (B); rather, their decision-making is influenced by the feedback they receive (C).

41. A: Multiple research studies repeatedly demonstrate that cardiovascular diseases, diabetes, and colon and breast cancer risks are lowered by regular physical activity (PA). Researchers recommend 30 to 60 minutes a day of PA to reduce the risks of breast and colon cancer significantly, and 150 minutes a week to decrease risks of cardiovascular diseases and diabetes. Thirty minutes a day for five days a week equals 150 minutes a week; therefore, the amounts needed are similar to lower the risks of these diseases. (Sixty minutes is double this and may afford some people greater cancer risk reduction.) Hence, risks for all these diseases are lowered, not some (B). The amounts necessary to reduce risk do not vary greatly among these diseases (C). Regular PA in adequate amounts does lower disease risk (D).

42. D: Current (2014) research finds that exercising in temperatures up to 62 to 65 degrees Fahrenheit maximum increases the odds of producing and activating healthy brown fat, which promotes building lean muscle tissue and burning more calories and keeps the internal organs warm. New research suggests brown fat may enhance glucose control and decrease insulin resistance. Studies find whole foods effective as opposed to supplements (A) for controlling blood sugar and weight because vegetables and fruits contain enzymes that activate antioxidants the body needs for controlling blood sugar and weight (as well as preventing cancers). Supplements lack these enzymes. A meta-analysis of multiple studies recently found people 28 percent more apt to develop diabetes when sleeping below 5 to 6 hours nightly,

compared to those sleeping 6 to 8 hours. Insulin sensitivity also improved greatly in people who slept 6 hours on weeknights but caught up by sleeping 10 hours on weekend nights (B). Studies also show stress raises levels of the hormone cortisol and of inflammatory cytokines, which both cause insulin resistance (C).

43. C: Milestones of physical growth and development include that, from birth to three years, children typically grow to twice their previous height and that, during puberty, they typically attain around 25 percent of their growth in height.

44. A: The seriousness of health risks from smoking cigarettes is driven home by the statistic that it causes more deaths in America every year than alcohol use, drug use, car accidents, human immunodeficiency virus (HIV), and gunshots combined—that is, around one in five people, exceeding 480,000. Another statistic to put smoking deaths in perspective is that they equal more than ten times the number of all casualties of war in American history. Moreover, one of every three deaths from cancer in America is caused by smoking.

45. B: Researchers find that, over time, avoiding discussion of important issues causes stress, damaging health and well-being, rather than affording more control over them (A). Instead, they find we attain more control over problems when we can explain them (B). Studies also find we overestimate the outcomes of sensitive discussions, which are emotionally safer and have more productive outcomes than we expect (C). Investigators also find quality supersedes quantity of discussion (D); that is, more is not better. They also find discussing important issues in the wrong way (e.g., by emphasizing quantity over quality) can cause more harm than not discussing them at all.

46. C: Whereas historically, type 1 diabetes involved children and teens more and type 2 involved onset in adulthood, today this is not true (A): More and more children and adolescents are developing type 2 diabetes due to lifestyle factors. Both types of diabetes are influenced by genetic and lifestyle factors; however, genetic elements contribute more to type 1, while lifestyle behaviors contribute more to type 2 (B). In type 1, the pancreas fails to produce insulin; in type 2, the pancreas produces insulin, but the body loses its sensitivity (C) and fails to respond to it. Obesity, inactivity, and poor nutrition all contribute to type 2 diabetes (D).

47. C: Piaget's theory identifies progressive stages of cognitive development; hence, it focuses most on intellectual development. While cognitive development interacts with and affects emotional development (A), relationship development (B), and the development of independence (D), and Piaget does explain how it does, his primary concern is how the intellect develops from birth to adulthood.

48. D: It is recommended that the teacher speak with the student in private (A) if at all possible rather than discipline the student in front of the whole class (B). This can backfire in two ways: (1) Humiliating the student in front of the entire class can have a negative impact on the student's attitude, making the misbehavior worse, or (2) making the student the center of attention can reinforce the misbehavior if it is motivated by attention seeking. It is also important for the teacher to make clear to the student that it is the behavior, not the student him- or herself, which the teacher finds unacceptable.

49. C: None of these is correct. Neither a condom nor a spermicide by itself is effective enough (A); the two should be used in combination. Vasectomy is often reversible, but not every time; tubal ligation is often reversible, but not in every case (B). While some women may ask a physician to insert a diaphragm for them, at least initially, they usually insert diaphragms themselves prior to intercourse once they have learned how. However, intrauterine devices (IUDs) are inserted for long-term use by physicians and removed by physicians as needed. Women swallow birth control pills orally rather than inserting them (D).

50. A: Students high in Gardner's interpersonal intelligence style learn best through social interactions with others. Those high in intrapersonal (B) intelligence are loners who would not learn best through group activities. Those high in visual-spatial (C) intelligence learn best through visual instructional activities and materials, for example, looking at, using, and making drawings, charts, graphs, photos, images, models, videos, multimedia, illustrations, and jigsaw puzzles and using videoconferencing and TV. Those high in logical-mathematical (D) intelligence learn best through solving mysteries and puzzles, conducting experiments, learning and formulating concepts, learning and applying logic, identifying and exploring patterns and relationships, and performing calculations.

51. B: The School Health Index (SHI) was developed jointly by the Centers for Disease Control (CDC) and national health and education nongovernmental organizations (NGOs), school staffs, school health experts, and parents as a self-assessment (C) and planning (D) guide. Schools use it to help conduct needs assessments to identify the strengths and weaknesses of their health and safety policies and programs, develop action plans for enhancing health to include in their School Improvement Plans (SIPs), and engage students, teachers, parents, and communities in health-promoting, health-enhancing behaviors.

52. B: Brainstorming can be done alone by individual students, or together by more than one student, and with or without the teacher's active involvement. Role-playing (A) can be done with or without the teacher's active involvement but requires more than one student. Guided discovery (C) can be done by individual or multiple students but requires the teacher's active involvement to guide students. Cooperative learning (D) may be done with or without active teacher involvement but requires more than one student. (Note: For all techniques that can be done without active teacher involvement, it is assumed that the teacher has previously instructed the students in the procedures involved when necessary, e.g., if students were not already familiar with them.)

53. B: Erikson described the nuclear conflict of infancy as basic trust versus mistrust: A baby whose needs are met fully and consistently develops trust in the world, while a baby whose needs are inadequately or inconsistently met develops mistrust. Erikson found that the positive outcome of this stage was hope. He identified will (A) as the positive outcome of successfully resolving the nuclear conflict of autonomy versus shame and self-doubt during toddlerhood. He identified purpose (C) as the positive outcome of successfully resolving the nuclear conflict of initiative versus guilt during the preschool years. He identified competence (D) as the positive outcome of successfully resolving the nuclear conflict of industry versus Inferiority during the elementary school years.

54. A: Legumes, that is, beans, split peas, and lentils, are classified in both the vegetables and the proteins food groups by the U.S. Department of Agriculture (cf. ChooseMyPlate.gov) because they have much higher protein content than other vegetables. Seafood (B) is in the protein food group only. Cheese (C) is in the dairy food group only. Eggplant (D) is in the vegetable food group only.

55. C: As of 2014, 48 U.S. states, the District of Columbia, plus Puerto Rico, the Virgin Islands, Guam, American Samoa, and the Northern Mariana Islands school, health care, child care, mental health, social services, and law enforcement employees are all mandated reporters of child maltreatment. Probation or parole officers are mandated reporters in 17 states; substance abuse counselors are in 14 states; and commercial film processors are in 12 states, Guam, and Puerto Rico (A). Employees, directors, and volunteers of camps and recreation and youth centers (B) are mandated reporters in 11 states. Domestic violence workers and humane or animal control officers are mandated reporters in 7 states and Washington, D.C.; college and university, technical and vocational school faculties, administrators, and other employees and volunteers (D) are mandated reporters in 4 states. Clergy are mandated reporters in 27 states and Guam.

56. B: *Explain* is an observable behavior that others can see and hear a student do; hence, it is also measurable. *Learn* (A) and *understand* (C) are verbs that refer to internal states, which others cannot observe students doing and which are also open to variable interpretations. The SMART acronym lists the characteristics of ideal learning objectives: specific, measurable, attainable, relevant or results oriented, and targeted (to learner and learning level). *Identify, define, describe, compare, contrast, analyze, classify, list,* and so on are some additional examples of measurable verbs. Therefore, (D) is incorrect.

57. B: This scenario describes the relationship pattern involving impairment of one or more children. The parent projecting anxiety onto the child becomes overly concerned that something is wrong with the child; this becomes a self-fulfilling prophecy as the child comes to believe something is indeed wrong with him or her and behaves accordingly. The dysfunction in one spouse (A) pattern involves one spouse overcompensating for, criticizing, and dominating the other, who becomes more dependent and dysfunctional in response. The emotional distance pattern (C) involves emotional withdrawal or isolation by one or more family members when their interactions with others become too intense for comfort. The marital conflict pattern (D) involves projection of their unmanageable personal anxiety by both partners into their marital relationship.

58. B: For teachers to self-analyze and adjust their own body language and movements within the classroom, video recordings would enable them to observe where they were positioned in the classroom; whether and how they moved around; and their posture, body language, and so on and make changes accordingly. Journals or diaries (A) help teachers reflect on what took place during class, their own reactions and feelings, student reactions they observed, and related questions that occur to them. Teachers may or may not recall their physical positions and movements, but they cannot view them as they can in videos. Audio recordings (C) give teachers a record of what was said but no visual recording. Peer observation (D) allows teachers to hear observations from colleagues about their physical positions and movements but not to observe and analyze these themselves.

59. A: Body mass index (BMI) is the ratio of weight to height squared, which shows the relationship between a person's weight and height. It is not the ratio of abdominal to total fat (B), fat to muscle (C), or fat to weight (D). Healthy BMIs are generally between 18.5 and 24.9. Below 18.5 is considered underweight, and 25 to 29.9 is considered overweight (with a few exceptions; e.g., some people with very high muscle mass rather than fat may have higher BMIs). A BMI of 30 or above is considered obese.

60. A: Physical education (PE) teachers find that their students are enthusiastic about apps that allow them to view their and classmates or teammates' athletic performance. This enthusiasm makes it easier for teachers to create positive learning environments wherein students are more appreciative of constructive criticism and more motivated to improve their performance. PE teachers find that, after only a brief demonstration, students can easily use them (B) for recording one another, viewing the recordings, and giving each other feedback. Teachers find student athletes really enjoy watching their performance postgame (C) in the locker room. They can much more easily identify which strategies and tactics they used were most and least effective through this viewing. Also, when PE teachers use apps to record video and they play it back, students get much more immediate feedback (D).

61. D: The skin is a part of the integumentary system, along with the hair, nails, nerves, and glands. The skin controls fluid loss, protects deep tissues, and synthesizes vitamin D. The skeletal system (A) gives the body its bony supporting structure, protects vital organs, collaborates with muscles in body movement, stores calcium, and produces red blood cells. The muscular system (B) maintains posture, collaborates with the bones in body movement, uses energy, and generates heat. The lymphatic system (C) retrieves fluids leaked from capillaries and contains white blood cells, and parts of it support parts of the immune system.

62. D: When physical education (PE) teachers want to hold events with Olympics themes for students, their local colleges are good places for them to find students willing to volunteer their time and work to help. PE teachers whose schools are short on funds for sports equipment can solicit financial assistance from local health and wellness agencies, which is not inappropriate (A) as these organizations may be able and often want to help. PE teachers also can ask local trophy companies to donate some of their products—and even refreshments as well—to student athletic events; these businesses frequently welcome the good public relations and advertising they can get by helping out schools (B). Local governments do have a department where PE teachers can recruit representatives to present to students about the use of community resources (C): their county and city Parks and Recreation Departments.

63. A: The breaststroke uses the frog kick. The frog kick is also used in self-contained underwater breathing apparatus (SCUBA) diving and can be used for treading water. The butterfly (B) stroke uses the dolphin kick. The crawl (C) typically uses the flutter kick. Therefore, (D) is incorrect.

64. B: Physical education (PE) teachers can provide kindergarten through Grade 2 (K–) students with log sheets with a prepared left column and an empty right column. The left side uses simple statements like "I have a strong heart," "I have strong muscles," "I can do movements over and over again," and "I can stretch," accompanied by graphic pictures (a heart, a bicep, a figure with arrows indicating repeated movement, and a figure with arrows or lines depicting stretching) to represent cardiovascular endurance, muscular strength, muscular endurance, and flexibility, respectively. In the blank right side, children make drawings or cut and paste pictures illustrating their activities (e.g., running, lifting, dancing, stretches, etc.) in each category. Teachers can guide this activity and collect the products to get assessment information. Writing journal entries (A), notes (C), or cards (D) is inappropriate for students with the limited writing skills of K–2 levels, as is independently turning in records regularly (C) or periodically (D) on a schedule at these ages.

65. B: Handling a hockey puck is an example of a performance skill that would be affected most by individual differences in the perceptual-motor ability of control precision. Football quarterbacking (A) is an example of a performance skill that would be affected most by individual differences in the perceptual-motor abilities of response orientation or choice reaction time. Dribbling a basketball (C) is an example of a performance skill that would be affected most by individual differences in the perceptual-motor ability of manual dexterity. Driving a race car (D) is an example of a performance skill that would be affected most by individual differences in the perceptual-motor ability of rate control.

66. A: Structured observations involve informing both teacher and student of the observation and applying specific criteria for evaluating student performance in physical education (PE) assessment. Naturalistic observations involve not informing students of the observation to capture typical student behavior, such as during their daily practice in regular PE classes. Though naturalistic observations are more realistic regarding behaviors than structured observations, not vice versa (D), they have been criticized for being more subjective, whereas structured observations are more objective, not vice versa (B). Structured observations are equally good for assessing social skills, motor skills (C), and movement skills.

67. C: In effective cooperative learning activities, the students engage in productive, face-to-face interactions frequently and substantially, not occasionally (A). They are accountable and responsible for their group goals not only collectively but also personally and individually (B). They frequently do apply their interpersonal and small-group skills that pertain to their specific cooperative learning activity (C). They regularly, frequently conduct group processing of how their group currently functions in order to improve their group's future effectiveness, not simply to sustain its current effectiveness (D).

- 180 -

68. C: Throwing at a stationary target (B) represents a beginner level of throwing skill. Throwing lead passes (A) represents an intermediate level of throwing skill. Throwing to teammates while being defended (C) by another player represents an advanced level of throwing skill. Therefore, these do not all represent similar levels of throwing skill (D).

69. A: Experts advise coaches that they must first determine whether they have athletes' attention before communicating with them successfully, and second, whether they are explaining in a way that athletes can understand easily. Third, coaches must determine whether the athletes have in fact understood what they said, and fourth, whether the athletes believed what they told them (B). Fifth, coaches must determine whether their athletes have accepted what they told them (C) as well as understanding and believing it. To control a team or group of athletes, coaches also must be sensitive to the nonverbal cues they give (D), while the coaches are talking. These cues communicate whether the athletes are puzzled, confused, disbelieving, bored, resentful, disrespectful, and so on toward a coach and what he or she is saying.

70. B: Musical hoops is played like musical chairs, except children must jump into hoops instead of sitting on chairs when the music stops. This is appropriate for younger children. Freeze tag or blob tag (A) is more appropriate for children older than 5 years, up to 12 years old. Children must try to tag others while holding hands with those in their blob. This demands higher levels of coordination than younger children have. Follow the leader (C) is better as a warm-up activity for children age 5 to 12 years, as younger children can have difficulty with leading and following and with the variations in leaders and locomotor skills that teachers can use with older children. Therefore, (D) is incorrect.

71. D: In spatial awareness, locations and levels (A) of the body or body parts can be high, middle, or low. Personal space (B) refers to the space immediately surrounding an individual person, as opposed to general space, which refers to the total space available or playing area. Directions (C) of movement in space include forward, backward, up, down, and sideways. Planes of movement in space include vertical, horizontal, and circular paths (D).

72. D: A teacher using reflection to inform instruction is less likely to use (A) as placing the responsibility for meeting the objective entirely with the students betrays a lack of reflection. Reflective teachers evaluate how students respond to their instruction, analyze their own design and implementation of lessons, evaluate the results, and determine how they can change what they do to promote the best outcomes for their students. Thus, the teacher using reflection might see whether having the students play the next game faster (B) will increase their heart rates to the target range, or change the game rules to enhance more active participation by all students (C), or even both of these.

73. B: Compared to regular baseball, softball has a bigger ball, a smaller infield, fewer innings, and a different pitch. Softballs are 11 to 12 inches around, whereas baseballs are 8 to 9 inches around. Softball infields have their bases 60 feet apart, whereas baseball infields have their bases 90 feet apart. Regulation softball games consist of seven innings, whereas regulation baseball games consist of nine innings. Softball requires underhand pitching, whereas baseball typically uses overhand pitching.

74. B: Of the activities named, swimming is ideal for students with joint problems because it puts no weight or stress on the joints. The buoyancy of the body in water keeps weight and impact off the joints. Students can be active and get exercise without aggravating joint conditions or pain. Skiing (A) requires a lot of knee bending and turning, hip swiveling, and bearing weight on the joints, so it is not compatible with joint problems. Skateboarding (C) also involves much knee bending and turning, as well as jumping and landing, and would be hard on joint problems. Playing soccer (D) requires running and kicking, again putting too much impact on the joints. These other sports also are done on the ground and subject to gravity, whereas swimming relieves the joints of weight.

75. C: When physical education (PE) classes involve a baseball, for example, injuries are much more likely when fielding teams include 30 or more students instead of only 9 as in regulation games. Teachers must instruct students wanting to field fly balls to call for them and other students to back away from them. Experts with legal and PE experience warn teachers to limit any gymnastics to only basic vaulting and tumbling and these only with individual spotters (A). Most average students cannot support their bodies or hang by their arms, making falls likely; falling from inverted positions risks spinal damage, paralysis, and death. Experts additionally warn PE teachers never to include trampolines in PE classes and also not in extracurricular activities (B) like gymnastics, cheerleading, and so on unless school insurance includes trampoline accidents, which are often not covered or incur excessive premiums. PE teachers should never discipline students using strenuous exercise (D), which is unsafe.

76. B: In addition to referrals, criteria indicating that a student should be evaluated to determine eligibility for adapted physical education (APE) include that the student performs below his or her ability level in group settings (A); has social behaviors that interfere with his or her or others' learning more than one-third of class time (B); has scored below average in two or more parts of the state physical fitness test used by the school district (C); and scored 1.5 or more standard deviations below the norm on the norm-referenced test used (D) by the school or district.

77. A: These steps are sequenced in order of ascending severity: First, the teacher gives the noncompliant student an oral warning that he or she is not following class rules. If the student fails to comply, second, the teacher gives the student a brief time-out from class to refocus his or her attention. If the student is still not complying upon returning, third, the teacher assigns another time-out wherein the student must write a response, for example, identifying the rules he or she broke and what he or she will do now to follow the class rules.

78. D: Teachers can give students cards with adverbs they recently learned, have them look up synonyms and antonyms for these, and write them on the cards. The teacher then directs the students to perform movements in ways described by the adverbs on their cards. The teacher then has students pass their cards to classmates and repeat the activity with new words. This lesson integrates physical education (PE) and English language arts (ELA) skills. Performing movements and then working with words separately or vice versa, (A) and (B), do not integrate PE and ELA skills together into the same activity. Describing movements using the adverbs (C) makes a mental connection between words and movement, but the students are not actually performing any body movements; they are only describing them verbally, so this is an ELA activity rather than an integrated PE and ELA activity.

79. C: TARGET stands for task, authority, recognition, grouping, evaluation, and timing. Varying difficulty levels (A) refers to task. Giving students some responsibility for choice of activities (B) refers to authority. Acknowledging process and improvement rather than product (C) and outcome refers to recognition. Avoiding peer comparison through strategies that get students to form groups quickly and switch groups frequently (D) refers to grouping.

80. C: When Cooper and Potts developed and named aerobics in the late 1960s, it originally focused on the ability of the heart and lungs to use oxygen in sustained physical activity. Cooper was the first to differentiate aerobic capacity from body flexibility (A) and muscular strength (B) and to notice that some people who were very flexible or very strong still did not have good endurance for running, biking, or swimming long distances. Although aerobics initially focused on cardiorespiratory endurance exclusively, today's aerobics classes combine all the elements of fitness (D), incorporating stretching for flexibility and strength training for the muscles along with movements that raise heart and breathing rates for cardiovascular fitness in their exercises.

81. D: For effective class behavior management plans, physical education (PE) teachers should define their expectations positively in terms of what they want the students to do, not negatively in terms of what they want them not to do (C). They should limit expectations to five at most, as students will be unable to remember more than that, and put them in writing, not orally (A), posted visibly in locker rooms and on classroom bulletin boards. They also should enforce their stated expectations consistently, not just occasionally (B).

82. C: The National Board for Professional Teaching Standards (NBPTS) include creating an environment of respect and rapport with students. The board provides an example for addressing student problem behaviors of having the misbehaving student describe his or her behavior, state what made it disruptive, and identify solutions for the problem. This standard's example does not advise for the teacher to do these things (A): The student must do them for ownership, responsibility, and understanding of his or her behavior. Neither should the teacher ask a classmate (B) to do them for the same reasons. The standard does not recommend giving concrete consequences and solutions instead of discussing the problem (D).

83. B: In exercise science, the principle of specificity means that, to improve certain body parts, muscles, or sports movements and techniques, one must exercise those specific parts, muscles, or movements and techniques. Exercising the lower body will not strengthen the upper body or vice versa. Specificity also means that one must practice football skills, for example, to improve in football rather than only exercising for general body conditioning: The latter may be required for and benefit playing football but will not improve specific football skills; only practicing those skills specifically will. The principle of overload (A) means extra or unaccustomed stimuli are required to make the body respond beyond its normal levels. If the question had said someone bench presses more weight than usual to make the upper body stronger, this would illustrate overload as well as specificity. The principle of adaptation (C) means the body adjusts to processes and demands, making activities easier over time and eventually requiring variation for continuing progress. The principle of progression (D) means individuals must progress at certain rates natural to them to achieve results and avoid injuries.

84. C: Fitbit devices can help physical education teachers to support and increase student motivation and also include a line of designer fashion accessories. They can be used for both controlling weight and monitoring sleep quality (A). Students can self-monitor their own progress using Fitbit devices; they also can use them to challenge and compete with friends (B). They are not just stand-alone progress trackers (D); they also sync wirelessly with mobile smartphones and tablets and with charts, graphs, and badges available online for documenting improvements and gaining insights about physical fitness.

85. B: Our respiratory systems inhale air, of which oxygen is one component. From that inhaled air, the respiratory system delivers oxygen to the body. Through gas exchange, it then expels carbon dioxide ($CO_2$) from the body as we exhale. The respiratory system obtains oxygen from the air we inhale; it does not create it, and it expels $CO_2$ rather than absorbing it (C). We do not use our respiratory systems to exhale oxygen or inhale $CO_2$ (D).

86. C: Kinetics is the division of biomechanics that studies the forces causing motion. Newton's First Law of Inertia, Second Law of Momentum, and Third Law of Reaction are most closely related to kinetics. Coplanar vectors (A) belong in the biomechanics division of vector algebra. Kinematics (B) is the biomechanics division that describes motion. Kinematics involves physics concepts including mass, center of gravity, inertia, displacement, linear and angular motion, linear and angular velocity, and acceleration. The biomechanics division of forces (D) involves concepts including center of pressure; force line; resultant force; muscular forces, joint forces, joint reaction forces, ground reaction forces, resisting forces, inertial forces, and gravitational forces; and fulcrums, levers, rotation, couples, equilibrium, weight, friction, and mechanical advantage.

87. B: Physical education (PE) instructors can address negligence in instruction (A) by ensuring they teach students the correct procedures and protocols for safety and for equipment setup, use, and takedown and ensuring students understand and practice how to execute sport and movement activities beforehand. Because PE classes often are large and getting larger, they can address negligence best in supervision (B) by ensuring they continually and actively supervise students throughout all activities and enlisting students to practice peer supervision in addition to supplement teacher supervision. In transportation (C), teachers and coaches are liable outside of school and must obtain written parental consent; follow all school policies, practices, and procedures; and supervise student behavior on buses. In class environments (D), teachers and coaches must be alert for possible dangerous conditions, which can vary daily, and space students to limit hazards.

88. D: Labeling a diagram is an example of a traditional assessment approach. Other traditional approaches include short-answer, constructed-response, and fill-in-the-blank written questions; written matching tests or worksheets; and written multiple-choice or true–false questions. Writing down a personal fitness plan (A) is an example of a written alternative assessment. Additional examples include research papers, essays, stories, poems, anecdotes, journals, logs, checklists, rating scales, brochures, advertisements, rubrics, performance records, newspapers, magazines, projects, pre-assessment inventories, surveys, questionnaires, interviews, editorials, and reflections. Performing dance movements (B) and playing sports games (C) are examples of alternative performance task assessments. Additional examples include locomotor or gymnastics routines, officiating games, making fitness assessments or oral reports, teaching lessons, warm-up routines, showcases, debates, skits, role-plays, or interviews.

89. C: Research studies find that motor skills, endurance, and strength training all modify the spinal reflexes according to the specific behaviors each task requires. New blood vessels are formed (A) through endurance training but not motor skills or strength training. Motor maps are reorganized (B) through motor skills training but not endurance or strength training. New synapses are generated (D) through motor skills and strength training but not endurance training.

90. D: "Match up" as a defense cue in basketball means that students should defend other players who are as similar to them in size, fitness, and skill level as possible—not just in size (C). This cue does not mean to pair up with another player (A). Staying near to the offensive players they are defending wherever they move on the court (B) is indicated to students with a cue of "Shadow" rather than "Match up."

91. A: Researchers have found that smaller class sizes and student–teacher ratios correlate with larger quantities of activity time, activity level, safety, and learning for students, whereas larger class sizes and student–teacher ratios correlate with smaller quantities of student activity times, levels, safety, and learning—that is, an inverse correlation. Studies show that students receive more and better physical education (PE) from teachers who teach only PE rather than dividing their teaching time and attention between PE and other subjects (B). Researchers are coming to increasing consensus that standards-based PE curriculum results in greater student physical activity (C). Well-maintained, safe, appropriate, and aesthetically appealing PE facilities and equipment also are found to increase and improve student activity (D).

92. D: Recently, the issue that has become the greatest challenge to kindergarten to Grade 12 (K–12) school physical education (PE) is that time in school curricula for PE classes and activities has been reduced significantly to make time for other academic classes. Inadequate resources and parental support (A); overly large class sizes and teacher burnout (B); and violence, student drug abuse, and discipline problems (C) are also challenges to K–12 PE, but these are also equal challenges to other school subjects and to education in general.

93. B: "Follow through!" is an example of prescriptive feedback, which is specific. It specifies an instruction that corrects or improves what the student or athlete is doing or needs to do. In this example, it tells the student or athlete that, when batting, kicking, throwing, and so on, he or she must follow t]he movement through for it to be effective rather than stopping it abruptly upon contact or release. The other examples are all descriptive feedback, which is general. It gives students or athletes positive social reinforcement by encouraging or praising their performance in general but does not specify exactly what it was that they did well or need to do better or differently.

94. C: The three main categories of fundamental movement skills (FMS) are locomotor (A), manipulative, (A and, (B), and stability (D). Within the main category of stability are included the subcategories of rotation, (B) and (C), and balance, (C) and (D). Activities like spinning, twirling, rocking, bending, and turning demonstrate rotation. Balance can involve both stationary and movement activities. Both rotation and balance are components of stability. Locomotor skills involve activities like walking, running, and so on. Manipulative skills include activities like throwing, catching, hitting, batting, kicking, and transporting objects.

95. C: Summation of forces refers to producing the maximum possible force from any movement using multiple muscles. Adding up the forces generated by each individual muscle yields the total force or summation of forces. Related to this, the order of use is that the largest body parts are slowest, and being stronger and hence the initiators of power, they move first; the smallest body parts are fastest, and being in charge of coordination and refinement, they move last. Thus, the largest, slowest parts do not move last (A), and the smallest, fastest parts do not move first (B). Therefore, (D) is also incorrect.

96. D: Physical education teachers report that apps like Apple's GradeBookPro enable them to spend much more of their class time actually teaching by reducing the time it takes them to perform administrative tasks like taking attendance (C); using standard or weighted grading systems; and displaying assignment, absence, percentage, and other student data all on one page, making disputes at the end of the course or year less likely (B). This app and similar ones enable teachers to create reports and assignments easily; e-mail current attendance and grade status to students; send copies of assignments across classes; quickly take and attach student photos to files, helping them learn students' names sooner; record grades with far greater speed and ease; and overall, streamline and make more efficient all of the tasks that used to be cumbersome, even irrelevant, yet are necessary.

97. A: When we exercise, our bodies access their stored glycogen supplies for energy; glycogen depletion triggers the release of endorphins, hormones that generate feelings of euphoria. These feelings of well-being are short-term effects of exercise. The prevention and relief of depression through regular exercise are long-term effects. So are lower risks of heart attacks and strokes (C), which result from consistent aerobic exercise over time. While a short-term effect of exercise is an immediate increase in blood circulation, a reduction of blood pressure and pulse (D) can be a long-term effect of exercising regularly for at least a few months.

98. A: Other than terms that have been translated into English for use by English-speaking people, a great deal of ballet terminology is in French because, historically, the dance form was popularized in France. While ballroom dance uses many Spanish (C) terms, especially related to Latin ballroom styles and techniques, ballroom also incorporates many French terms taken from ballet to describe steps also taken from ballet, for example, the passé step, chaîné turns, pirouettes, and so on. Italian (B) is not shared in common by ballet and ballroom dance. Although ballet technique was highly developed in Russia later in its history after its early popularization in France, and Russia remains a stellar center of the ballet discipline today, ballet does not use Russian (D) terms, and neither does ballroom dance.

99. C: Activities that require agility and lower-body strength, which do not involve body contact (A), are most appropriate for coed participation and are less dependent on team assignment by student skill levels. For activities that require more upper-body strength (B), it is more important for physical education teachers to assign teams according to individual student skill levels to prevent injuries. Therefore, (D) is incorrect.

100. C: Formative assessments measure student progress during the instructional process. They enable teachers to use the assessment results to inform ongoing instruction and adjust it to meet their students' particular needs and strengths, for example, making their pace faster or slower according to student learning rates; spending more or less time on different skills or areas according to which students have already mastered or are struggling with more; or replacing teaching methods that are ineffective for some students with different ones. Showing accountability (A), comparing student achievement to state or national population averages (B), and assessing whether instruction has helped students meet curriculum standards (D) are all functions of summative assessments rather than formative assessments.

101. B: Human babies actually display coordinated arm–hand movements in the womb before birth, such as moving their thumbs to their mouths. The amniotic fluid provides buoyancy to make this easier. After birth, gravity makes arm and hand movements harder for newborns, who initially exhibit arm flapping and jerky arm extensions (C) before progressing to successfully reaching for objects (A) around four to five months old. At this age, they only adjust their hand shapes to object shapes after touching them. They develop the ability to use visual information to change their hand shapes before touching objects (D) around the age of eight months.

102. A: When physical education (PE) teachers pose think-about questions to students, for example, asking them what the pros and cons are of certain playing formations, positions, or strategies or where they should be aiming their shots, and so on, they give the students a mental advantage by getting them to consider, analyze, and then plan their playing strategies. Thinking about what they just did in one practice session enables them to plan ahead for the next one and improve their game. When PE teachers read aloud the tasks or steps of a practice session, they ensure that player setup is timely rather than delayed (B). They should not alternate the sequence of practice plans (C) but always follow them in the sequence they are written. PE teachers should both verbally describe and physically demonstrate movements or actions, not do only one or the other (D).

103. A: The Institute of Medicine recommendation is for children to spend an hour a day in moderate to vigorous physical activity (MVPA). But studies show that, in actual schools, physical education (PE) classes last about 23 minutes a day, with only 10 of those minutes spent in MVPA. In other words, children get about one-sixth the MVPA that is recommended from school PE classes. Researchers conclude that not only must children be physically active outside of PE classes, but also schools must increase how much children are active during PE class times.

104. C: National Association for Sport and Physical Education (NASPE) recommends that elementary school students should receive a minimum of 150 minutes per week of quality PE time in schools, meaning that somewhat more than this would not be too much. Thirty minutes per day most reflects the recommendation of 150 minutes per week as school is in session five days per week. A minimum of 15 minutes per day (A) is not enough. A maximum of 30 minutes per day (B) implies that more than this is bad, which does not reflect the NASPE recommendation. A maximum of 60 minutes for an entire week (D) is also far too little: This would break down to only 12 minutes daily, or two 30-minute classes per week, or three 20-minute sessions, four 15-minute sessions, and so on.

105. D: Physical education (PE) teachers must always conduct regular safety inspections of facilities and equipment on a consistent basis. Rather than using extrinsic motivations (A) like external punishments or

rewards, PE teachers are advised to enhance intrinsic student motivations to be responsible for learning. When student behaviors are inappropriate, PE teachers should not ignore them (B) but address them immediately. PE teachers do need to obtain and regularly renew certification in cardiopulmonary resuscitation (CPR) and automated external defibrillator (AED) use (C).

106. D: It is not a good idea to keep class rules from parents in a misguided attempt to gain student trust (A). Parents need to be informed of the rules, so they know what is expected of their children and can make sure their children understand the rules. Teachers also protect themselves by informing parents of rules in advance: In the event of student behavior problems, injuries, or disputes, parents cannot subsequently deny knowledge or accuse teachers of not informing them. Giving the students copies of the rules to take home to parents (B) often means the parents never receive them. Postal mail (C) is much slower when today's technology enables almost instant transmission of e-mails (D), eliminating the potential for events to occur before parents receive the information.

107. B: Center of gravity (COG) is not in the same location in every human body (A); neither is it always in a certain location of every individual body (C). Rather, it shifts corresponding to changes in the positions of the body parts (B). COG is not precisely the same as center of mass, but their difference is negligible, so for all practical purposes they are considered synonymous; however, center of gravity or mass is not the same as center of pressure (D).

108. A: MyFitnessPal is an app that features healthy recipes (B) and an extensive food database, whereby users can enter meals to calculate caloric and nutritional content. The Endomondo Sports Tracker features Audio Coach feedback (C) on user exercise performance. Endomondo and Fitbit both include social networking (D) capabilities for sharing fitness motivation, goals, progress, support, and reinforcement with friends. One thing these apps share in common is that they all sync (A) with each other as well as with other apps, devices, and online tools. MyFitnessPal and Endomondo sync with heart-rate monitors as well as with each other and Fitbit.

109. C: Good nutrition provides the body with more energy, which enables and motivates people to exercise. Reciprocally, getting regular exercise can help to control the appetite and prevent overeating. Exercising does not mean you can eat anything you want (A). Both calcium and other nutrients in the diet and weight-bearing exercise can prevent loss of bone density and osteoporosis (B). A combination of exercise and a nutritious diet, not one or the other, prevents high blood pressure, high cholesterol (D), diabetes, and other diseases that unhealthy lifestyles often contribute to or cause.

110. D: Working together with the principal to develop an exercise program that benefits student learning by enhancing the environment is an example of using administrator support and collaboration. (A) is an example of collaborating with an English language arts (ELA) teacher by using a novel to study a sport for the physical education (PE) component and character development and relationships for the ELA component. (B) is also an example of how to collaborate with an ELA teacher by watching a movie, studying its dance movements for the PE component and its themes for the ELA component. (C) is an example of collaborating with a Family and Consumer Sciences teacher by combining nutrition with exercise—a very natural and valuable combination as good nutrition and physical activity interact and mutually support one another in healthy lifestyles.

111. D: Ectomorphs have long, narrow, thin body shapes with little muscle or fat. The high jump (D) and long-distance running are examples of appropriate sports for this somatotype. Wrestling (A) and shot-putting (C) are more suitable for endomorphic body types, which tend to be pear-shaped with more fat on the torso and limbs but small wrists and ankles. Gymnastics (B) is more appropriate for mesomorphs, who tend to have triangular shapes and strong limbs with more muscle and less fat.

112. C: According to the description, the test is reliable, meaning that it gives the same results every time it is administered, but it is not valid, meaning that it does not measure what it was intended to measure. Therefore, it is not correct that the test is neither reliable nor valid (A). It is not true that the test is valid but not reliable (B) but, rather, vice versa. The test is not both valid and reliable, and it is not simply misused (D); it is actually not valid because it does not test what it means or claims to test but assesses something else instead.

113. C: Kayaking is an activity that most involves the physical proficiency of dynamic strength. Static strength (A) is most involved in an activity like weight lifting. Trunk strength (B) is most involved in an activity like pole-vaulting. Explosive strength (D) is involved most in an activity like the standing long jump.

114. A: The first step in the volleyball activity is for students to assume rotational positions, that is, with one setter in front and one in the back row, without overlapping. The second step is for a student to serve the ball. In the third step, following the serve, students move from their rotational positions to their base positions. The fourth step is for players to defend against attack by watching, calling, and passing the ball.

115. C: In the first, cognitive stage of motor learning, learners understand the activity's goal and nature (A) and make initial attempts to perform it that include major errors (B). In the second, associative stage, learners engage in practice to master the timing of the skill, and they make fewer errors that are more consistent in nature (C). In the third, autonomous stage, learners perform the activity effortlessly and automatically (D), enabling them to redirect their attention to other aspects of the skill.

116. A: Atlantoaxial instability consists of excessive movement at the junction of the atlas, or first cervical vertebra (C1), and axis, or second cervical vertebra (C2), due to bone or ligament abnormality. It includes neurological symptoms when the spinal cord also is involved. This condition would make it unsafe for a student to perform a forward roll (B). However, to meet a learning objective, a physical education teacher could substitute a log roll, which would be safe for a student with this condition (A). Therefore, it is incorrect that no kind of roll should be assigned (C). Atlantoaxial instability is not necessarily that rare (D): It is caused by Down syndrome, a number of metabolic diseases, birth defects, traumatic spinal injuries, upper respiratory infections, rheumatoid arthritis, and surgeries to the head or neck. With so many different etiologies, the chances for a student to have this condition are not so remote.

117. A: According to social psychologists, nonverbal communication has these primary functions: performing social rituals (A) like greetings, farewells, and so on; revealing personalities as well as interpersonal relationships (B); supporting verbal interactions (C); and expressing feelings (D).

118. B: When the teacher writes a task on the board that students can begin upon entry to physical education (PE) class, this supports high expectations for students to take responsibility for classroom procedures and routines. While it encourages their independence in starting the activity, this does not mean the teacher will not be supervising them (A) thereafter. This teacher practice not only supports student independence in initiating activities; it also helps them comprehend their learning objectives and expectations (C) by the teacher's structuring the learning activities (D) he or she has provided for them.

119. A: In quality of movement, the flow of movement can be bound, that is, interrupted, or free, that is, sustained. Effort (B), or the amount of force in a body movement, can be strong, medium, light, or other increments within each of these. Speed (C) of movement can be quick, slow, or any degree in between these. Rhythm (D) of body movement can be constant, accelerating, or decelerating.

120. B: The best professional development not only improves a teacher's own expertise (A) and that of the teacher's colleagues (C) but both mutually as well as enabling physical education teachers to promote

their own discipline. It enables teachers to improve instruction not only at the classroom level (D) but also at schoolwide and districtwide levels.

121. C: Posture has played an equally significant role in classical and contemporary theories of motor development. In classical theories attributing motor skill development to neuromuscular maturation, increasingly vertical posture was evidence of babies' progress as their cerebral cortices developed more control over their abilities to overcome gravitational pull. In contemporary theories attributing motor development to dynamic systems and relationships between perceptions and actions, posture became the stable biomechanical basis for action and was evidence of learning about new perception–action systems. Hence, posture was not more important to either classical theories (A) or contemporary theories (B). Neither did these theories regard its role in motor development as minor (D).

122. B: Differentiation is a calculus technique for finding a quantity's rate of change, used in biomechanics to get derivatives of curves or functions like velocity, acceleration, and jerk, which are derivatives of displacement. Integration is a calculus technique to determine the area between an x-axis and a curve, used in biomechanics to obtain integrals like velocity as an integral of acceleration, displacement as an integral of velocity, and work as an integral of power. Composition and resolution of vectors (A) in biomechanics are ways of combining coplanar and concurrent vector quantities by using vector algebra, not calculus. The parallelogram method (C) is a method for resolving vectors in different directions in biomechanics that is based on geometry, not calculus: The parallelogram is a geometric shape. Because (B) is correct, (D) is incorrect.

123. D: Alcohol, cocaine, Prozac, and other substances temporarily can reduce inhibitions so that students who are usually shy or introverted behave more sociably around peers (A). When students see substance use as a solution to being socially awkward and unpopular, they repeat it, which can lead to addiction. Conversely, students who were normally extroverted often withdraw socially when they become addicted to substances (B). Students who normally demonstrate self-control often behave more impulsively under the influence of substances (C).

124. A: Large-scale state research has found that student cardiovascular fitness achievement and healthy body mass index (BMI) scores correlate positively with student scores on the state academic achievement test of knowledge and skills. Other research has found that children who are more physically fit demonstrate not only quicker reaction times but also more accurate responses (B). Another investigation found that children burn more calories and take nearly twice as many steps during teacher-led fitness activities as during active gaming, not vice versa (C). Other studies show that intense exercise is followed by improvement in cognitive function (D).

125. B: This is a description of the command or direct method, which uses teacher-centered task instruction to promote psychomotor learning. The contingency or contract method (A) is a behavioral approach that uses specified rewards that are contingent on student task completion to reinforce psychomotor behaviors. The task or reciprocal method (C) uses stations whereby student learning of specific psychomotor tasks is integrated into the learning setup. Because (B) is correct, (D) is incorrect.

126. B: The Heimlich maneuver should be performed only on someone who is choking and cannot breathe. This means the person cannot speak, so the Heimlich maneuver should not be performed on a student who says he or she is having trouble breathing (A). Someone who is choking and cannot breathe also cannot cough, so the Heimlich maneuver should not be performed on a student who is coughing (C), which means he or she can breathe. The Heimlich maneuver should be done first if someone is choking; cardiopulmonary resuscitation (CPR) should be started after that if the victim loses consciousness (D).

127. B: To enhance students' perceived physical competence, it is better for physical education (PE) teachers not to specify how many trials to complete during a certain time period (A) but rather to specify the time period for practicing without requiring any specific number of trials (B). This allows students to focus not on how many times they complete the actions but rather on perfecting their technique. Rather than emphasizing technical errors they make (C), it is better to emphasize which things students do well technically, providing positive reinforcement that increases their motivation to practice. Varying assigned activities is more effective to minimize off-task student behavior than not varying them (D).

128. D: When learning to fall sideways and land on the hands, students should first learn to fall sideways from a kneeling position (A). Then they can practice rolling sideways down a wedge (B) to simulate falling down an incline. Then they learn while moving to fall, roll sideways, stand up (C), and keep moving. They begin this exercise from a walking speed and gradually increase to jogging then running (D). Thereafter, they can practice this activity with dodging. After mastering these activities, students can try in pairs to pull each other off balance and take turns tipping each other sideways from an all-fours position.

129. A: While feedback is important in physical education (PE) instruction, knowing when and when not to provide feedback is equally important to effective teaching. PE teachers need to give feedback to give students specific corrections to incorrectly performed techniques, for example. However, when a task furnishes inherent environmental feedback (B),—for example, a student throws a basketball, and it goes through the hoop—additional feedback may be unnecessary. When a student already has enough experience with a skill (C), sometimes PE teachers need not give them feedback. Also, when a teacher's demonstration enables students to see easily how to perform a skill correctly (D), they may need little or no additional feedback.

130. B: A time-lapse bulletin board can begin with the physical education (PE) teacher labeling a board's theme (e.g., balance, strength, speed, teamwork, sportsmanship, a certain sport, etc.) posting about a dozen pictures to provide examples and ideas for students and get them started. The teacher then assigns students to bring in pictures—drawings, photos, diagrams, art, and so on that they have found or made—that apply to the board's identified theme. Over time, student contributions fill the board with pictures, which students can view, discuss, and use as illustrations to help them understand aspects of a learning unit or topic. PE teachers need not even have schools provide (A) or have to buy their own real bulletin boards; they simply can create a board by hanging large pieces of paper, poster board, or fabric on the wall. This project is completed by students, not just teachers (C). Students do not ignore such boards (D), especially when they contain their own and classmates' contributions.

# Thank You

We at Mometrix would like to extend our heartfelt thanks to you, our friend and patron, for allowing us to play a part in your journey. It is a privilege to serve people from all walks of life who are unified in their commitment to building the best future they can for themselves.

The preparation you devote to these important testing milestones may be the most valuable educational opportunity you have for making a real difference in your life. We encourage you to put your heart into it—that feeling of succeeding, overcoming, and yes, conquering will be well worth the hours you've invested.

We want to hear your story, your struggles and your successes, and if you see any opportunities for us to improve our materials so we can help others even more effectively in the future, please share that with us as well. **The team at Mometrix would be absolutely thrilled to hear from you!** So please, send us an email (support@mometrix.com) and let's stay in touch.

If you'd like some additional help, check out these other resources we offer for your exam:

http://MometrixFlashcards.com/WEST